KING'S COLLEGE LONDON

MEDIEVAL STUDIES

VI

King's College London
Centre for Late Antique and Medieval Studies

Director: Roy Wisbey

KING'S COLLEGE LONDON MEDIEVAL STUDIES

BOOKS AND GRACE
ÆLFRIC'S THEOLOGY

LYNNE GRUNDY

King's College London

Centre for Late Antique and Medieval Studies

1991

ISSN 0953-217X

ISBN 0 9513085 5 6

British Library Cataloguing in Publication Data

Grundy, Lynne
Books and grace: Aelfric's theology.
1. Christianity. Theology, history
I. Title
230.092

ISBN 0-9513085-5-6

Printed on

Acid-free long life paper

by

Short Run Press

Exeter

1991

CONTENTS

For Martin

ACKNOWLEDGEMENTS

I gladly acknowledge the encouragement, help and advice that friends and colleagues have given so freely. Among them, in particular, I would like to thank my editors, Jane Roberts and David Hook, who have sought with Ælfrician zeal to combat error, together with Janet Bately, Brian Horne and George Mathews, who have read the text at various stages in its development. I would also like to thank members of the Computing Centre at King's College London for their help in preparing the text for camera-ready copy.

My greatest debt is to Martin Grundy, whose support has been unfailing.

NOTE

In the case of primary sources, all references include line numbers where a line count is provided by the edition; these are preceded where necessary by a page number. For convenience, sermons in Old English works are referred to by the editor's name followed by sermon number. For full bibliographical information relating to the editions of Ælfric's works and of other Anglo-Saxon sermon writers, please see the bibliography (Primary sources, section II: Old English works). Line numbers, not provided by Thorpe in his edition of *Catholic Homilies*, have been supplied for the sake of precision, the line count beginning anew at the top of each page. Spelling, word division and punctuation follow the method of each text cited. For modern works, short references are used after the first; this system also applies to the citation of material from editorial introductions or commentaries.

Where Ælfric discusses a point in other places in addition to the lines referred to in the text, cross-references are given in the footnotes.

All translations from Old English are my own. Where quotations from the Bible are given in English, they are taken from the Douay/Rheims version. The Vulgate is the norm for the Latin. English versions of patristic texts are taken from modern translations: the English version may readily be found by reference to the bibliography where translations are listed alongside Latin originals. Where no published translation is known to me I give my own.

1

INTRODUCTION

In his English Preface to the *Catholic Homilies*, Ælfric, concerned to forestall anxiety about the tribulation to be faced at the end of the world, declares:

Gehwa mæg þe eaðelicor ða toweardan costnunge acuman, ðurh Godes fultum, gif he bið þurh boclice lare getrymmed; forðan ðe þa beoð gehealdene þe oð ende on geleafan þurhwuniað. (Thorpe English Preface p. 4. lines 7-10)[1]

Each person will be able, by God's help, to confront the more easily the temptation which is to come, if he is strengthened by book-learning; for those who continue in faith until the end will be preserved.

Two things are of paramount importance. The first is that nothing anyone can do will be of any profit to the soul without God's help: this help is grace, which Ælfric perceives to be essential for every aspect of the Christian life. But secondly, the faithful may also help themselves, within the sphere of grace, by learning about their faith, so that they are equipped with a powerful weapon against temptation. Books contain a body of knowledge which represents the sum of human resource against the terror to come.

Ælfric's confidence in the knowledge to be gained from the study of books, which stems from his very high regard for the tradition of the church Fathers, is everywhere apparent in his writings. To transmit that tradition, and the security which it affords, is Ælfric's purpose in these sermons. The teachings of the Fathers, at present concealed from ordinary people because they are written in an inaccessible language, are to be the protection of the faithful

---

1. Benjamin Thorpe, editor, *The Homilies of the Anglo-Saxon Church: the first part, containing the Sermones Catholici, or Homilies of Ælfric, in the original Anglo-Saxon, with an English version*, 2 vols (London, 1844-46). Volume I is cited below as 'Thorpe', while Volume II is used only for *De penitentia*, which is cited under this title.

in the time of crisis. Such a time will certainly come to every Christian, for death brings everyone to a confrontation with the truth. But perhaps the greatest crisis will be that faced by all those still living at the end of time, when tribulation and persecution will confound and weaken those without the strength to persevere. Then it will be essential to distinguish the wicked inventions of Antichrist from the truth of Christ, and this will be easier for those who are 'strengthened by book-learning.' Supported by the knowledge of the true faith, Ælfric believes, the faithful will be able to withstand the rigours of the last days. Survival depends on understanding: the diligent teaching of 'boclice lare' to ordinary people is the way to ensure they have the benefit of that understanding.

Ælfric's most important function, in his own eyes at least, both as priest at Cerne Abbas and later as abbot at Eynsham, appears to have been that of the teacher. Ælfric went to Cerne in 987.[2] He moved there from Winchester, where he had been educated under Æðelwold. It was apparently after he had moved to the new foundation that he conceived the idea of making his collection of sermons (Thorpe English Preface p. 2. line 6). This carefully constructed series of sermons was intended to serve the needs of people who lacked the benefits of education. In the two-year cycle, the sermons offer a reliable account of the basic tenets of the Christian faith.

By 992 the two volumes of sermons had been issued; in their original form, then, they were the product of five years' work at most, written in the new (and perhaps ill-equipped) monastery.[3] But if the material resources available to him were small, they were well chosen, for he clearly had around him suitable collections of sermons and lives of saints.[4] Apparently

2. P.H. Sawyer, *Anglo-Saxon Charters* (London, 1968), no. 1217.

3. The dating of Ælfric's homilies is discussed by Kenneth Sisam, *Studies in the History of Old English Literature* (Oxford, 1967) pp. 157-60; P.A.M. Clemoes, 'The Chronology of Ælfric's Works', *Old English Newsletter*, Subsidia, 5, (Binghamton, New York, 1980), *passim*; and in the introductions to their editions, by John C. Pope, *The Homilies of Ælfric: a supplementary collection*, EETS, 259-260, 2 vols (London, 1967-68), I, 146-50, and Malcolm R. Godden, *Ælfric's Catholic Homilies, the Second Series: Text*, EETS, Supplementary Series, 5 (London, 1979), pp. lxxxvi-xciv.

4. Cyril L. Smetana, 'Ælfric and the Early Mediæval Homiliary', *Traditio*, 15 (1959), 163-204; 'Ælfric and the Homiliary of Haymo of Halberstadt', *Traditio*, 17 (1961), 457-69.

too, Ælfric's clear memory of his own studies allowed him to range freely over a number of works, placing at his disposal a considerable body of teaching.[5] Even after Ælfric became the abbot of the Benedictine house at Eynsham he continued to enlarge, correct and reissue his sermons. His strong awareness of the responsibility of the teacher, who is the guardian of the souls placed in his keeping, remained with him and may be discerned in the background of all his work.

The Latin and English Prefaces to Ælfric's first series of sermons were not originally part of the issue. They were added at the time of the first major revision of the sermons, and were subsequently removed, at which point the homiletic material of the English Preface became a sermon in its own right. The prefaces are of value in that they provide Ælfric's observations concerning the task of translating the sermons of the Fathers. In his Latin Preface, addressed to Archbishop Sigeric, Ælfric's first concern is to give his reasons for undertaking this work. This collection of sermons is 'ob ædificationem simplicium' ('for the edification of the humble', Thorpe Latin Preface p. 1. line 6) and 'ad utilitatem animarum suarum' ('for the profit of their souls', lines 9-10). He explains his method briefly, and emphasizes that even in the process of transmission his intention is to avoid all possibility of error:

Nec ubique transtulimus verbum ex verbo, sed sensum ex sensu, cavendo tamen diligentissime deceptivos errores, ne inveniremur aliqua haeresi seducti seu fallacia fuscati. (lines 11-14)

We have not everywhere translated word from word, but sense from sense, yet guarding most diligently against deceptive errors, that we may not be found to be seduced by any heresy nor darkened by deceit.

Ælfric cites as his sources (lines 15-18) a combination of major patristic figures (Augustine, Jerome, Bede and Gregory), for whom he has the highest respect, and of two homilists who may be regarded primarily as compilers, assembling material from Augustine, Gregory and Bede in particular. Haymo and Smaragdus in large measure did in Latin what Ælfric achieves

---

5.   On this aspect of Ælfric's method see, for example, J.E. Cross, 'Ælfric — Mainly on Memory and Creative Method in Two *Catholic Homilies*', *Studia Neuphilologica*, 61 (1969), 135-55.

in the vernacular. Of Haymo, John Pope observes, 'it appears that Haymo was constantly at his elbow' (*Homilies*, p. 193); Joyce Hill has recently shown the extent of Ælfric's debt to Smaragdus.[6] Ælfric uses these authorities with a degree of freedom, substituting and rearranging where necessary, admittedly with some diffidence, in order to present an orthodox viewpoint which at the same time is relevant and useful to the contemporary church.

Ælfric's regard for tradition is matched by a concern for accuracy. His sermons are to be widely disseminated, which means that unknown scribes are expected to take part in the task. He is evidently familiar with the mistakes that can creep into a text as a result of careless copying, and so makes a stern injunction to the scribe whose own manuscript will become the exemplar for another. His instructions are given in English. All scribes are to take extreme care to ensure that their texts are accurate transmissions of the original text (Thorpe English Preface p. 8. lines 9-16).

In the English Preface Ælfric enlarges on his stated purpose in undertaking the translation of patristic writings, already briefly recorded in the Latin Preface. Education, with particular attention to the usefulness of that education to the soul, is here seen to have a twofold urgency.

In the first place, widespread ignorance of Latin has significantly reduced the accessibility of wise, orthodox teaching, and as a result, Ælfric observes, people are increasingly falling prey to error and deception:

> Ic geseah and gehyrde mycel gedwyld on manegum Engliscum bocum, þe ungelærede menn þurh heora bilewitnysse to micclum wisdome tealdon. (p. 2. lines 8-11)

> I have seen and heard of much error in many English books which ignorant people, because of their simplicity, have esteemed as great wisdom.

Ælfric's very high regard for tradition is the foundation for his planned assault on the errors currently circulating. He seems to make little distinction between heresy and error. The degree to which people may be wrong matters little to him; he is merely concerned to correct that error. He appears to be especially conscious of ignorance about the nature of God: his

---

6. 'Ælfric and the Smaragdus Problem' (unpublished paper delivered at Kalamazoo, May 1991: forthcoming).

sermons show that he takes a particular interest in those heresies relating to the doctrine of God, although he cannot have encountered many Arians or Sabellians. But he must have discerned all kinds of confusion resulting from the decline in Latin scholarship; further, the vernacular sermons already available were not, perhaps, as accurate in their transmission of patristic teaching as Ælfric could have wished.

In the second place, instruction is deemed to be essential in view of the calamities and tribulations which are soon to assail the world:

> menn behofiað godre lare swiðost on þisum timan þe is geendung þyssere worulde, and beoð fela frecednyssa on mancynne ærðan þe se ende becume, swa swa ure Drihten on his godspelle cwæð to his leorningcnihtum. (p. 2. lines 16-20)

> people need good teaching, especially at this time which is the ending of this world, and there will be many dangers among mankind before the end comes, just as our Lord said to his disciples in his gospel.

Ælfric quotes Christ's warnings about the future tribulations and the miracle-working false christs, two manifestations of the devil's power newly unleashed upon the world (Matthew 24. 4-13). Recognizing the reality of the danger to which all will be exposed, he seeks to offer protection for those who might literally be the world's last inhabitants ('us endenextum mannum', 'us, the last people', Assmann I. line 117).[7] Although the gospel promises that even the elect might become entangled in the snares of the false christs, the scholar clings obstinately to the belief that with God's help, a sound education in orthodox truths will strengthen them to keep their faith, 'forðan ðe þa beoð gehealdene þe oð ende on geleafan þurhwuniað' ('for those who continue in faith until the end will be preserved', Thorpe English Preface p. 4. lines 9-10). Ælfric proceeds immediately to a brief account of the tribulation to be faced, particularly in the person of Antichrist, and gives full warning of the punishment which will await all those who submit to his lies and believe in his miracles.

---

7. Bruno Assmann, editor, *Angelsächsische Homilien und Heiligenleben*, Bibliothek der angelsächsischen Prosa, 3 (Kassel, 1889), reprinted with a supplementary introduction by Peter Clemoes (Darmstadt, 1964). For this line, compare Thorpe XXXII. p. 476. line 18.

Ælfric conveys with some force the individual's requirement of a solid grounding in truth to enable him to withstand the engulfing falsehood of the end: in doing so he acknowledges his own awesome responsibility in undertaking to provide that foundation, recognizing that if he fails in this task he will have to answer for his negligence before the judgement seat of Christ. His purpose in writing is therefore partly to ensure that he has discharged his own responsibility by providing for the needs of others.

The Latin and English Prefaces appear only in one manuscript of Ælfric's homilies, Cambridge University Library MS Gg.3.28, dated by Ker and Pope to around the year 1000.[8] The Cambridge manuscript represents one of two major stages of revision which are visible in the collections that have survived. The earliest state of Ælfric's text is that represented by British Library MS Royal 7 C. xii, a manuscript which includes some editorial markings of such authority that they are very likely to be in Ælfric's own hand. He marks passages for excision which he has treated more fully since the compilation of that issue. Gg.3.28 embodies the revisions of Royal 7 C. xii and makes the significant addition of the prefaces.

The coincidence of this reissue with the approaching millennium may perhaps indicate a heightened anxiety about eschatological matters on Ælfric's part. Although not expecting the second coming of Christ with any precise time in mind (for he is expressly forbidden to do so by the Gospel), he is nevertheless increasingly aware of the people's needs. This is why he is particularly concerned that his sermons should be copied accurately and transmitted without distortion. The armoury of the Christian in the last days must be completely trustworthy.

Ælfric did not allow the eschatological content of the English Preface to go to waste after he had cancelled the prefaces, which also had a dedicatory purpose, in succeeding issues. He used this material to expand a sermon on the last days provided for Advent, now preserved in Corpus Christi College Cambridge MS 188, representative of Ælfric's second-stage revision. This set includes a number of expansions, in which Ælfric adds some new material and offers sermons for days which had previously been left untreated. His later revisions show increasing concern that people be well-informed about the last days: in addition to the Advent homily, a long sermon on eschatology is included for the Octave of Pentecost (Pope XI). To the modern reader Thorpe's inclusion of the homiletic preface to the Gg.3.28 issue has the

---

8. N.R. Ker, *Catalogue of Manuscripts containing Anglo-Saxon* (Oxford, 1957), no. 15; Pope, *Homilies*, p. 34.

effect of throwing a peculiar light over the whole collection: it enhances the sense both of the proximity of judgement and of the urgency of Ælfric's task. But it was only when the preface became a homily, and the sermon for the Octave of Pentecost was added to the collection, that Ælfric's audience can have become sensible of this.

Whether as preface or sermon, this account of the last days does draw attention to the conviction with which Ælfric viewed his work. It offers an unintended self-portrait, revealing a man of spiritual wisdom and discernment, humbly conscious of the size of his task and energetically ready to undertake it. Ælfric also reveals himself in his letters to be ready to spend any amount of time to explain something, or to provide an authoritative account of some aspect of the priesthood, whether practical or spiritual.

In the introduction to his edition of Ælfric's homilies, Pope observes, 'For the history of ideas what matters most is the originator of the idea and secondarily the extent of its dissemination and its persistence' (*Homilies*, p. 155). This observation forms the guiding principle of the following discussion, which assumes that the content of the sermons is of interest, and that the transmitted idea and its life in a new time and place constitute a proper object of enquiry.

Pope remarks in his prefatory note to Ælfric's sermon *Nativitas Domini*, which discusses the opening verses of John, that Ælfric 'begins his own exegesis of the gospel with explicit mention of Augustine, "se wisa and se wordsnotera bisceop", the expositor of John *par excellence* by whom, directly or indirectly, he is more profoundly affected in these homilies than by any other, even Bede' (p. 195).[9] That profound influence may be discerned in all of Ælfric's writings. It is no exaggeration to say that almost all the ideas contained within Ælfric's sermons are to be found in Augustine, who was either their originator or their refiner. Augustine is the direct source of much of what Ælfric teaches, and, additionally, Pope identifies many points at which Ælfric turns from a commentator, whose work derives from Augustine, to Augustine himself (see, for example, p. 305). Equally importantly, Ælfric is the inheritor of a set of ideas which are recognizably Augustine's. In his own way, he is also the developer, nourisher and disseminator of these ideas, as Gregory the Great, Bede, Alcuin, Haymo and Smaragdus had been before him. The new life which Ælfric gives to them is appropriate to his own time and place. Milton McC. Gatch rightly draws attention to the way in which new circumstances reshape the original ideas: 'It has not always been understood

---

9. Augustine, 'the wise and eloquent bishop': Pope I. 55.

by those who have commented on Anglo-Saxon theology that, derivative though it may be, any body of thought is unique by virtue of the historical moment in which it was produced and by which it was conditioned'.[10] This uniqueness makes Ælfric's theology worth examining for its own sake, as well as for what it may have to say about the understanding and dissemination of Augustine's ideas.

The way in which Ælfric represents Augustine's teaching can vary considerably from one doctrine to another, depending on a number of factors. Yet it is generally true to say that his teaching fits into the Augustinian tradition, broadly perceived, and is heightened by direct reference to Augustine himself. Both his acceptance of the tradition and his use of pertinent illustration or embellishment from Augustine lend an air of authority to Ælfric's sermons. He is confidently secure in their orthodoxy, convinced that the doctrine he is passing on is precisely the kind which will guarantee safety on the day of judgement. This teaching is secure without being unadventurous or uninspired, and Ælfric's direct recourse to some of Augustine's most startling insights contributes to the sense that these are not such basic sermons after all. Repeatedly, they turn to a sacramental understanding of the church and its participation in the life of Christ. Most strikingly, they recognize the importance of the individual as a member of 'the body of Christ', each of whom takes part in and partakes of the mystery of Christ. Ælfric's theology is one which strives to offer, explain and strengthen exactly this participation for even the meanest of God's servants.

My purpose in examining Ælfric's teaching in comparison with Augustine's is not to offer a source study. It is rather to take one body of thought and compare it, in depth as well as in detail, with another; to explore the generic relationship between the two, which may be at least as important or interesting as an exact correspondence. In making this comparison, I do not mean to imply that Ælfric ever saw a copy of *Confessiones* or *De trinitate*, for example. I wish only to suggest the importance of Augustinian teaching as the foundation of Ælfric's theology and, incidentally, to accord Ælfric the status he deserves as a theologian.

In *The Monastic Order in England* Dom David Knowles gives an account of the achievement of Dunstan, Æðelwold and Oswald, Ælfric's forerunners in the task of religious education in England. In restoring to England the life and devotion of the Benedictine Rule,

---

10. Milton McC. Gatch, *Preaching and Theology in Anglo-Saxon England: Ælfric and Wulfstan* (Toronto, 1977), p. 64.

they gave 'to Englishmen what they had almost wholly lacked for more than a century, an ordered scheme, based on the soundest traditions of the past, for a life devoted to the service of God. They gave this in an epoch which for the rest of Europe was very dark, and almost a century before the Gregorian reform and the intellectual renaissance began to transform the Western Church'.[11] It was in this framework that Ælfric's teaching found a place, extending the knowledge of God beyond the confines of the monastery to the ordinary people. Knowles' description of him is generous and respectful, comparing him with Bede: 'In his diligent absorption of the inheritance of the past, in the sobriety and breadth of his teaching, in his responsiveness to all calls made upon him, in his strong national feeling and in the quiet life passed within the walls of a monastery, he inevitably recalls his great forerunner, and is, when all his gifts are taken into the reckoning, one of the most distinguished figures in the history of Western theological learning in the centuries immediately before the renaissance of the eleventh century' (p. 63).

Both the respect inspired here by Ælfric's achievement and the affection evidently awakened by the man himself are also pervasive within Milton McC. Gatch's work on Ælfric. He takes seriously Ælfric's standing as a theological teacher, and, in *Preaching and Theology in Anglo-Saxon England*, looks not merely at the historical and literary context of Ælfric's work (particularly in relation to preaching customs on the continent) but also at its theological content. He concentrates on the eschatological teaching of Ælfric and Wulfstan, deliberately selecting only part of the 'Theology' of the title. The book is important, not least for its recognition that Ælfric's theology merits proper study.

Preaching and Theology provides detailed summaries of those sermons in which Ælfric's theme is eschatological. For each, Gatch gives a very close account of the text, drawing attention to individual ideas and their expression. Where he discusses Ælfric's source, however, it is Ælfric's immediate source he has in mind (usually Julian of Toledo, or rather the 'Boulogne Excerpts', a collection of passages taken from Julian's *Prognosticon futuri sæculi*). The account of Ælfric's teaching on eschatology given below seeks instead to make that comparison not with Julian's text, at one remove from Ælfric, but with the ideas which

---

11. David Knowles, *The Monastic Order in England: a history of its development from the times of St Dunstan to the Fourth Lateran Council, 940-1216*, second edition (Cambridge, 1963, reprinted 1966), p. 48.

informed both of these teachers, and which are to be found in Augustine. As Gatch suggests, Ælfric's interests, generated by his time and place, make of his source material a new and unique body of teaching. Augustine provides the basis for much later exploration of the ideas of hell, a place of purgatory, and heaven itself, and it is essentially his vision which permits Ælfric to speak with such assurance. As with all his theology, he makes Augustinian doctrine his own.

I seek to give to the whole of Ælfric's theology serious attention, following the leads offered by Knowles and Gatch. The 'boclice lar' offered by Ælfric for the strengthening of the people is examined below under four main headings, corresponding to the principal preoccupations of Ælfric's sermons: the doctrine of God, grace, the church and sacraments, death and judgement. Books are the source of the education necessary, while the grace of God, which may be depended upon for necessary help, supplies the proper conditions for learning, the will to understand and the desire to respond. Ælfric's understanding of grace colours all his other teaching. In all cases, he is guided by a belief in the supreme power of God's mercy, the source of all divine interaction with creation. This belief insists that grace, rather than judgement, determines God's relationship with mankind.

Plate 1

'The Quinity of Winchester'
London, British Library MS Cotton Titus D XXVII, folio 75v.

Reproduced by permission of the British Library.

2

THE DOCTRINE OF GOD

When he composed his sermons, Ælfric must have considered his audience to have a reliable grounding in the Christian faith, on which he felt confident he could build. His preface to the *Catholic Homilies* indicates that there are certain errors and misunderstandings to be combatted; but his primary concern is not to convert, but to strengthen faith. He provides a sound orthodoxy which may serve as a refuge in times of challenge and difficulty. His teaching on the doctrine of God is basic but presupposes an understanding of the concept of one God. Ælfric shows a particular interest in the idea of trinity, for which he offers a number of simple analogies.

As well as offering an orthodox doctrine of God, Ælfric also has observations to make about paganism, idolatry and heresy. Paganism causes him little anxiety: it is a spent force manifested mainly in the entrenched (and possibly unthinking) superstitions of the ill-educated. In *De falsis diis* (Pope XXI) the gods of the Danes (and their classical counterparts) are dismissed with no sense of dread that paganism may revive. Apparently it represents no threat to the church. Wulfstan also offers a critical appraisal of the ancient gods (Bethurum XII).[1] He and Ælfric are triumphant rather than fearful: the histories of pagan gods merely underline the folly of those who worshipped them, for the wise worshippers of the true God are directly contrasted with the foolish pagans of the past. Like Ælfric, Wulfstan has plenty to say about the 'hæðendom' ('heathenism') of superstition but again this represents folly rather than danger.

Ælfric's sermons are not without significant reference to idolatry, however. He distinguishes two kinds of idolatry or devil worship: one is literal, the other metaphorical. Literal idolatry, he warns, will characterize the last days, and will be personified in Antichrist: he will appropriate the worship due to God and will deceive apparently true followers of Christ (Pope XVIII. 296-99). The predicted power of Antichrist is viewed with proper fear, for it will signify a fundamental retrogression to heathenism. However, although Ælfric often speaks of the proximity of the last days, Antichrist's idolatry is still a future problem. The

---

1. Dorothy Bethurum, editor, *The Homilies of Wulfstan*, corrected reprint of 1957 edition (Oxford, 1971).

11

idolatry which is the object of Ælfric's campaign is the 'devil-worship' implied by sin. For Ælfric it is essentially insulting to God, a negative rejection of the true God rather than a positive choice for some other divine power. Paul includes idolatry in a list of the works of the flesh, among which are to be found adultery, witchcraft, heresy and drunkenness (Galatians 5. 19-21), and Ælfric explains that idolatry, the rejection of Christianity, dishonours the Creator. But he suggests that there is a still more insidious idolatry which equally, by implication, dishonours the Creator:

> Oðer deofolgild is derigendlic þære sawle.
>
> ðonne se man forsihð his scyppendes beboda.
>
> and þa sceandlican leahtras begæð. þe se sceocca hine lærð. (Skeat XVII. lines 49-51)[2]

A second pagan practice is injurious to the soul: then the man despises his creator's commands, and practises the shameful sins which the evil spirit teaches him.

He contrasts with these 'sceandlican leahtras' the virtues of the man who truly seeks to please God, the fruits of the Spirit dwelling within him.

If real idolatry is a problem of the past and the future, the present is not without its superstitions. Ælfric advises that all superstitious practices, innocuous as they seem, are in reality deeply harmful, and should be eschewed. If Christians seek protection, they may pray or cross themselves (Skeat XVII. 67-99). Consulting witches for prophecy or advice may produce apparent success, for they draw on the devil's wide knowledge of the world. But their advice always ends in disaster (108-23). As Ælfric proceeds, looking at practices which are identifiably non-Christian, in each case he provides an alternative Christian habit to be cultivated. The sign of the cross is a specially potent protection: Ælfric calls it 'ure sige-beacn ongean þone sceoccan' ('our victory-sign against the devil', line 147).

---

2. W.W. Skeat, editor, *Ælfric's Lives of Saints: being a set of sermons on saints' days formerly observed by the English Church, edited from British Museum Cott. MS Julius E.vii with variants from other manuscripts*, EETS, 76, 82, 94, 114, 4 vols (London, 1881-90); reprinted as 2 vols (London, 1966). For the lines quoted here compare Pope XXX. 25-28.

Ælfric's unexpectedly detailed discussion of superstitious practices, even taking into account the preoccupations of his source, Caesarius, serves as a reminder that in these aberrations from acceptable behaviour were the vestiges of paganism. The superstition Ælfric meets is mostly harmless, but even in subconscious repetition these habits always imply the danger of becoming estranged from God. In this lies the reality of idolatry.

In addition to his condemnation of idolatry Ælfric speaks of heresy and error. He condemns the heretics of the past (such as Arius) and the mistaken or credulous people of the present (such as those who read too much into stories about Mary) in the same terms: he uses 'gedwola' or 'gedwolman' for both. Thus it is difficult to tell whether he regards some of his erroneous contemporaries as heretics in the true sense of the word. It has been suggested that the mediæval church condemned heresy out of habit, lacking contemporary experience of it but continuing to believe that it was the devil's work.[3]

Certainly Ælfric's sermons support this view. 'Gedwola', apparently, may describe anyone whose beliefs and practices are eccentric. Nevertheless, there is no doubt that Ælfric is sufficiently worried by eccentricity to work hard to correct it. He directs his energies against the non-standard, the fanciful, the excessive, the superstitious, and perhaps the truly erroneous. But he is confident that the orthodox doctrine of God is no less wonderful than the fanciful would have it, and he is securely upheld by the authority of the church. That authority is enhanced, moreover, by setting truth against the heresies and errors of the past, which, like the old paganism, may serve to delineate more clearly the worship of the true God.

Ælfric teaches that the true God is the creator and preserver of the empirical universe. Creation is the foundation of the knowledge of God's nature available to the mind, and as he sees it, creation declares God's unity and trinity. Ælfric allows no misconceptions to cloud the clear picture of one God; at the same time he directs the faithful to a discovery of the three persons of the trinity within their own experience.

In Ælfric's doctrine of God, God as the essence or origin of all life is simply affirmed. He understands the substantial unity of the three-personed God, and uses Augustine's concept of relation to speak of God without subordination of one person to another. Like Augustine, he looks first at the unity of God before exploring the personal mystery of the trinity, guided

---

3. M.D. Lambert, *Mediæval Heresy: popular movements from Bogomil to Hus* (London, 1977), p. 10.

by Augustine's images from the created world, which culminate in the image of the trinity in the soul. Ælfric's Christology, like Augustine's, asserts the perfect union of God and man in Christ. Because of this union he insists on the elevation of humanity to the Godhead by the incarnation and resurrection of Christ, and thus centres his attention on the redemptive life and death of the Son. Reproducing the Augustinian formula he declares that the Spirit proceeds from both the Father and the Son and that as he is the personal love expressed between them, uniting them, so also he unites the believer with God in love.

Ælfric seeks to introduce the Christian to a relationship with God as trinity, looking to God as Father and exploring the implications of sonship; recognizing the Son as brother and Lord; enjoying the indwelling love of the Holy Spirit. Nevertheless, by far the greatest devotional attention is given to the person of the Son, the divine agent of creation and of recreation. The Son's gracious redemptive work, not only in restoring humanity to a lost knowledge of God but also in offering a true communion with God, is at the centre of Ælfric's teaching.

I. THE KNOWLEDGE OF GOD

For Augustine, knowledge of God begins with creation, in which the creator is immanent as the omnipotent, omnipresent, sustaining life-force. All things have their being in him:

> sic est Deus per cuncta diffusus, ut non sit qualitas mundi; sed substantia creatrix mundi, sine laborare regens, et sine onere continens mundum . . . in solo coelo totus, et in sola terra totus, et in coelo et in terra totus, et nullo contentus loco, sed in seipso ubique totus. (*Epistula* CLXXXVII.iv.14)

> Yet God so permeates all things as to be not a quality of the world, but the very creative substance of the world, ruling the world without labor, sustaining it without effort . . . wholly in heaven alone and wholly in the earth alone, and wholly in heaven and earth together; not confined in any place, but wholly in Himself everywhere.[4]

---

4. Quoted in the translation by Sister Wilfred Parsons.

The creator is different from all created things, for in him resides the being or essence which is bestowed in the act of creation. He cannot be defined: the statement 'God is' is already complete, and needs no concluding definition, for in God is all that can possibly be expressed by the verb 'esse'. God is being itself (*De trinitate* V.ii.3. line 13). His continued provision of being for his creatures is necessary; their preservation is thus a continuation of the creative impetus. The absence of God's provision of being would mean that creation would tend to non-being, to nothingness. God is never other than creator in his sustaining activity:

> Neque enim, sicut structor aedium, cum fabricauit, abscedit, atque illo cessante atque abscendente stat opus eius, ita mundus uel ictu oculi stare potuit, si ei Deus regimen sui subtraxerit. (*De Genesi ad litteram* IV.xii.22)

> When a builder puts up a house and departs, his work remains in spite of the fact that he is no longer there. But the universe will pass away in the twinkling of an eye if God withdraws His ruling hand.[5]

This is the nature of God as Ælfric also describes it.

The divine and unfathomable Origin is approached preeminently in his act of creation, in which his nature begins to be revealed. Ælfric affirms that God is eternal: only on one occasion does he envisage a time when there was no creation to manifest his glory and power (Crawford 34-43).[6] Such a time is foreign to the imagination, and it is the creating God that the creature recognizes:

> An Scyppend is ealra ðinga, gesewenlicra and ungesewenlicra; and we sceolon on hine gelyfan, forðon ðe he is soð God and ana Ælmihtig, seðe næfre ne ongann ne anginn

---

5. Quoted in the translation by John Hammond Taylor.

6. S.J. Crawford, editor, *Ælfric's Exameron Anglice; or, The Old English Hexameron*, Bibliothek der angelsächsischen Prosa, 10 (Hamburg, 1921). For this point, compare Augustine, *De civitate Dei* XII.xv.

næfde; ac he sylf is anginn, and he eallum gesceaftum anginn and ordfruman forgeaf, þæt hi beon mihton. (Thorpe XX. p. 274. lines 8-12)[7]

There is one creator of all things, visible and invisible, and we must believe in him, for he is true God and he alone is almighty, he who never began nor had beginning, but he himself is Origin, and he gave beginning and origin to all created things, that they might exist.

The unoriginate nature of God distinguishes him from his creatures, all of which recognize a moment when they came into existence. God's divinity is seen in his uncreatedness:

He wæs æfre, and æfre he bið þurhwunigende on him sylfum and þurh hine sylfne. Gif he ongunne and anginn hæfde, butan tweon ne mihte he beon Ælmihtig God; soðlice þæt gesceaft ðe ongann and gesceapen is, næfð nane godcundnysse; forði ælc edwist þætte God nys, þæt is gesceaft; and þæt þe gesceaft nis, þæt is God. (p. 276. lines 17-22)[8]

He was ever, and he ever continues to remain in himself and through himself. If he had begun and had beginning, without doubt he could not be almighty God; truly the created thing which began and is created has no divinity, for every substance which is not God, is a created thing, and that which is not a created thing, is God.

This is the eternal, holy Lord, never changing, undiminished by time or labour, one immutable truth. God's self-sustaining nature is the highest being, the essence, of whom all things have their being (Thorpe XIX. p. 262. 13-14).

The name 'I am' expresses God's eternality of being (Exodus 3. 14). He is the entirely self-contained life-force to whom all time is present and changeless:

---

7. Compare Thorpe I. p. 8. 1-4 and p. 14. 27-34; XXXI. p. 458. 33-34 and p. 474. 6-9; Godden XII. 260-67; XXIX. 47-50; Pope XI. 276-77; XIa. 1-3, 44-47 and 197-98; Skeat I. 10-19, 31-33 and 62-64; XVI. 1-3; Crawford 49-57 and 379-86.

8. Compare Thorpe XV. p. 228. 27-8; XX. p. 284. 5-7; Skeat I. 64-69; and in Augustine, *De trinitate* I.vi.9. 16-19.

Ne cwæð se hælend. ær ðan ðe abraham wære ic wæs. ac he cwæð. ær ðan þe abraham gewurde. Ic eom; Þæt word belimpð synderlice to gode anum. Ic eom. for ðan ðe he is ana butan anginne. and ende. (Godden XIII. lines 210-13)[9]

The Saviour did not say, 'Before Abraham could be, I was', but he said, 'Before Abraham could come to be, I am'. That utterance, 'I am', pertains exclusively to God alone, for he alone is without beginning and end.

Ælfric counters any proto-existential murmurings by referring the name 'I am' to the existence which is proper only to God, for the created thing's existence is derivative. It lacks the self-determination of the Godhead. God alone is 'þurh hine sylfne wunigende' ('existing through himself', line 218).[10]

Pelikan describes Exodus 3. 14 as 'the proof text for the ontological absoluteness of God'.[11] Augustine uses it as such in his discussion of 'essence'. He first aligns his teaching with the orthodoxy established by the oecumenical councils, which is that God is one 'ousia', translated into Latin as 'substantia' or 'essentia'.[12] Essence is understood as the infinite possession and expression of the quality of being, and in the name 'I am' Augustine finds God's just claim to exactly this perfection of being:

Sicut enim ab eo quod est sapere dicta est sapientia et ab eo quod est scire dicta est scientia, ita ab eo quod est esse dicta est essentia. Et quis magis est quam ille qui dixit famulo suo, 'Ego sum qui sum.' (*De trinitate* V.ii.3. lines 2-6)

---

9. I refer to these lines again on pages 54 and 58. Compare Augustine, *In Ioannis Evangelium tractatus* XLIII.17, which may be a direct source for this passage.

10. Compare Thorpe XXVI. p. 366. 32-33; Godden XXXIV. 331-32; Pope XXI. 674-75.

11. Jaroslav Pelikan, *The Christian Tradition*, volume III, *The Growth of Medieval Theology 600-1300* (Chicago, 1978), pp. 110-11.

12. Augustine decides in *De trinitate* VII.v.10 that 'essentia' is more appropriate than 'substantia' in speaking of God, since 'essentia' is expressive of an unchanging nature.

For just as wisdom is so called from being wise, and knowledge is so called from knowing, so essence is so called from being. And who possesses being in a higher degree than He, who said to His servant Moses: 'I am who am.'[13]

The essence of God is also expressed in his goodness: the creator is the supreme good, from which all goodness is derived. Ælfric comments:

soðlice nis nan ðing god butan Gode anum. Gif ænig gesceaft is god, þonne is seo godnys of ðam Scyppende, seðe is healice god. (Thorpe XVII. p. 238. lines 8-10)[14]

truly nothing is good excepting God alone. If any created thing is good, then its goodness is derived from the creator, who is supremely good.

Here Ælfric asserts not merely that God alone is good. He is also saying that God the creator is the source of all goodness. God's essential goodness is expressed in his work of creation, which is therefore a revelation of the mind of God. Without creation God's goodness would have remained unknown. Ælfric also suggests that it is as a part of God's expression of his goodness that the created thing itself is good: created by the Good, it thus partakes of his goodness. That man as a creature has this basic God-derived goodness is fundamental to his doctrine of man. With Augustine he insists that humanity is good, in spite of the fact that it has been spoiled by original sin. Even sin cannot take away the goodness inherent in creation.

Satisfied to attribute supreme goodness to God, Ælfric does not explain how the mind may grasp this concept, but it is extensively discussed by Augustine. In *De trinitate* he speaks first of the mind's difficulty in understanding the nature of God. Materialistic images crowd in, and must be rejected. It is impossible to understand God simply by magnifying or multiplying all things known to the mind, but rather the mind must grasp the truth at the heart of these things. The mind's materialism may seek almost immediately to constrain and define exactly what that truth is, to examine and possess it, but Augustine says that the flash of

---

13. Quoted in the translation by Stephen McKenna.

14. Compare Thorpe XVII. p. 238. 15-19; XVIII. p. 254. 8-9; Godden XXIX. 50-51; Skeat I. 88-90.

illumination which in its first purity is bestowed on the mind by the word 'truth' is what it must cling to:

> Ecce in ipso primo ictu qua uelut coruscatione perstringeris cum dicitur ueritas mane si potes. (*De trinitate* VIII.ii.3. lines 35-37)

> See, remain in that first flash in which you were dazzled as it were by its brightness, when it was said to you 'Truth'. Remain in it, if you can.

But it is not possible to maintain the flash of illumination with any permanence. So instead Augustine offers another route to an understanding of God through the nature of goodness. Goodness in anything inspires admiration and love, and a great number of examples come immediately to mind. But once they are represented in thought, Augustine asks for the things themselves to be set aside, and their inherent goodness to be separated and revealed. A glimpse of the source of all goodness is the reward of this effort:

> Bonum hoc et bonum illud. Tolle hoc et illud, et uide ipsum bonum, si potes; ita Deum uidebis, non alio bono bonum, sed bonum omnis boni. (VIII.iii.4. lines 15-17)

> This good and that good; take away this and that, and see good itself if you can; so you will see God who is good not by another good, but is the good of every good.

This course of inquiry is extremely fruitful for Augustine: such a glimpse inspires love for this good, the establishment of faith, and the building up of the Christian's relationship with God. Ælfric merely notes that this is a way of describing God, in whom is found the quintessence of goodness, approached not by multiplying together all known goods but by finding a principle of goodness in which all good things participate. Philosophy's account of God's essence is of the greatest interest where it is realizable in human experience. Beyond this it is only in the context of praise and worship that deeper penetration to the essence of God — his aseity, eternity, unity and trinity — is desired and achieved, and these glimpses of God's nature are especially located in the countless doxologies in the sermons.

These elemental expressions can be greatly persuasive in the context of prayerful worship, in which the act of praise may free itself of human limitations. Ælfric's *De falsis diis*, the sermon which dismantles the hierarchy of the heathen gods, opens with a triumphant proclamation of the worship of the true God. The splendid, rhythmic Latin of Ephesians 4. 5-6 and Romans 11. 36 is translated with declamatory force:

> Eala ge gebroðra ða leofostan, þæt godcunde gewrit us tæhte þone biggeng anes soðes Godes, þisum wordum cweþende: An Drihten is, and an geleafa, and an fulluht; an God and Fæder ealra þinga, se ðe is ofer ealle þing, and þurh ealle þing, and on us eallum. Of þam synd ealle þing, and þurh þone synd ealle þing, and on þam synd ealle þing; sy him wuldor a to worulde, amen. (Pope XXI. lines 6-11)[15]

> O ye dearest brothers, holy scripture has taught us the worship of one true God, speaking in these words: There is one Lord, one faith, and one baptism; one God and Father of all things, who is above all things, and throughout all things, and in us all. All things are from him, all things are by him, and all things are in him; to him be glory for ever and ever, amen.

Such incantatory and all-encompassing language is peculiarly powerful in its capacity not only to extol the known, but also to point beyond it to a God who is above all imagining. God's power, eternal reign and glory are repeatedly extolled, as they are here, in closing doxologies, which praise God in trinity and unity.[16] Doxology may allow a deeper penetration of the mystery of God, but does so by deepening faith rather than knowledge. A developing understanding of God's control of creation, the pre-eminent witness to his power in daily experience, is a readily accessible route to knowledge of God.

In his early works Augustine places considerably less emphasis on the whole creation as a means of revelation: rather, he is confident in the power of reason to come to a knowledge of God. In *De ordine* he explores the search of the reasoning mind for an understanding of God's created world, in which it draws ever closer to God's own understanding of it,

---

15. Compare Augustine in *De vera religione* lv.113 and *De doctrina Christiana* I.v.5 (Pope, *Homilies*, 713).

16. Compare, among many examples: Thorpe II. p. 44. 4-6; XXV. p. 364. 5-9; XXXIII. p. 500. 26-29; Godden I. 299-303; XIV. 354-56; Pope XI. 572-74.

eventually achieving 'an identity of content with the divine Understanding'.[17] That this identity is at best only rarely achieved is finally acknowledged by Augustine (*De civitate Dei* XI.ii). This points him towards humanity's need of a Mediator, to enable the desired communion with the divine. But first, creation has much to teach the attentive mind about the nature of God, especially in providing images of the divine trinity, and may serve to guide the seeker to a welcoming acceptance of the Mediator. So also in Ælfric there is found a series of stages leading the mind from awe to worship. It learns of the forbidding exclusiveness of God's otherness, and then that God welcomes not merely the worship but also the love of his created subjects.

God is seen at work in his creation: its magnitude speaks of his greatness. He has perfect knowledge of all aspects of creation hidden to human eyes; his effortless control of the entire system speaks of his immeasurable power:

> He hylt mid his mihte heofonas and eorðan, and ealle gesceafta butan geswince, and he besceawað þa niwelnyssa þe under þyssere eorðan sind. He awecð ealle duna mid anre handa, and ne mæg nan þing his willan wiðstandan. (Thorpe I. p. 8. line 5-p. 10. line 1)[18]

> He sustains with his power heavens and earth and all created things, without toil, and he looks upon the depths which are beneath this earth. He raises all hills with one hand, and nothing can oppose his will.

The intimacy with which the life of God and the life of his creation are bound together is praised by Augustine. In this infusion of God's presence, sustaining and developing his gift of life, his creation may be differentiated from something made by an earthly craftsman. For the carpenter may make his cabinet, and set it in another place: it does not require his continued presence in order that it may exist. The world, however, is God's place, defined by his shaping power and suffused with the maker's own Spirit:

---

17. E. TeSelle, *Augustine the Theologian* (London, 1970), p. 87.

18. Compare Godden XXIII. 144-46; Pope XI. 79-80; XIa. 195-96; XXI. 91-98 and 664-66; Skeat I. 41-44; XVI. 117; Crawford 173-80.

Praesentia maiestatis facit, quod facit; praesentia sua gubernat, quod fecit. (*In Ioannis Evangelium tractatus* II.10. lines 11-12)

By the presence of his majesty he makes what he makes; by his presence he governs what he has made.[19]

The controlling God indwells his creation, unlimited by any constraints or laws, yet imposing the necessary order on the created world. Creation exhibits the orders of measure, number and weight, constraints of which the increate God is free:

He is butan gemete, forðy he is æghwær. He is butan getele, forðon ðe he is æfre. He is butan hefe, forðon þe he hylt ealle gesceafta butan geswince; and he hi ealle gelogode on þam ðrim ðingum, þæt is on gemete, and on getele, and on hefe. (Thorpe XX. p. 286. lines 10-15)[20]

He is without measure, for he is everywhere. He is without number, for he is always. He is without weight, for he sustains all created things without toil; and he disposed all of them according to these three properties, that is, in measure, number and weight.

God is immanent in his creation, intimately involved in its life, and yet he remains separate from it. He is Lord, and yet it is due to his careful sustaining that creation continues to exist. In a very profound sense, therefore, God is very close, yet to human perception such all-pervading power must render him immensely distant. This means that God is only imperfectly accessible to his creatures: even the angels, who are closest to him, cannot know him completely (Thorpe I. p. 10. 2-5).[21] If the angels cannot know God perfectly, then the constraints of mortality are likely to be great impediments to human understanding of the immortal; human words must fail in speaking of God, who is beyond understanding:

---

19. Quoted in the translation by John W. Rettig.

20. Compare Pope I. 177-78; in Augustine, for example *De trinitate* XI.xi.18.

21. Compare Skeat I. 32-33.

We sprecað ymbe God, deaðlice be Undeaðlicum, tyddre be Ælmihtigum, earmingas be Mildheortum; ac hwa mæg weorðfullice sprecan be ðam ðe is unasecgendlic? (Thorpe XX. p. 286. lines 8-10)

We speak about God, the mortal of the Immortal, the weak of the Almighty, wretched ones of the Merciful; but who can speak worthily of that which is unspeakable?

It is in the witness of creation that human vision finds confirmation of the vast difference between the creator and the created thing. The mind is moved to praise, yet can give only inadequate expression to what it perceives, leaving unspoken countless things beyond its comprehension (15-22).[22]

Creation is itself a potent witness to the reality of God: a proof, where it is needed, of his existence. Even in communities where the faith has never been taught, creation declares the presence of God:

þæt hi mihton tocnawan þone ælmihtigan God
þurh þa gesceafta þe he gesceop on worulde,
þæt he is ana to wurðigenne þe geworhte ealle þing. (Pope XX. lines 413-15)[23]

that they might discern the almighty God through the created things which he has made in the world, that he who created all things is alone to be worshipped.

So it is as creator that God is distinguished as worthy of worship. No creature may receive worship, for this is idolatry, but God alone is worthy of this offering (Thorpe XI. p. 174. 4-9).[24] In the Hexameron, such worship is seen as the purpose of creation. In creating the world, God has provided both a manifestation of his own lordship and the means of his eternal glorification:

---

22. Compare Augustine in *In Ioannis Evangelium tractatus* I.9.

23. Compare Augustine in *De civitate Dei* XI.iv. 22-26.

24. Compare Godden XII. 265-67; Pope XX. 33-37.

wæs æfre æt fruman on his ecum ræde

ðæt he wolde gewyrcan ealle ðas woruld

and ealne middaneard mid his agenre mihte

him sylfum to lofe. (Crawford lines 389-92)[25]

at the beginning it was always in his eternal purpose that he would make all this world and all the earth by his own power to his own glory.

Ælfric places humanity in the context of a glorifying creation: in worship its potential is realized. Implicit here is the belief that God wishes to be known by his creation, and that he seeks a relationship with each person. Nevertheless, the division perceived between God and his creation suggests that however successfully mankind realizes its potential in worship, the step towards true communion with God must be a very great one, necessitating some kind of concession or condescension on the part of God. Direct revelation is the full completion of what creation only begins to make known.

The Old Testament records occasions when God approached his people directly, rather than speaking through his creation. Addressing individual human minds, God showed his desire to be personally and intimately involved with the Jewish people. God spoke, admonished, guided, promised: above all, he made covenants with his people. The covenants had immediate reference to the historical community, but also looked forward to a fuller realization in Christ. The promise to Abraham of blessing for himself and his descendants (Genesis 22. 17-18) is made universal in its fulfilment in the birth of Jesus, descended from Abraham through David and Mary (Matthew 1. 1-16), and through whom all the faithful are blessed (Galatians 3. 29).[26] This blessing rests upon the spiritual heirs of Abraham after the institution of the new relationship with God in Christ, the new covenant with his people:

Ne synd we na Abrahames cynnes flæsclice, ac gastlice, swa swa se apostol Paulus cwæð, 'Witodlice, gif ge cristene synd, þonne beo ge Abrahames ofspring, and yrfenuman æfter behate.' Þæt æftermyste word is ðises lofsanges, 'On worulda;' forðan

---

25. Compare Crawford 42-46 and 162-64.

26. Thorpe VI. p. 90. 15-19 and p. 92. 24-29; XIII. p. 204. 17-21; Godden IV. 154-60; XIII. 196-99.

ðe ure behat, þe us God behet, ðurhwunað a on worulda woruld butan ende. (Thorpe XIII. p. 204. lines 21-27)[27]

We are not physically of Abraham's race, but spiritually. As the apostle Paul said, 'Truly, if you are Christians, then are you the offspring of Abraham, and inheritors according to the covenant.' The last word of this song of praise is 'for ever', for our promise, which God has promised us, will last eternally for ever, world without end.

The new covenant is made possible by the mediation of the humanity of Christ, whose redemptive work is effectively a recreation of the community of God, a second work of creation. In Ælfric's glorification of God the creator he does not fail to make clear the trinitarian dispensation of that work in which the agent of creative impetus is the Word of God. Creation through the Son thus prefigures the recreation through the Son which is necessary after the first creation has been spoiled. In each case, therefore, God makes himself known to humanity through the medium of his Son, who acts as the channel of power.

II. THE TRINITY

The concept of trinity is the subject of a long discussion by Ælfric in his sermon *De fide Catholica*. Not so much an exposition of the faith as an essay exploring one particular aspect of it, its real subject is the nature of the trinity. Perhaps in Ælfric's experience this was the most difficult concept for people to grasp, for the sermon offers many different ways of approaching the mystery.

Trinity for Ælfric is no merely intellectual concept: it is real and living. This is quite different from the purely formulaic approach made by other Old English homilists. Ælfric's treatment of the doctrine is unique for its time and place. It must be admitted that Ælfric's account of the doctrine of the trinity, when compared with the minutely exhaustive and philosophically demanding exposition of Augustine, is disappointing in its brevity. He also compounds image upon image in his sermon on the trinity, which might suggest anything

---

27. Compare Godden IV. 173-78; and in Augustine, *In Ioannis Evangelium tractatus* CXVIII.5.

from fascination to desperation. However, when Ælfric's writing on the trinity is compared with that of other Old English homilies, it is clear that he went to far greater trouble than anyone else to teach this doctrine in a coherent and lively form. The Vercelli Homilist, for example, offers a single analogy (with no discussion) to help with this difficult concept (Szarmach XVI. 120-26).[28] The doctrine is virtually absent from the Blickling collection, in which even trinitarian doxology is rare (occurring only at the end of XV and XIX).[29] Wulfstan's sermon *De fide Catholica*, a short exposition of the whole creed, devotes just a few lines to the doctrine of the trinity (Bethurum VII. 29-33).[30] He gives no analogical explanations, using a trinitarian doxology only once, at the close of a Latin sermon (Bethurum Xb. 152-54).

Ælfric the teacher is concerned to expound the concept of the trinity. Often, too, it is in the context of discussion concerning the trinity that the question of heresy is raised. Again, among the Old English homilists Ælfric is alone in showing any interest in heresy. Wulfstan, preoccupied with Christian practice rather than doctrine, does not discuss it, although any real threat of heresy or schism would certainly have been noted as further evidence of Antichrist's growing influence. No anxieties about heresy disturb the sermons in the Vercelli and Blickling collections.

Heresies concerning the nature of the trinity are mentioned by Ælfric with surprising regularity: Arianism is especially singled out.[31] Ælfric was worried by error, as his prefaces

---

28. Paul Szarmach, editor, *The Vercelli Homilies IX-XXII*, Toronto Old English Series, 5 (Toronto, 1981).

29. R. Morris, editor, *The Blickling Homilies of the Tenth Century*, EETS, 58, 63, 73, 3 vols (London, 1874-80).

30. Compare Bethurum XII. 81-93.

31. Heretics who opposed the Catholic doctrine of the trinity, mentioned by Ælfric are: Arius: Thorpe IV. p. 70. 3-22; VII. p. 116. 15-17; XX. p. 290. 3-24; Pope I. 151-53; X. 159-69; Skeat I. 5-9; XVI. 206-7; Assmann IV. 195-202; Sabellius: Thorpe XX. p. 290. 25-29; Olympius: Pope X. 170-76; Assmann IV. 203-12. Others mentioned are: Manichees: Thorpe VII. p. 116. 17-21; Pope I. 410-12; IV. 276-77; 'the masspriest who said that Christ never ate': Pope V. 230-32 (his identity is not known: Pope suggests he might have been a local heretic, *Homilies*, p. 302).

indicate, but it is not likely that he had to deal with actual heresy. The situation was different for Augustine, who illustrates his experience with the image of the church as a ship steering a course through the hazards of heresy (*In Ioannis Evangelium tractatus* XXXVI.9). Since it is particularly with trinitarian heresy that Ælfric takes issue, it is, of course, possible that he adopted the condemnation of heresy along with information about orthodoxy, without proper consideration of the relevance of such material. But he did not include the quantities of irrelevant material about Donatism or Pelagianism, to be found in contemporary Latin homilies, in spite of his interest in Augustine's teaching on the church, baptism and grace. His references to trinitarian heresies are apparently intended to reinforce the true faith, the false throwing the true into relief. He offers the choice between clear folly on the one hand and logically satisfying truth on the other.

Arius, in particular, may be taken as symbolic of all heresy and all error. His figure appears in this light in a miniature in the New Minster Offices, or Prayer Book of Ælfwine (written for Ælfwine in Winchester, 1023-35).[32] The miniature is known as the 'Quinity of Winchester'. It depicts the divine trinity, joined by Mary who is portrayed holding her child. The Father and Son are seen in conference together, seated in majesty. Beside them the Virgin is crowned but not nimbed. The Holy Spirit, in the form of a nimbed dove, rests on Mary's crown. Mary carries her child, behind whose head is the cross element of the cruciform nimbus worn by the three Persons. Spirit-dove, Mother and Child together form a concise evocation of the doctrine of the incarnation. Beneath the feet of the Son the devil lies in submission, while two notorious men represent human powers conquered by Christ: these are Judas Iscariot and Arius. Judas apparently stands for the Jews, understood by the Anglo-Saxon church to have cut themselves off irrevocably from the mercy of God in their willing embrace of the crucifixion of Jesus (Matthew 27. 25). Judas' presence in the picture speaks of the widening of God's 'chosen people'. In his turn, Arius seems to represent all heretics: all who would in any way deny or belittle the glory expressed in the group portrait above. The superior and triumphant Virgin, by her position above the heretic, simultaneously affirms the humanity of the Child in her arms and identifies him with the Son: not two persons, chronologically distinct, but one. The Virgin's eminence over Arius also makes her the symbol of the church, whose orthodoxy finally conquered the errors of all 'Arians'.

---

32. British Library MS Cotton Titus D XXVII, folio 75v. See plate facing page 11.

Arius seems to serve a similar purpose in Ælfric's homilies. From the perspective of several centuries, Arius appeared to perform the work of the devil in the life of the early church in much the same way as Antichrist was expected to do in the last days. Through the false teachings of Antichrist even the faithful would be deceived and would turn away from faith in the true God; this was the effect of Arius' teaching on the early church.[33] Just as many false prophets were to be subsumed in the person of Antichrist, so 'Arius' could stand for all heresy in its various manifestations but single intent. Heresy is a sign of uncertain ground: it represents dangerously uncharted territory. Arius may serve as a symbol for the folly of those who are wrong about God.

Since it is not necessary to be heretical to be puzzled about God who is both three and one, Ælfric is careful to explain the truth of this doctrine. Always, before opening any discussion on the nature of the trinity, Ælfric begins with the authoritative assertion that God is one. That there is one God is taught by stressing his omnipotence: there cannot be lesser beings possessed of any share in the Godhead without that omnipotence being destroyed. Thus any expression of threeness is referred back to the singularity of almighty God:

> Se God wunað on Ðrynnysse untodæledlic, and on annysse anre Godcundnysse, soðlice oðer is se Fæder, oðer is se Sunu, oðer is se Halga Gast; ac þeah-hwæðere ðæra ðreora is an Godcundnys, and gelic wuldor, and efen-ece mægenðrymnys. (Thorpe XX. p. 276. lines 23-27)[34]

> God exists in indivisible trinity and in the unity of one Divinity; truly one is the Father, one is the Son, one is the Holy Spirit, but yet of these three there is one Divinity, and equal glory, and co-eternal majesty.

---

33. See Jaroslav Pelikan, *The Christian Tradition*, volume I, *The Emergence of the Catholic Tradition (100-600)* (Chicago, 1971), pp. 195-201, for an account of the verbal battles which preceded the statement of faith promulgated by the Council of Nicaea in 325.

34. Compare Thorpe I. p. 10. 7-10; VIII. p. 134. 3-8; IX. p. 150. 15-17; XX. p. 278. 1-6; XXII. p. 324. 16-20 and p. 326. 17-27; XXXIII. p. 500. 3-14; Godden III. 127-29; XIII. 185-89; *De penitentia* p. 604. 21-p. 606. 2; Pope VIII. 194-99; X. 177-80; XI. 85-87; XIa. 216-19; XVIII. 214-16; XXI. 20-24 and 664-66; Skeat I. 31-33. (*De penitentia* is found in the second volume of Thorpe's edition of *Catholic Homilies*.)

Because threeness must not be taken to mean any diminution or fragmentation of power, the omnipotence of the one God in three persons is the next point to be grasped. As though to establish the truth by its very repetition, Ælfric continues:

> Ælmihtig God is se Fæder, Ælmihtig God is se Sunu, Ælmihtig God is se Halga Gast; ac þeah-hwæðere ne sind ðry Ælmihtige Godas, ac an Ælmihtig God. (lines 27-30)

> Almighty God is the Father, almighty God is the Son, almighty God is the Holy Spirit; but nevertheless there are not three almighty Gods, but one almighty God.

These statements are reminiscent of a passage in Augustine's commentary on John, part of a paragraph of highly rhetorical structure containing no explanation of doctrine but only repeated pattern:

> Deus est Pater, Deus est Filius, Deus est Spiritus sanctus; et tamen Pater non est qui Filius, nec Filius est qui Pater, nec Spiritus sanctus Patris et Filii Spiritus aut Pater est aut Filius. Trinitas unus Deus; Trinitas, una aeternitas, una potestas, una maiestas; tres, sed non dii. (*In Ioannis Evangelium tractatus* XXXIX.3. lines 13-18)

> The Father is God, the Son is God, the Holy Spirit is God: and yet He is not the Father who is the Son, nor He the Son who is the Father, and the Holy Spirit, the Spirit of the Father and the Son, is neither the Father nor the Son. The Trinity is one God. The Trinity is one eternity, one power, one majesty; — three, but not (three) Gods.[35]

Later he adds, 'Non tres dii? Non. Non tres omnipotentes? Non.' ('Are They not three Gods? No. Are They not three Almighties? No.' XXXIX.4, line 22).

Ælfric's words bear comparison not only with Augustine but with the *Quicunque vult* as well. Can this also have influenced him? In his history and discussion of the Creed, Kelly shows that by the time of the Carolingian reform it was widely used for teaching clergy and testing their orthodoxy.[36] Unfortunately, he gives no details of its use in the Anglo-Saxon

---

35. Quoted in the translation by James Innes.

36. J.N.D. Kelly, *The Athanasian Creed* (London, 1964), p. 41.

church, and it is not among the creeds and prayers collected by Thorpe at the end of his second volume of homilies.

Kelly points out numerous parallels in the text of the Creed with Augustine's writings, especially from *De trinitate*. A comparison between Ælfric's sermon and the Creed indicates that most of the points at which he is closest to the *Quicunque vult* coincide with verses which closely resemble Augustine, although sometimes the Creed provides an equally close linguistic parallel where the thought is contained in both; there are also instances where similar parallels are available from writers after Augustine. The closest coincidence is between the two passages just quoted from Ælfric's sermon *De fide Catholica* (Thorpe XX. p. 276. 23-27 and 27-30) and these passages in the Creed:

(a) Alia est enim persona Patris, alia Filii, alia Spiritus sancti; sed Patris et Filii et Spiritus sancti una est divinitas, aequalis gloria, coaeterna maiestas. (5-6)

(b) Similiter omnipotens Pater, omnipotens Filius, omnipotens Spiritus sanctus; et tamen non tres omnipotentes, sed unus omnipotens. Ita Deus Pater, deus Filius, deus Spiritus sanctus; et tamen non tres dii, sed unus est deus. (13-16).[37]

(a) For the Father's person is one, the Son's another, the Holy Spirit's another; but the Godhead of the Father, the Son and the Holy Spirit is one, their glory is equal, their majesty coeternal.

(b) In the same way the Father is almighty, the Son almighty, the Holy Spirit almighty; yet there are not three almighties, but one almighty. Thus the Father is God, the Son God, the Holy Spirit God; and yet there are not three Gods, but there is one God.

Either the Creed or Augustine in his commentary on John could have been the model for Ælfric's lines on the triune nature of God. The passages cited by Kelly as parallel texts from Augustine are, I believe, less likely to have been Ælfric's model; neither is as close to the Creed verses as the lines quoted above from the commentary on John.[38]

---

37. References are to the affirmations of the Creed as numbered by Kelly in *The Athanasian Creed*.

38. The passages cited by Kelly are respectively 'Trinitas est, sed una operatio, una maiestas, una æternitas, una coæternitas' ('He is trinity, but one work, one majesty, one eternity,

In contrast with these closely-related passages, there are others in Ælfric which are developments of ideas stated only simply in the Creed, such as the passage which distinguishes the increate creator from the creature (Thorpe XX. p. 276. 17-22); this may be compared with the patterned statement of the Creed (8), part of the section listing the qualities which describe God as unity and as trinity ('increatus Pater', etc.). Some elements which are quite lacking in the *Quicunque vult* repeatedly occur in contexts which otherwise might point to a parallel with the Creed text. For example, the verses on the 'origins' of the Father, Son and Holy Spirit read as follows in the Creed:

> Pater a nullo est factus nec creatus nec genitus. Filius a Patre solo est, non factus nec creatus sed genitus. Spiritus sanctus a Patre et Filio, non factus nec creatus nec genitus sed procedens. (21-23)

> The Father is from none, not made nor created nor begotten. The Son is from the Father alone, not made nor created but begotten. The Holy Spirit is from the Father and the Son, not made nor created nor begotten but proceeding.

This may be compared with Ælfric's treatment of the same article of faith:

> Se is Fæder, seðe nis naðer ne geboren ne gesceapen fram nanum oðrum. Se is Fæder gehaten, forðan ðe he hæfð Sunu, ðone ðe he of him sylfum gestrynde, butan ælcre meder. Se Fæder is God of nanum Gode. Se Sunu is God of ðam Fæder Gode. Se Halga Gast is God forðstæppende of ðam Fæder and of ðam Suna. (Thorpe XX. p. 278. lines 7-13)[39]

---

one co-eternity', *Sermo* CXXVI.viii.10) and 'Itaque omnipotens pater, omnipotens filius, omnipotens spiritus sanctus; nec tamen tres omnipotentes, sed unus omnipotens' ('Therefore the omnipotent Father, the omnipotent Son, and the omnipotent Holy Spirit, yet there are not three omnipotents, but one omnipotent', *De trinitate* V.viii.9, 31-33) (*Creed*, p. 28).

39. I make reference again to this account of the trinity on pages 36 and 47.

He is the Father who is neither born nor created from any other. He is called Father, because he has a Son, who was begotten from himself, without any mother. The Father is God from no God. The Son is God from the Father God. The Holy Spirit is God proceeding from the Father and from the Son.

Where the Creed stresses only the absence of origin for God, Ælfric adds the important defining concept of his relationship with the Son. Here too, as always when discussing the person of the Holy Spirit, he adds that the Spirit is the Will and Love of the Father and Son jointly (p. 280. 8-15). This definition is not offered by the Creed. That the Spirit is Love is taught by Augustine (for example in *De trinitate* XV.xix.37. 133-44), while the concept of the Spirit as Will is part of his trinitarian image of memory, understanding and will, the principal image adopted by Ælfric.

Whilst Ælfric may have known and used the *Quicunque vult* he supplemented it with what he knew of Augustine's teaching. Certainly its anxiety for precision in its affirmation of the trinity is emulated by Ælfric. If, as it seems, he did take a special interest in the nature of the trinity, then this Creed would have provided a precisely-worded account of that nature. Its preoccupation with the nature of the three-personed God, to the relative neglect of other articles of faith, might even have given him licence to preach a sermon 'on the Catholic faith' which was almost exclusively about the trinity.

The faith declares that as a unity the power of the Godhead is manifested, with all attributes of each person in the trinity to be predicated of the one God:

Ælc ðæra þreora is God, þeah-hwæðere hi ealle an God; forðan ðe hi ealle habbað an gecynd, and ane godcundnysse, and ane edwiste, and an geðeaht, and an weorc, and ane mægenðrymnysse, and gelic wuldor, and efen-ece rice. (Thorpe XX. p. 284. lines 17-21)[40]

---

40. Compare Thorpe IX. p. 150. 15-17; XX. p. 278. 1-2 and p. 282. 21-23; XXII. p. 326. 18-21 and 26-27; XXXIII. p. 500. 3-6; Godden III. 125-30; XIII. 187-89; XXII. 130-32 and 170; Pope I. 159-66; IV. 166-72; VI. 247-49 and 266-68; VIII. 194-98; X. 118-19 and 177-80; XI. 78-87; XIa. 17-19; XXI. 20-24; Crawford 70-80.

Each of the three is God, yet they are all one God, for they all have one nature, and one divinity, and one substance, and one purpose, and one work, and one majesty, and equal glory, and co-eternal rule.

According to the truth that only the uncreated may create, the work of creation shared by the three persons confirms that God is one. Each person of the trinity is the uncreated creator. Each exists without the necessity of any creative impetus from another. It is to the triune creator that faith responds:

> . . . we gelyfað on þone lifiendan God,
>
> on ða halgan Þrynnysse, þe heofonas gewylt
>
> and ealle gesceafta, an ælmihtig Scyppend. (Pope XI. lines 78-80)[41]

we believe in the living God, in the holy trinity, who governs the heavens and all created things, one almighty Creator.

The unitary work of the trinity is seen in the particular roles within the act of creation appropriated by each Person. God the Father is understood to be the origin of all things. Christ is the medium of the creative act, the expression of that power:

> Hwæt is se Sunu? He is ðæs Fæder Wisdom, and his Word, and his Miht, þurh ðone se Fæder gesceop ealle ðing and gefadode. (Thorpe XX. p. 278. lines 17-19)[42]

What is the Son? He is the Father's Wisdom, and his Word, and his Power, through whom the Father created all things and set them in order.

---

41. Compare Thorpe I. p. 10. 10-12; Godden XII. 261-67; XXIX. 49-50; Pope XIa. 17 and 194-96; XXI. 28-30.

42. Compare Thorpe I. p. 10. 5-6 and p. 24. 31-32; II. p. 40. 13-14; XIII. p. 192. 2-3; XV. p. 228. 22-23; XXVI. p. 366. 34-35; XXXII. p. 500. 21-22; Godden I. 7-8; III. 123-24; XII. 285-86; XXII. 92-94; *De penitentia* p. 604. 27-88; Pope I. 72-87, 167-76 and 282-83; IV. 150-51; V. 103-4; VI. 243-45; XIa. 1-4, 15-16 and 202-8; XII. 99; XXI. 13-14; Crawford 54-57.

The word is the manifestation of wisdom, the speech which proclaims the truth. The wise Father is eternally in possession of his wisdom, and therefore never without its expression and effect (Thorpe II. p. 40. 6-12).[43] As the Father is never separated from his creating Word, so the Father and the Son are never without the Love which binds them eternally together, and they always possess the Will to effect and complete their creative actions. This mutual Love-Will is the Holy Spirit, present in the Godhead from the beginning. Like the other persons, he may be called 'angin':

> se halga gast is angin. æfre of þam fæder. and of þam sunu. na acenned ac forð-stæppende forðan þe se sunu is þæs fæder wisdom. of him. and mid him. and se halga gast is heora begra wylle. and lufu. of him bam. and mid him bam. (Skeat I. lines 35-38)[44]

> the Holy Spirit is the beginning, eternally from the Father and from the Son, not begotten but proceeding. For the Son is the Wisdom of the Father, from him and with him, and the Holy Spirit is the Will of them both, and their Love, from them both and with them both.

The creating God bestows life on all things through the effecting will of the Holy Spirit, finishing his creative work (Pope XIa. 14-16).[45]

Creation gives active expression to the relations which bind the three persons in unity of substance. The concept of relation was a realistic attempt by Augustine to respond to the

---

43. Compare Thorpe XXV. p. 358. 11-16 and p. 362. 1-3; Pope I. 86-87; X. 67-73; and in Augustine, *In Ioannis Evangelium tractatus* XLII.8.

44. Compare Thorpe XIII. p. 196. 23-24; XX. p. 282. 2-6; XXXIII. p. 498. 31-34 and p. 500. 11; Godden IV. 75-78; XXII. 71-73; *De penitentia* p. 604. 28-31; Pope VI. 240-41; VII. 210-14; IX. 110-13; X. 41-42; XIa. 11-13, 213-15 and 221-22.

45. Compare Thorpe I. p. 10. 6-7; II. p. 40. 14-15; XIII. p. 192. 3-4; XV. p. 228. 23-25; XXVI. p. 366. 35-p. 368. 1; XXXII. p. 500. 22; Godden XII. 287; *De penitentia* p. 604. 31; Pope IV. 154; VI. 245-46; X. 118-19; Crawford 57-59 and 176.

challenge of philosophical concepts and terms seized upon by heretical opponents.[46] An argument employed by Arians to support their case that the Father and the Son were substantially different made use of the claim that no property of God could pertain to accident. Their use of logic clearly offended Augustine: he refers to their 'callidissimum machinamentum' ('very cunning argument', *De trinitate* V.iii.4. lines 4-5). They claimed that if 'begotten' and 'unbegotten' both refer to substance, this 'proves' that the substance of the Father and Son are different because to be begotten is different from being unbegotten.

In *De trinitate* Augustine counters this with his concept of relation. The fatherhood and sonship of the first two persons of the trinity pertain to the mutual relation between the two: they are not called 'Father' and 'Son' according to substance, nor yet according to accident, but these names represent eternal truths which subsist between them and bind them inseparably. Each name has a unique referent, whilst the relation is the sign of unity. The relation between the two, by which one is Father and the other Son, is therefore a quality in itself, being neither substance nor accident,

> quia hoc non secundum substantium dicuntur sed secundum relatiuum, quod tamen relatiuum non est accidens quia non est mutabile. (*De trinitate* V.v.6. lines 20-22)

> The names . . . do not refer to the substance but to the relation, and the relation is no accident because it is not changeable.

The relation also exists between the Holy Spirit and the other two persons, affirming his consubstantiality with them. In this regard it is important that the relation between the Spirit and the Father, and that between the Spirit and the Son, is one and the same relation, not two, affirming Augustine's doctrine of the double procession of the Spirit.[47] Kelly summarizes: 'Thus in relation to the Holy Spirit the Father and the Son form a single principle: inevitably so, since the relation of both to Him is identical, and where there is no difference of relation their operation is inseparable' (*Doctrines*, p. 275).

---

46. For a helpful exposition of this concept, see J.N.D. Kelly, *Early Christian Doctrines*, fifth edition (London, 1977), pp. 274-75.

47. On the 'filioque', see Kelly, *Doctrines*, pp. 275-76.

Translation of Greek terminology into Latin poses problems for Augustine. Although the proper translation of 'mian ousian treis hypostaseis' is 'unam essentiam tres substantias' ('one essence, and three substances', *De trinitate* V.viii.10, lines 45-47), the use of 'substantia' in this context is misleading to the Latin mind; therefore the word 'personas' is to be preferred. Augustine admits that the concept is virtually inexpressible, so that any solution is bound to be inadequate; but, as he remarks, the heretics require a response so the effort must be made. It is necessary to say more than that the members of the trinity are three in one: the question 'In what way are they three?' must be addressed. So 'tres personae' must suffice:

> Dictum est tamen 'tres personae' non ut illud diceretur sed ne taceretur. (V.ix.10 lines 10-11)

> the formula three persons has been coined, not in order to give a complete explanation by means of it, but in order that we might not be obliged to remain silent.

Augustine's response to the obligation to put an answer into words, and his creative solution to the problem posed by the heretics, found ready acceptance as an appropriate way of describing the Godhead. Ælfric uses Augustine's doctrine of relation with confidence, though without reference to the substance-accident dichotomy. Relation for Ælfric appears to be most important as a means of affirming the equal divinity of each member of the trinity, as in the following passage, already quoted:

> Se is Fæder, seðe nis naðer ne geboren ne gesceapen fram nanum oðrum. Se is Fæder gehaten, forðan ðe he hæfð Sunu, ðone ðe he of him sylfum gestrynde, butan ælcre meder. Se Fæder is God of nanum Gode. Se Sunu is God of ðam Fæder Gode. Se Halga Gast is God forðstæppende of ðam Fæder and of ðam Suna. (Thorpe XX. p. 278. lines 7-13)

> He is Father who is neither born nor created from any other. He is called Father, because he has a Son, whom he begat from himself without any mother. The Father is God from no God. The Son is God from the Father God. The Holy Spirit is God proceeding from the Father and from the Son.

36

Various analogies taken from Augustine's sermons illustrate these relations. Ælfric introduces two which are helpful for an understanding of the Father-Son relation but are misleading in that they do not include the person of the Spirit.[48] Although Augustine sometimes limits his discussion to the relation between Father and Son (for example, in *Sermo* CXVIII and *In Ioannis Evangelium tractatus* XX), Ælfric usually prefers to speak of all three persons of the trinity to avoid giving the impression that the first two are more important than the Spirit. In doing so, he follows Augustine's teaching that the Spirit proceeds from both the Father and the Son.

Ælfric offers the analogy of the sun, which produces light and both together produce warmth (Thorpe XX. p. 282. 15-18).[49] This analogy also illustrates the way in which the members of the trinity may be understood to appropriate certain work, such as becoming incarnate:

> seo hætu drygð, and seo beorhtnys onlyht. Oðer ðing deð seo hætu, and oðer seo
> beorhtnys; and ðeah ðe hi ne magon beon totwæmde: belimpð, hwæðere ðeah, seo
> hæðung to ðære hætan, and seo onlihting belimpð to ðære beorhtnysse. Swa eac Crist
> ana underfeng ða menniscnysse, and na se Fæder, ne se Halga Gast: þeah-hwæðere hi
> wæron æfre mid him on eallum his weorcum and on ealre his fare. (p. 284. line 35-
> p. 286. line 7)[50]

> the heat dries and the brightness illuminates. The heat performs one function, the
> brightness another; and though they may not be separated, the heating nevertheless
> belongs to the heat and the illumination belongs to the brightness. So also Christ alone
> assumed humanity, and not the Father or the Holy Spirit; yet they were ever with him
> in all his works and on all his journey.

---

48. The first is drawn from human fathers and sons (Thorpe XX. p. 278. 21-66), the second, from fire and its brightness (27-31); see also Augustine *Sermo* CXVIII.2.

49. Cited below on page 80.

50. The source of the analogy of the sun has not been identified. Because it describes the double procession of the Holy Spirit it is basically Augustinian, whatever its route down to Ælfric. Ælfric uses the analogy again in *De penitentia* p. 606. 9-21.

Better than this analogy is that found by Augustine in the mind. This image is the culmination of Augustine's quest for an appropriate interpretation of the assurance that man is created in the image of God. In his exploration of this idea, *De trinitate*, the quest for God in his creation is carried to an inspired extreme. It drives the reader's understanding of the created image of God to the point where the origin of the image is discernible. On the premise that God is to be sought and found in places where he has left his image, Augustine finds trinity-images all through creation, ending in the mind.

The trinity-images of the mind approach ever more nearly the nature of the Original. It is in the human mind, with its capacity to grow toward God, that the image is dynamically present. Growth in understanding continues all through the Christian life, reaching a culmination with the beatific vision, which is the reward of the blessed: this reunion with God after the resurrection of the flesh completes the soul's progress. Then understanding will be unclouded:

> Imago uero quae renouatur in spiritu mentis in agnitione Dei, non exterius sed interius de die in diem, ipsa perficietur uisione quae tunc erit post iudicium facie ad faciem, nunc autem proficit per speculum in aenigmate. (*De trinitate* XIV.xix.25. lines 14-17)

> But the image which is being renewed day by day in the spirit of the mind and in the knowledge of God, not outwardly but inwardly, from day to day, will be perfected by the vision itself which will then be after the judgment face to face, but it is making progress towards it now through a mirror in an obscure manner.

In resurrection image is transcended. Then for the faithful the last barrier of understanding will be removed, because they will be present before the truth, of which until that moment they have both seen and been only a distorted image. The development of the mind up to that moment of revelation and understanding is what Augustine explores, finding increasingly appropriate trinity-images in the mind as the proximity of image to Original increases. Indeed, at the beginning of Augustine's exploration these images are no more than excellent analogies. However, a transition is made from analogy to image as Augustine is led to the recognition of what it is in man which corresponds to the divine impulse to create him 'to our image and likeness' (Genesis 1. 26). This is the point at which the mind turns towards God in love, here fulfilling its highest earthly purpose. J.E. Sullivan summarizes the development from analogy to image in these words: 'It is only in knowing and loving God that the trinity in man becomes more and more like God, and here is the "return" of the image upon its exemplar, that is the activation of the essential tendency of the image'.[51]

Augustine first finds a true image of God in three elements of the mind which he considers to be substantial, consubstantial, separate and equal: 'mens, notitia sui, amor sui' ('the mind itself, its love and its knowledge', *De trinitate* IX.iv.4-xii.18). In examining this group for patterns of the life of the trinity Augustine probes something of the timelessness of its mystery. He finds that in the mind, its knowledge and love cannot be understood to proceed in a linear fashion, because love is discerned in the birth of knowledge (IX.xii.18). The image therefore guards against a materialistic misunderstanding of the interrelation of the trinity: no temporal expansion is found there. The uniting love of the Father and the Son is illustrated by the love which both precedes the acquisition of knowledge and unites the mind with its acquired knowledge; it cannot be said that one precedes another. The mystery is further explored in this analogy by the way in which love is not seen to be objectified in the mind as knowledge may be: the mind's knowledge can readily be perceived as a body of knowledge, but love cannot be so confined by boundaries. Its unifying bond is one of complete permeation.

Next, Augustine finds the image of 'memoria, intelligentia, uoluntas' ('the memory, the understanding, and the will'), in which he finds a unity of life and substance, equality and interrelation (*De trinitate* X.xi.18-xii.19). The image is most completely realized, however, when the soul is concentrated not upon itself but upon its creator. The soul's trinity which has God at the centre is the closest the earthly soul can come to its purpose of union with God. The inward-looking soul is, in effect, still only a potential image of the trinity; this potential is brought to the greatest possible realization when the soul turns in recognition and contemplation to God. Then it may properly be called an image of God,

quia potest etiam meminisse et intellegere et amare a quo facta est. Quod cum facit sapiens ipsa fit. (XIV.xii.15. lines 3-4)

---

51. J.E. Sullivan, *The Image of God: the doctrine of St Augustine and its influence* (Dubuque, Iowa, 1963), p. 147.

because it can also remember, understand and love Him by whom it was made. And when it does so, it becomes wise.

The contemplation of the trinity is necessarily imperfect in earthly life, but the discovery of the image of the divine trinity in oneself is possible and is the logical end of the gift of the mind. The one who uses the mind to fulfil its divine purpose will certainly discover and love the trinity, and there find joy:

> Ad quam summam trinitatem reminiscendam, uidendam, diligendam ut eam recordetur, eam contempletur, ea delectetur totum debet referre quod uiuit. (XV.xx.39. lines 57-59)

> Man ought to direct all that lives in him to remember, to see, and to love this highest Trinity, in order that he may recall it, contemplate it, and find his delight in it.

Ælfric chooses only one of Augustine's image-trinities: that of memory, understanding and will, 'gemynd, and andgit, and willa' (Thorpe XX. p. 288. line 19). He explains what he means by these terms:

> Þurh þæt gemynd se man geðencð þa ðing ðe he gehyrde, oþþe geseah, oþþe geleornode. Þurh þæt andgit he understent ealle ða ðing ðe he gehyrð oððe gesihð. Of ðam willan cumað geðohtas, and word, and weorc, ægðer ge yfele ge gode. (lines 19-20)

> Through the memory, the man reflects upon the things that he has heard, or seen or learned. Through the understanding, he understands all the things that he hears or sees. From the will come thoughts, and words, and deeds, both evil and good.

Ælfric concentrates here on the mind's perception of external things and the translation of that perception into action. In this case he is not interpreting the mind-trinity exactly as Augustine does, lacking Augustine's sense that the mind's consciousness is essentially self-consciousness. Ælfric, by contrast, is certainly referring to the mind's response to external stimuli. Here, 'memory' refers to an active recollection of what is in the memory; 'understanding' to the interpretation of things heard or seen; 'will' to the product of this interpretation, in an activity of some kind. There is an outward progression in operation, rather than the inward self-reference which Augustine explores.

A slightly different interpretation is offered in a Christmas sermon composed for the *Lives of Saints* collection. First Ælfric makes the familiar point about the unity of the soul's nature: that it has three things, memory, understanding and will, and that these are one soul, or life, or substance. He draws the distinction between substance and relation. It now seems clearer that the relations discussed are internal rather than external:

> Seo sawul. oððe þæt lif. oððe seo edwist. synd gecwædene to hyre sylfra. and þæt gemynd. oððe þæt andgit. oþþe seo wylla. beoð gecwædene to sumum þinga. edlesendlice. and þas ðreo þing habbað annysse him betwynan. (Skeat I. lines 117-120)

> The soul or the life or the substance are named with respect to themselves, and the memory, or the understanding, or the will are named relatively with respect to certain things and these three things possess unity between them.

The name of the soul describes its substance: it exists *per se*. Memory, understanding and will are the names given to the relations within the soul which together have the soul's unity of substance. They coinhere perfectly:

> Ic undergyte. þæt ic wylle undergytan and ge-munan. and ic wylle þæt ic under-gyte and gemune. Þær þær þæt gemynd bið, þær bið þæt andgyt and se wylla. (lines 120-22)[52]

> I understand what I want to understand and to remember; and I wish for what I understand and remember. Where the memory is, there is understanding and will.

At least part of Augustine's point is preserved.

In *De fide Catholica* Ælfric reminds his listeners that although the soul provides an instructive analogy of the nature of the divine trinity, there is an important dissimilarity between the kinds of unity which may be predicated of each. The soul is indeed a unity of

---

52. Compare Augustine, *De trinitate* IX.v.8.

life and substance, exhibiting the functions of memory, understanding and will operating inseparably. Yet none of these contains the essence of the soul; each relates to the life of the whole but does not define it. Moreover, the soul is not the whole of the person, only that part of it which shows most likeness to the trinity. The human being is not a trinity, therefore, as God is:

> Is hwæðere se man an man, and na ðrynnys: God soðlice, Fæder and Sunu and Halig Gast, þurhwunað on ðrynnysse hada, and on annysse anre godcundnysse. Nis na se man on ðrynnysse wunigende, swa swa God, ac he hæfð hwæðere Godes anlicnysse on his sawle þurh ða ðreo ðing þe we ær cwædon. (Thorpe XX. p. 288. line 32-p. 290. line 2)

> Yet the man is a single man, and not a trinity; truly God, Father, Son and Holy Spirit, continues in a trinity of persons and in the unity of one Godhead. The man does not continue in trinity as God does, yet he has God's likeness in his soul because of the three things of which we have spoken.

Augustine also makes the point that there is no real comparison between the unity of one man and the unity of God. The inseparable trinity has a unity more perfect than is possible in anything created (*De trinitate* XV.xxiii.43. 1-23). Augustine warns against the dangerous supposition that the presence of an image-trinity in the mind means that something of God's very nature is to be found there. Instead, a properly oriented understanding, with love, directed to the service of God, will lead to increasing humility as God takes the central place of the soul's attention. Again, Augustine points out that the human trinity differs from the divine in that it is only a part of the whole body, whereas the divine trinity is God in his totality:

> Trinitas uero illa cuius imago est nihil aliud est tota quam Deus, nihil aliud est tota quam trinitas. (XV.vii.11. lines 18-20)

> But that Trinity, of which the mind is an image, is nothing else in its totality than God, nothing else in its totality than Trinity.

Setting aside analogy and turning to the clear relationship of the Christian with the holy trinity, it is clear that Ælfric has a strong sense of the necessity for faith in God as trinity, which, he says, will lead to eternal life. Analogies may help to elucidate the nature of the relations inherent in the trinity, but understanding must inspire faith. To illustrate this point Ælfric takes an exposition from Augustine of the parable of the friend at midnight, Luke 11. 5-11. This interprets the three loaves of bread, begged from the friend, as faith in the trinity. Midnight signifies the darkness of ignorance, and out of this darkness the one who seeks understanding should rise from sleep to beg for this essential bread,

> þæt is, þæt he sceal gebugan to Criste mid ealre geornfulnysse, and biddan þære ðreora hlafa, þæt is, geleafan þære Halgan Ðrynnysse. (Thorpe XVIII. p. 248. lines 4-6)[53]

> that is, he must turn to Christ with all eagerness, and ask for the three loaves, that is, for faith in the holy trinity.

This faith is provision not only for the suppliant soul, but also for the needs of others: he who receives may teach, just as the bread is shared with the visitor (11-13). The necessity of this faith in the trinity is also drawn by Ælfric from John 17. 3, but specifically in the reading which Augustine favours in his commentary on John, where he changes the word order of this verse:

> Haec est autem vita aeterna . . . ut te et quem misisti Iesum Christum cognoscant solum verum Deum. (*In Ioannis Evangelium tractatus* CV.3. lines 1-4)[54]

> And this . . . is eternal life . . . that they may know Thee, the only true God, and Jesus Christ whom Thou hast sent, as the only true God.

Augustine deliberates on the meaning of this verse in *De trinitate*, trying different interpretations, puzzling over the apparent meaning of the verse that only God the Father is the true God, and questioning why the Holy Spirit is not obviously included in this

---

53. Compare Augustine, *Sermo* CV.iii.4, an exposition of Luke 11. 5-13.

54. Quoted by Ælfric in Godden XXII. 69-71.

confession. He suggests that perhaps the answer is that the cohesion within the trinity means that the presence and co-equality of the three is constantly presupposed:

> An quoniam consequens est ut ubicumque nominatur unum tanta pace uni adhaerens ut per hanc utrumque unum sit, iam ex hoc intellegatur etiam ipsa pax, quamuis non commemoretur? (VI.ix.10. lines 25-28)

> Is it because it logically follows that wherever one is named, who adheres to one by a harmony so great that by virtue of it both are one, the harmony itself must also be understood, even though it is not mentioned?

In the commentary on John, this 'pax' is asserted with confidence, and the presence of the whole trinity readily affirmed. Augustine uses his variant word order to support this interpretation:

> Consequenter enim et Spiritus sanctus intellegitur, quia Spiritus est Patris et Filii, tanquam caritas substantialis et consubstantialis amborum. (*In Ioannis Evangelium tractatus* CV.3. lines 5-7)

> Consequently, therefore, the Holy Spirit is also understood, because He is the Spirit of the Father and Son, as the substantial and consubstantial love of both.

He now rehearses familiar formulae: God is three, yet there are not three gods; there are three persons, but one God.[55] It is knowledge of this God in trinity which is eternal life, and, Augustine says, the more we grow in knowledge, the more we grow in life:

> Porro si cognitio Dei est uita aeterna, tanto magis uiuere tendimus, quanto magis in hac cognitione proficimus. (lines 17-19)[56]

---

55. Compare Ælfric in Godden XXII. 71-77.

56. Augustine makes the same point about growing in life and knowledge in *De trinitate* XIV.xvii.23. 24-40, but the quotation from John is lacking.

Accordingly, if the knowledge of God is eternal life, we are making the greater advances to life in proportion as we are enlarging our growth in such a knowledge.

Ælfric's version of this passage is ponderous. It is clear that he has understood Augustine's point, but the translation is difficult, the 'tanto-quanto' parallel resulting in a laboured phrase:

Ðeos tocnawennys is ece lif. for ðan ðe we habbað þæt ece lif. ðurh geleafan. and oncnawennysse. þære halgan ðrynnysse. gif we ða oncnawennysse mid arwurðnysse healdað; Witodlice gif godes oncnawennys us gearcað þæt ece lif. swa miccle swiðor we efstað to lybbenne swa micclum. swa we swiðor on ðissere oncnawennysse ðeonde beoð. (Godden XXII. lines 77-83)

This understanding is eternal life, for we have eternal life through faith in and knowledge of the holy trinity, if we keep that knowledge with reverence. Truly if the knowledge of God prepares for us eternal life, so much the more we hasten to live, by as much as we keep on prospering in this knowledge.

Ælfric's phrase 'swa micclum' suggests that he has in mind the fullness or abundance of life which is the gift of Christ in his revelation of God. Augustine continues here by equating perfect knowledge with the perfection of eternal life (*In Ioannis Evangelium tractatus* CV.3). Although such life begins for Christians as soon as they dedicate themselves to God, still it is only in the life to come that death is eliminated. So too Ælfric brings together vision and perfection:

Soðlice ne swelte we on ðam ecan life. þonne bið us godes oncnawennys fulfremed. þonne þær nan deað ne bið. þonne we god geseoð. and butan geswince ecelice heriað. (Godden XXII. lines 83-85)

Truly we shall not die in that eternal life, when the knowledge of God is perfected in us; then there will be no death, when we see God and praise him eternally without toil.

Ælfric's eternal, toilless praise corresponds to Augustine's vision of heaven, where the completion of knowledge and life are the perfection of God's glory. Then the purpose of creation is realized:

> Ibi erit Dei sine fine laudatio, ubi erit Dei plena cognitio; et quia plena cognitio, ideo summa clarificatio uel glorificatio. (*In Ioannis Evangelium tractatus* CV.3. lines 28-30)

> There will God's praise continue without end, where there shall be the full knowledge of God; and because the full knowledge, therefore also the complete effulgence or glorification.

Ælfric's teaching on the trinity is soundly based upon Augustine's, and offers useful analogies of the trinity to help people to grasp this difficult concept. Like Augustine, he progresses from a study of image-trinities to an awareness of what the image of God in man may truly be said to be. He does not draw attention to Augustine's very powerful recognition that the truest image of God in man is the soul's memory, understanding and will when these faculties are directed towards God. Nevertheless, his own vision of the perfection of heaven is a clear indication that he understood this to be so, for in that bliss he perceives that knowledge of God is the same as eternal life: there, he sees that the perfect expression of knowledge is the praise offered unceasingly by the blessed to God.

III. GOD THE FATHER

The Father is the origin of all: for although the Son and Spirit exist in a certain eternal relationship with the Father, begotten by the Father or proceeding from him, the Father himself derives his nature from no other. So the Father is in some mysterious sense the 'Ur-origin' of the Godhead, and while Ælfric confesses a trinitarian God of whom all persons are equal and inseparable he finds in the Father the beginning of all beginnings. So does Augustine: in commenting on Jesus' promise that he would send his disciples the Holy Spirit 'from the Father' he observes that the Son is acknowledging the Father to be Principle whilst at the same time preserving his own place in the work of sending the Spirit together with the

Father. In using these words the Son indicated both the double procession of the Holy Spirit, and his own generation by the Father as principle of the Godhead:

> uidelicet ostendens quod totius diuinitatis uel si melius dicitur deitatis principium pater
> est. 'Qui' ergo 'ex patre procedit et filio' ad eum refertur a quo natus est filius. (*De*
> *trinitate* IV.xx.29. lines 121-23)

> thus He clearly showed that the Father is the principle of the whole divinity, or to speak
> more precisely, of the whole Godhead. He, therefore, who proceeds from the Father and
> the Son, is referred back to Him of whom the Son was born.

As the Origin, the Father may be described only according to what he is not. But the name 'Father' reveals his nature through the sonship of the Son. Ælfric finds it is the relationship between them which invites human contemplation:

> Se is Fæder, seðe nis naðer ne geboren ne gesceapen fram nanum oðrum. Se is Fæder
> gehaten, forðan ðe he hæfð Sunu, ðone ðe he of him sylfum gestrynde, butan ælcre
> meder. Se Fæder is God of nanum Gode . . . Hwæt is se Fæder? Ælmihtig Scyppend,
> na geworht ne acenned, ac he sylf gestrynde Bearn him sylfum efen-ece. (Thorpe XX.
> p. 278. lines 7-16)[57]

> He is the Father who is neither born nor created from any other. He is called Father,
> because he has a Son, who was begotten from himself, without any mother. The Father
> is God from no God . . . What is the Father? The almighty creator, neither created nor
> born, but he himself begot a Child co-eternal with himself.

This passage may be compared with Augustine's account of the relation between Father and Son in his commentary on John: the being of God is life itself, pure existence, but the Fatherhood of God is defined by the Son. Through this relation both the Father and the Son

---

57. Compare Thorpe XX. p. 284. 10-11; XXXIII. p. 500. 6-7; Godden III. 121-23; XXII. 74-
    75; *De penitentia* p. 606. 6-7; Pope III. 177-78; VI. 228-30; XIa. 201-4; XXI. 12-17;
    Skeat I. 33-34.

can be said to be life: the begetting of the Son engenders in him the life of the Father. Life is therefore not added to the nature of the Son, but is in him in the same perfection as in the Father because of their unity:

> Pater uita est non nascendo; Filius uita est nascendo. Pater de nullo patre, Filius de Deo Patre. Pater quod est, a nullo est; quod autem Pater est, propter Filium est. (*In Ioannis Evangelium tractatus* XIX.13. lines 8-11)

> The Father is life, not by a 'being born'; the Son is life by a 'being born'. The Father (is) from no father; the Son, from God the Father. The Father, in that he is, is from no one, but in that he is the Father, he is in regard to the Son.

Later Augustine adds that although God's name was known before the coming of Christ, the name of 'Father' remained unknown until the Son revealed God as Father. The Jews were specially blessed with the knowledge of God's name, but only with the advent of Christ was the greatness of the name 'Father' revealed (CVI.4).[58]

For Ælfric, it is God as Father who contemplates his creation, and plans its redemption. Ælfric draws attention to the fact that mercy is the impulse of the new creation:

> Ac se mildheorta Fæder, ðe us to mannum gesceop
>
> þurh his ancennedan Suna, wolde eft alysan
>
> ðurh ðone ylcan Suna eall manncynn
>
> of deofle 7 fram ðam ecan deaðe. (Pope XIa. lines 53-56)[59]

> But the merciful Father, who created us as men through his only-begotten Son, afterwards desired through that same Son to redeem all mankind from the devil and from the eternal death.

---

58. Compare Ælfric's comment that people did not know about the trinity until the Son came to them and spoke to them of the Father and the Holy Spirit: Pope IX. 89-95.

59. This passage is cited again below on page 104. Compare Thorpe XIII. p. 192. 9-13 and 18-21; XV. p. 228. 22-29; XIX. p. 258. 24-p. 260. 2; XX. p. 292. 1-4; Godden I. 12-14; Pope V. 103-12; XVII. 311-14.

God's solution to the problem of sin reveals not only the Father's authority over the Son (corresponding to the Son's obedience) but also the fact that in redemption, his fatherhood extends to all, even though it means the sacrifice of the princely Son. Here, as on many occasions, the creating Son is linked with the Son who recreates by his redemptive act.

The portrayal of the God-Man as intercessor with the Father underlines this association of humanity in sonship with Christ, all dependent upon the Fatherhood of God. Offering prayer with mankind, the Son also receives prayer with the Father:

> On þære menniscnysse þe he mid is befangen,
> he bit for his halgum his heofenlican Fæder;
> and on his godcundnysse, on þære þe he God is,
> he getiþað ealle þing æfre mid þam Fæder;
> and we habbað on þam Suna swiðe godne þingere. (Pope VIII. lines 208-12)[60]

In the humanity with which he is invested, he prays to his heavenly Father for his saints; and in his divinity, in which he is God, he grants all things eternally with the Father, and in the Son we have a very good intercessor.

Here Christ is seen continuing his work as Mediator, enabling communication between the Father and his sons. Because he is at once the suppliant and the giver, the faithful may confidently appropriate for themselves his intercession for them and the gifts bestowed.

Human relation to the Father is possible because the Son of God became human. His humanity was directed and perfected by grace, as is the sonship of all believers:

> Þurh ða gife þe se mennisca crist wearð godes bearn. þurh ða ylcan gife bið gehwilc cristenra manna gode gecoren. fram ðam anginne his geleafan. (Godden XXXV. lines 68-70)[61]

Through that grace by which the human Christ became God's child, through that same grace every Christian is chosen by God, from the beginning of his belief.

---

60. Compare Godden XXIV. 131-33.

61. Cited again on page 76. Compare Thorpe XIX. p. 258. 17-p. 260. 2; Pope I. 393-402.

After being chosen, the children of God, now joint heirs by grace with the Son, are assured that God will provide the grace necessary for sonship. The condition in which grace may be received, that of love, is also granted. The children need not fear the possibility that their hearts will prove hard, unable to respond to the grace of the Father, for even the will to respond to God is provided:

> And ðu nelt ðinum bearne syllan stan for hlafe, nele eac God us syllan heardheortnysse for soðre lufe. Ac se goda Heofonlica Fæder forgifð us geleafan, and hiht, and ða soðan lufe, and deð þæt we habbað godne gast, þæt is, godne willan. (Thorpe XVIII. p. 252. line 33-p. 254. line 2)[62]

> If you will not give to your child a stone instead of bread, no more will God give us hard-heartedness instead of true love. But the good heavenly Father gives us faith and hope and true love, and ensures that we have a good spirit, that is, good will.

The Fatherhood of God forms the supreme bond of unity in his children. All, rich and poor, slave and freeman, are of equal value, equally deserving of love. Love, Ælfric says, unites each one to God and to his brothers in Christ; here again Christians are associated with the Sonship of Christ:

> God is ure Fæder, þi we sceolon ealle beon gebroðru on Gode, and healdan þone broðerlican bend unforedne . . . Se ðe ðis hylt, he bið Godes bearn, and Crist, and ealle halige men ðe Gode geðeoð, beoð his gebroðru and his gesweostru. (Thorpe XIX. p. 260. lines 28-34)[63]

> God is our Father, therefore we must all be brothers in God, and hold the brotherly bond inviolate . . . he who maintains this is the child of God, and Christ and all holy people who prosper in God are his brothers and his sisters.

---

62. Compare Thorpe XVIII. p. 250. 10-14; XIX. p. 270. 10-12 and p. 274. 6-7.

63. Compare Thorpe XIX. p. 258. 24-p. 260. 11 and p. 272. 18-23; XXXV. p. 528. 16-18; Godden XII. 316-17; XIII. 71-72; Pope I. 352-63 and 386-90.

Brotherly love provides guidance and instruction in the love of God. The love is the same: there is no separate, higher plane of love for God, but love for the Father is contained within the response of the Christian to the Spirit's gifts. Ælfric explains that the double bestowal of the Holy Spirit upon the disciples (John 20. 19-22 and Acts 2. 1-4) speaks of this unity of love:

> An is se Halga Gast, þeah ðe he tuwa become ofer ða apostolas. Swa is eac an lufu and twa bebodu, Þæt we sceolon lufian God and menn. (Thorpe XXII. p. 326. lines 4-6)[64]

> The Holy Spirit is one, though he came twice over the apostles. So also there is one love and two commandments, that we must love God and men.

Love is always expressed in service: the child of God cannot ignore God's other children. Love offered through the Spirit to others is returned to its origin, the love of the Father.

Ælfric's discussion of the nature of God as Father is limited, its most important point being dependent on the best experience of the father-child relationship that is known to all, even if merely as an unrealized ideal. In the person of the Son is found exemplified the human response to such a Father, together with the means of making that response a reality for all.

IV. GOD THE SON

The second person of the trinity is the Son of God. The mutual Father-Son relation, dynamic and eternal, is revealed in the names of the first and second persons of the trinity: they presuppose and define each other, and each is necessary to the other. Their names encapsulate their essential nature:

---

64. Compare Thorpe XVI. p. 232. 17-22; XXII. p. 326. 6-10; XXIV. p. 346. 13-17; Godden XIX. 7-12 and 60-63. Based on Augustine in a point made in *De trinitate* XV.xxvi.46. 24-26 and also in *In Ioannis Evangelium tractatus* LXXIV.2.

Þonne ðu gehyrst nemnan þone Fæder, þonne understenst ðu þæt he hæfð Sunu. Eft, þonne þu cwyst Sunu, þu wast, butan tweon, þæt he hæfð Fæder. (Thorpe XX. p. 284. lines 10-12)[65]

When you hear the Father named, then you understand that he has a Son. Again, when you say 'Son', you know, without a doubt, that he has a Father.

The Son is the realization of the power of God. As a word is begotten in the thinking mind, in order to bring thought to expression, so is the Son born of the Father, bringing to expression his power. This word, Augustine asserts, is not transitory as is a word uttered in human speech. The Word eternally reveals the power of the Father and the unity of the Godhead:

Verbo enim quod genuit dicens est, non uerbo quod profertur et sonat et transit; sed uerbo quod erat apud deum et deus erat uerbum, et omnia per ipsum facta sunt, uerbo aequali sibi quo semper atque incommutabiliter dicit se ipsum. (*De trinitate* VII.i.1. lines 22-25)

For He speaks by the Word which He begot, not by the word which is spoken, produces a sound and passes away, but by the Word which was with God, and was God, and by which all things were made, by a Word equal to Himself, by which He expresses Himself always and unchangeably.

Ælfric says that just as the history of creation begins with God's Wisdom or Word, his creating medium, so also John's account of the history of salvation begins with the Word:

He is Wisdom gehaten, forðan ðe se Fæder ealle gesceafta þurh hine geworhte. He is Word gecweden, forðan þe word is wisdomes geswutelung. Be ðam Worde ongann se

---

65. Compare Thorpe XXXIII. p. 498. 28-29; *De penitentia* p. 604. 25-28 and p. 606. 7-8; in Augustine, *In Ioannis Evangelium tractatus* XIX.13.

godspellere Iohannes þa godspellican gesetnysse, ðus cweðende, 'On frymðe wæs Word'. (Thorpe XXV. p. 358. lines 11-15)[66]

He is named Wisdom, for the Father made all created things through him. He is called Word, for the word is the manifestation of wisdom. With the Word the evangelist John began the gospel account, saying thus: 'In the beginning was the Word'.

Ælfric treats the names Wisdom and Word as synonymous: both are names of the Son. Augustine, by contrast, draws a precise distinction between Wisdom and Word, the one an attribute of divine substance, the other a title of relation. He explains that wisdom is the same as being: the simplicity of the Godhead equates 'to be wise' with 'to be':

ita dicitur filius sapientia patris quomodo dicitur lumen patris, id est ut quemadmodum lumen de lumine et utrumque unum lumen, sic intellegatur sapientia de sapientia et utrumque una sapientia. Ergo et una essentia quia hoc est ibi esse quod sapere. (*De trinitate* VII.i.2. lines 158-62)

the Son is called the wisdom of the Father in the same sense as He is called the light of the Father. That is to say, just as He is the light of light, and both are one light, so He is understood to be the wisdom of wisdom, and both are one wisdom; therefore, they are also one essence, for to be and to be wise is one and the same.

Both may be called 'Wisdom' essentially, but 'Word' describes the relation between Father and Son, just as in speech the conceived word does not stand alone but only in relation to the speaker's generating mind:

uerbum non ad se dicitur sed tantum relatiue ad eum cuius uerbum est. (VII.ii.3. lines 9-11)

the Word is not spoken of in respect to itself, but only in relation to Him whose Word it is.

---

66. Compare Pope X. 65-73.

The begetting of the Word does, however, include the manifestation of Wisdom, which Ælfric suggests in his 'wisdomes geswutelung':

> Quoniam uero et uerbum sapientia est, sed non eo uerbum quo sapientia (uerbum enim relatiue, sapientia essentialiter intellegitur), id dici accipiamus cum dicitur uerbum ac si dicatur nata sapientia ut sit et filius et imago. (lines 12-16)

> The Word, however, is also the wisdom, but is not the Word by that by which it is the wisdom, for Word is understood as referring to the relation, but wisdom to the essence. And, therefore, when He is spoken of as the Word, let it be understood as though He were called the wisdom that was begotten, so as to be both the Son and the Image.

Since God's power can never be without its expression, the Son is necessarily co-eternal with the Father. In this regard it is interesting to note that Ælfric applies the 'proof text' of Exodus 3. 14, which properly describes the eternality of the Godhead, to the Son himself. Ælfric simultaneously affirms the divinity and the eternality of the Son here:

> Ne cwæð se hælend. ær ðan ðe abraham wære ic wæs. ac he cwæð. ær ðan þe abraham gewurde. Ic eom; Þæt word belimpð synderlice to gode anum. Ic eom. for ðan ðe he is ana butan anginne. and ende. (Godden XIII. lines 210-13)

> The Saviour did not say, 'Before Abraham could be, I was', but he said, 'Before Abraham could come to be, I am'. That utterance, 'I am', pertains exclusively to God alone, for he alone is without beginning and end.

Ælfric illustrates the concept of the Son's co-eternality with an analogy taken from Augustine which compares fire and the light that it generates with the relationship of Father and Son. The analogy demonstrates the unity of the two (for fire is never without brightness). It also illustrates the concept of principle within the relations: fire and brightness have an essential unity, but fire is certainly the principle of the two. Brightness cannot of its own power generate fire (Thorpe XX. p. 278. 27-31).[67] Though begotten by God the Son is nevertheless coeternal and coequal with him:

> Nu ðu gehyrst þæt seo beorhtnys is ealswa eald swa þæt fyr þe heo of cymð; geðafa nu forði þæt God mihte gestrynan ealswa eald Bearn, and ealswa ece swa he sylf is. (lines 31-34)[68]

> Now you have heard that the brightness is just as old as the fire from which it is derived; agree therefore that God could beget a child just as old and eternal as he himself is.

The co-eternality of the Son and Father must be believed even if imperfectly understood. It is affirmed against heresy and error, for there is a danger that the Son's condition of being born may seem to over-emphasize the pre-eminence of the Father. To some, the concept of the Father as principle within the trinity may imply the subordination of the Son (and of the Holy Spirit) to the Father. Conscious of the way in which orthodox beginnings may end in heresy, Ælfric insists on the priority of belief, to which understanding may be added at a later stage. Understanding is good, but for the Christian, faith is greater. Faith, once established, however, permits a new power of understanding:

> Se ðe mæg understandan þæt ure Hælend Crist is on ðære Godcundnysse ealswa eald swa his Fæder, he ðancige þæs Gode, and blissige. Seðe understandan ne mæg, he hit sceal gelyfan, þæt he hit understandan mæge; forðan þæs witegan word ne mæg beon aidlod, ðe þus cwæð, 'Buton ge hit gelyfan, ne mage ge hit understandan.' (Thorpe XX. p. 278. line 34-p. 280. line 4)

---

67. From *Sermo* CXVIII.2. Augustine uses the analogy in other sermons too, for example in *In Ioannis Evangelium tractatus* XX.8.

68. A similar analogy is that of the sun and its light, to which is added a third, the sun's heat, corresponding to the Holy Spirit, already referred to above (on page 37) in connection with Ælfric's teaching on the trinity (Thorpe XX. p. 282. 15-18).

He who is able to understand that our Saviour Christ is just as old in the Godhead as his Father, let him thank God for it and rejoice. He who is unable to understand must believe it, so that he may understand it; because the word of the prophet, who spoke thus, cannot be spoken in vain: 'Unless you believe it, you cannot understand it.'

The verse which Ælfric quotes, Isaiah 7. 9, is a favourite of Augustine, who is his source here:

Qui intelligit, gaudeat: qui autem non intelligit, credat. Quoniam verbum Prophetæ evacuari non potest: Nisi credideritis, non intelligetis. (*Sermo* CXVIII.2)

Whoso understandeth, let him rejoice: but whoso understandeth not, let him believe. For the word of the prophet cannot be disannulled; 'Unless you believe, you will not understand.'[69]

It is faith, then, which declares that Christ is co-eternal with the Father and is of the same majesty and glory. In the trinity and in his own person, he is almighty God. He is both the creating God and the Father's medium of creation. His work in creation confirms that he himself was not a product of God's creation of the world. On the contrary, he was begotten by God: had his birth been a part of creation (however superior a part) the Son could not be the creating God, for all that is created is not God. Nor is the birth of the Son confined within time, as creation is: the generation of the Son is eternal (Thorpe XV. p. 228. 21-23).[70]

As the Father's creative medium the Son revealed God in his omnipotence, and that same omnipotence is revealed for the second time in the recreation of mankind through the Son. This second creation achieved still more than the first, transforming man into the child of God, giving him a regenerate nature, because the Son allowed himself to be humbled to the acceptance of human nature. By his incarnation he allied humanity with his divinity in such a way that humanity was raised to the level of the divine. The Son's sonship was broadened

---

69. Quoted in the translation by R.G. Macmullen.

70. Compare Thorpe IX. p. 150. 13-14; XIII. p. 198. 14-16; Godden I. 6-11; XXII. 35-36; Pope VI. 228-30; XXI. 14-20.

to include the faithful by his acceptance of human nature, purifying it and making it worthy
of the honour by his own sinlessness:

> Se mann is godes bearn. for ðan ðe se godes sunu ðe æfre wæs acenned of ðam
> ælmihtigan fæder. underfeng ða menniscnysse buton synnum to soðre annysse his hades.
> and þæt ylce godes bearn. is mannes bearn. for ðære underfangenan menniscnysse.
> (Godden XXXV. lines 77-81)[71]

> Man is God's child, because God's Son, who was eternally begotten of the almighty
> Father, received humanity without sins to the true unity of his person, and that same
> child of God is the child of man, according to the humanity which he took.

Here is the inseparable unity of natures which works a miracle in the natures of men:

> Ealle cristene men sind his gastlican gebroðra, and he is se frumcenneda, on gife and
> on godcundnysse ancenned of ðam Ælmihtigan Fæder. (Thorpe II. p. 34. lines 25-28)[72]

> All Christian men are his spiritual brothers, and he is the first born, in grace and
> divinity, only-begotten of the almighty Father.

The incarnation of the Son is the new covenant, now no longer of law but of grace, in which
all may be sons and daughters. The astonishing implication of this is that the Son's divinity
is mysteriously shared with his brothers and sisters; so it may truly be said, 'You are gods'
(Pope XXI. 669-75).[73]

For Ælfric, the incarnation of the Son is the pivot of human history. It is the point at
which death is transformed to life, punishment to glory, exile to sonship. The magnitude of

---

71. Compare Thorpe II. p. 32. 34-p. 34. 1; XIX. p. 260. 2-11; Godden I. 29-31.

72. Compare Pope I. 386-90.

73. The reference is to Psalm 81. 6. Compare Thorpe XXII. p. 324. 11-16; Pope I. 357-63.
    Augustine also speaks of deification, but emphasizes that human beings are made gods
    by grace, not by nature (*Enarrationes in Psalmos* XLIX.2. 13-15).

the divine plan, the almost unbelievable truths which faith affirms, the marvellous paradoxes involved: all are explored as Ælfric strives to convey the miracle of incarnation adequately. His first task is to describe the divinity of the incarnate Son. Jesus, 'se Hælend' ('the healer', 'the saviour'), used the name 'I am' of himself, identifying himself with God whose eternal present comprehends all time: Jesus' proper claim to the name expresses the fullness of divinity in him (Godden XIII. 210-14). That the one whose eternal name is 'I am' could become a man, localized in time and place, was a powerful expression of God's grace, realized bodily in Christ and effecting a fundamental change in human potential. Ælfric speaks of the great grace given to the human nature of Christ; at the moment of his incarnation his humanity was received into the Godhead. Thus the man Jesus was never less than wholly divine:

Micel gifu wæs þæt ðære menniscnysse, þæt he wæs Godes Sunu and God sylf, swa hraðe swa he ongann man to beonne. (Thorpe IX. p. 150. lines 11-13)[74]

In respect of his incarnation, it was a great grace that he was God's Son and God himself, as soon as he began to be man.

Lest this be misinterpreted to mean that Christ was the Son of God only from the time of his incarnation, Ælfric immediately adds that he was eternally God, dwelling with the Father and the Holy Spirit.

Only one person of the trinity stepped from eternity into time: 'Se Sunu ana underfeng þa menniscnysse, and hæfde anginn, seðe æfre wæs' ('The Son alone received humanity and had beginning, he who was always', Thorpe IX. p. 150. lines 17-18). The paradox of the eternal Son's taking upon himself a temporal beginning is one of many in the mystery which unites two irreconcilable worlds. The life of God omnipotent, infallible, impassive, was voluntarily confined by the restrictions of humanity, with all the created being's natural weaknesses: the creator humbled himself to the level of creation. Ælfric enjoys the paradox of the creator's bringing himself to birth:

---

74. Compare Pope I. 456-60: in Augustine, *Enchiridion* xi.36. 8-13.

Se ylca godes sunu se ðe ealle ðing gesceop. he eac gesceop his agene moder. and on hire innoð sylf becom. and ðæron geworhte his agenne lichaman. and wearð of hire geboren. soð man on sawle and on lichaman. (Godden I. lines 70-73)[75]

That same Son of God who created all things also created his own mother, and came himself into her womb, and there created his own body and was born of her, a true man in soul and body.

Ælfric is careful to stress that Christ remained truly God when he became truly man:

ac se heofonlica Æþeling her on þas woruld com

7 þa menniscnysse genam of Marian innoðe,

soð man acenned on sawle and on lichaman,

7 wunode swaþeah God on þære godcundnysse,

an ælmihtig Hælend, us to alysende. (Pope I. lines 405-9)[76]

But the heavenly Prince came to this world, and took humanity from Mary's womb, true man born in soul and body, and yet remained God in his divinity, one almighty Saviour, as our redeemer.

Here Ælfric's expression of the Son's function, 'us to alysende', encompasses both of the things he did: he became man, and he remained God. Each was essential for salvation, and so it is as man and as God that he may properly be called 'an ælmihtig Hælend' ('one almighty saviour'). The saviour's nature reconciles two irreconcilables, and the circumstances of his humble birth speak with gentle irony to the human condition. Ælfric relishes the almighty Son of God's tolerance of the ignominies of babyhood for the sake of mankind:

---

75. Compare Thorpe XIII. p. 194. 7-9; XXX. p. 454. 2-4; XXXI. p. 458. 32-35; Godden I. 300-1.

76. Compare Thorpe XIII. p. 200. 7-9; XXIV. p. 350. 25; Godden I. 73 and 301-2; XIII. 124-26; XXII. 48-49 and 94; XXIII. 22-23; XXIV. 106-9; XXXV. 74-81; Pope I. 456-60; XIa. 76-79; and in Augustine, *De trinitate* XIII.xvii.22; *In Ioannis Evangelium tractatus* XXVIII.1.

He wæs mid wacum cild-claðum bewæfed, þæt he us forgeafe ða undeadlican tunecan, þe we forluron on ðæs frumsceapenan mannes forgægednysse. Se Ælmihtiga Godes Sunu, ðe heofenas befon ne mihton, wæs geled on nearuwre binne, to ði þæt he us fram hellicum nyrwette alysde. (Thorpe II. p. 34. lines 28-33)[77]

He was wrapped in humble swaddling clothes, so that he might give us the immortal garment which we lost in the transgression of the first-created man. The almighty Son of God, whom the heavens could not contain, was laid in a narrow manger, so that he might redeem us from the confines of hell.

In the paradoxes of the God-Man's birth are found the mysteries of redemption. The salvation of mankind was the only motive of the Son's incarnation. The very assumption of flesh achieved a healing of human nature. The sinlessness of Christ's humanity worked a transformation which made cleansing and restoration possible again. This lesson is drawn from the Gospel account of the healing of the leper (Matthew 8. 1-4). The picture of the disfigurement brought about by leprosy is only a suggestion of the loathsome distortion brought to the soul by the disease of sin (Thorpe VIII. p. 122. 16-24). It is to this disease that the incarnation brings healing:

His hand getacnaþ his mihte and his flæsclicnysse. Swa swa Crist mid his handa hrepunge þone hreoflian gehælde, swa eac he alysde us fram ure sawla synnum ðurh anfenge ures flæsces; swa swa se witega Isaias cwæð, 'Soðlice he sylf ætbræd ure adlunga, and ure sarnysse he sylf abær.' (lines 27-32)[78]

His hand betokens his power and his humanity. Just as Christ with the touch of his hands healed the leper, so also he redeemed us from our souls' sins by his assumption of our flesh. Thus the prophet Isaiah said, 'Truly he himself took away our diseases, and he himself bore our pain.'

---

77. Compare Thorpe IX. p. 136. 35-p. 138. 6; and in Augustine, for example *Sermo* CLXXXIV.ii.3.

78. The reference is to Isaiah 53. 4.

That the incarnation was for the healing of humanity, and not for any other purpose (such as the broadening of the divine experience) is repeatedly affirmed.[79]

In Christ dwelt 'eal gefyllednys þære godcundnysse' ('all the fullness of divinity'); grace dwelt bodily ('lichomlice') in him (Thorpe IX. p. 150. lines 9-11). This fullness of divinity in Christ distinguishes him from other people, for his is a unique grace:

> Drihten nis na oðrum mannum to wiðmetenne. ðeah ðe he mann sy geworden. ac his heofenlica fæder hine wurðode. toforan eallum his dælnymendum on ðære mennisc-nysse. þe he for manna alysednysse underfeng. (Godden XIII. lines 123-26)[80]

> The Lord is not to be compared with other men, though he be become man. But his heavenly Father glorified him above all the fellow-sharers in that humanity which he assumed for man's redemption.

Ælfric emphasizes that even in his humanity Christ is pre-eminent in honour.

Augustine finds that the names 'Son of God' and 'Son of Man', both equally proper, point to the fact that Jesus remained true God whilst being true man. His sonship of each nature ensures the perfect generation of the qualities inherent in each. The Word and the man co-exist in unity:

> Filius hominis habet animam, habet corpus. Filius Dei, quod est Verbum Dei, habet hominem, tamquam anima corpus. Sicut anima habens corpus, non facit duas personas, sed unum hominem; sic Verbum habens hominem, non facit duas personas, sed unum Christum. (*In Ioannis Evangelium tractatus* XIX.15. lines 25-30)

---

79. Thorpe I. p. 24. 32-33; XIII. p. 200. 18-22; XIX. p. 260. 1-2; XX. p. 284. 24 and p. 292. 2-4; XXII. p. 312. 17-18 and p. 320. 5-11; XXV. p. 358. 16-19; XXX. p. 454. 2-4; XXXIII. p. 494. 32-33; XXXIX. p. 600. 4-6; Godden I. 13-14; XIII. 125-26; XXVI. 144-45; Pope I. 409; III. 125-27 and 177-81; V. 110-12; XI. 7-9; XIa. 54-56, 73-78 and 226-30; XXI. 656-57.

80. Godden XIII. 140-43.

The son of man has soul, has a body. The Son of God, who is the Word of God, has human nature, as the soul has body. As a soul, having body, does not make two persons but one man, so the Word, having human nature, does not make two persons but one Christ.

Just as Ælfric finds that the person of Jesus, in whom two natures were perfectly united, was the embodiment of grace, Augustine distinguishes the special indwelling of God in Jesus from the divine omnipresence in creation by reference to this union, the result of a perfect response to grace (TeSelle, *Augustine*, p. 153). Grace must be received in order to be realized, and whilst God dwells in all who are capable of being influenced by his grace, the perfect receptivity of Christ allowed the bodily indwelling of grace:

> deus igitur, qui ubique praesens est et ubique totus praesens, nec ubique habitans sed in templo suo, cui per gratiam benignus est et propitius; capitur autem habitans, ab aliis amplius ab aliis minus. De ipso uero capite nostro apostolus ait: Quia in ipso inhabitat omnis plenitudo diuinitatis corporaliter. (*Epistula* CLXXXVII.xiii.38. p. 116. line 4-xiii.39. p. 116. line 10).[81]

> Thus, God, who is everywhere present and everywhere wholly present, does not dwell everywhere but only in His temple, to which, by His grace, He is kind and gracious, but in His indwelling He is received more fully by some, less by others. Speaking of Him as our Head, the Apostle says: 'For in him dwelleth all the fullness of the Godhead corporally.'

The grace which dwells in the Son is unique, therefore; not even the saints can claim this perfect indwelling:

---

81. The reference is to Colossians 2. 9. Compare *De trinitate* XIII.xix,24. lines 26-27, where the 'Word made flesh' is understood in terms of the operation of unique grace, 'dei et hominis ineffabili gratiae largitate coniunctum' ('both are united together into the one person of God and man by the ineffable liberality of grace').

de nullo enim sanctorum dici potuit aut potest aut poterit: Verbum caro factum est. (xiii.40. p. 117. lines 11-13)

of none of the saints has it been, is it, or will it be possible to say: 'The Word was made flesh.'

TeSelle sees in Augustine's understanding of the union of natures precisely the required balance of unity and discrimination: 'What is asserted here is not any less a theory of "real" or "hypostatic" union; but the reality involved is mind, and its actuality is gained through enactment, not through bare subsistence alone' (*Augustine*, p. 156).[82] Ælfric strives to reproduce Augustine's account of the vital union of the divine and human in Christ, which reveals that there is no superiority of one nature over the other, no subordination within the person which could disturb the perfect unity.

Ælfric discovers that language is scarcely subtle enough to describe this unique event. The words should encompass a complete equality of co-existence without suggesting any confusion or distortion. He offers the following: becoming flesh: 'þæt ylce Word wæs geworden flæsc' ('that same Word became flesh', Thorpe II. p. 40. line 17); assuming or receiving it: 'Se Sunu ana underfeng þa menniscnysse' ('the Son alone assumed humanity', Thorpe IX. p. 150. line 17); taking it: 'he genam ða menniscnysse of Marian innoðe' ('he took humanity from Mary's womb', Thorpe II. p. 42. lines 7-8); being invested with it: 'Næs þæt Word to flæsce awend, ac hit wæs mid menniscum flæsce befangen' ('The Word was not transformed into flesh, but it was invested with human flesh', Thorpe II. p. 40. lines 18-19); being clothed with humanity: 'mid þære menniscnysse gescrydd' (Thorpe XXXVIII. p. 578. line 29); or wrapped in it: 'mid flæsce bewæfed' (Thorpe III. p. 56. line 32). The best of these is the first: a simple, direct statement underpinned by mystery. Most other words are hampered by their association with ordinary experience. 'Receiving' or 'taking' express addition, rather than union, and the images of clothing or wrapping give the impression that there is something inessential about the human element. From the opposite point of view, Ælfric also comments on 'the divinity that received him': 'ðære godcundnysse þe hine underfeng' (Godden XXIV. lines 111-12), and 'the divinity that inhered in the man': 'seo

---

82. For an account of the theology of the hypostatic union, see Pelikan, *Tradition*, I, pp. 247-51.

godcundnys þe on ðam men sticode' (line 113). He offers the analogy of the human soul and body to suggest the unity of divine and human in Christ:

> Swa swa anra gehwilc manna wunað on sawle and on lichaman an mann, swa eac Crist wunað on godcundnysse and menniscnysse, on anum hade an Crist ... Nis þeahhwæðre seo godcundnys gemenged to ðære menniscnysse, ne ðær nan twæming nys. (Thorpe II. p. 40. lines 19-26).[83]

> Just as every man continues in soul and in body one man, so also Christ continues in divinity and humanity, in one person, one Christ. Nevertheless, the divinity is not mingled with the humanity, nor is there any separation.

Ælfric also offers the analogy of an egg, a single entity composed of yolk and white which are neither separated nor mixed together; but he apologizes that this might be too humble an image (lines 26-30). These attempts to describe the unity of the divine and human in Christ must necessarily fail because such a unity is unparalleled in human experience. But birth is familiar, and as God the Father guarantees the divinity of his Son, so the person of Mary, in her indisputable humanity, confirms the humanity of Jesus. Mary is unique, and therefore very special to the church, but she is still a real woman. Precisely because her humanity guarantees that of her Son, she must not be made supernatural by the pious devotions of the faithful: for this reason Ælfric calls a halt to speculation concerning both her birth and her assumption into heaven. The credal affirmation that Christ was born of the Virgin Mary is the sign of the precise equality of his flesh with hers, just as the birth of the Son within the relations of the trinity assures his divinity. These two births are equally miraculous: 'ægðer acennednys is wundorlic. and unasecgendlic' ('each birth is wonderful and indescribable'), the first without a mother and the second without a father (Godden I. lines 5-12).[84]

The unity of Christ's person is such that what is characteristic of one nature may be understood of the other without doing violence to the truth. For this reason it is possible for Jesus to say that he has descended from heaven and yet remains there (John 3. 13):

---

83. Compare Godden I. 43-46; and in Augustine, *Enchiridion* XI.36. 9-13.

84. Compare Thorpe I. p. 24. 27-31; Pope XIa. 226-28; Assmann III. 54-64; and in Augustine, *Sermo* CXC.ii.2.

Rihtlice is gecweden for ðære annysse þæt se mannes sunu of heofenum astige. and on heofenum wære ær his upstige. for ðan ðe he hæfde on ðære godcundnysse ðe hine underfeng. þæt þæt he on menniscum gecynde habban ne mihte; Witodlice seo godcundnys þe on ðam men sticode wæs ægðer ge on heofenum. ge on eorðan. and seo gefylde þysne earfoðan cwyde ðurh ða annysse cristes hades. (Godden XXIV. lines 109-15)[85]

Because of that unity it is correctly said that the Son of Man descended from heaven and was in heaven before his ascension, for he had in that divinity which received him that which he could not have in his human person. Truly the divinity which inhered in the man was both in heaven and on earth, and it fulfilled this difficult saying through the unity of Christ's person.

It is particularly important that Christ is referred to here as 'se mannes sunu', for this stresses that the deepest human qualities of Christ's person (which make him the pattern of humanity) are to be understood as wholly acceptable to the divine realm. Only the unity of the God-man could allow this to be so, bestowing the privileges of the divine upon the human, liberating one aspect of his nature by communication with the other.

Ælfric affirms that the divinity of Jesus was perfect from the beginning of his earthly life (Thorpe IX. p. 150. 11-13). Likewise, his was a true humanity in that he developed from childhood to adulthood, and suffered the weaknesses of the human frame. In spite of this, Ælfric, like Augustine, is unwilling to admit the possibility of any ignorance in Christ even as a child.[86] Of the baby presented to Simeon in the temple he says:

Sprecan he mihte, gif he wolde; and ealswa wis he wæs ða, þaþa he wæs anre nihte, swa swa he wæs, þaþa he wæs ðrittig geara; ac he wolde abidan his wæstma timan on ðære menniscnysse, swa swa hit gecyndelic is on mancynne. (Thorpe IX. p. 142. lines 26-30)

---

85. Compare Pope VIII. 219-35; XII. 212-18; and in Augustine, *In Ioannis Evangelium tractatus* XXVII.4.

86. Compare Augustine in *De peccatorum meritis et remissione* II.xxix.48 and *De trinitate* I.xii.23.

He could have spoken, had he wished to, for he was just as wise when he was one day old as when he was thirty years old; but he wished to wait for the time of his growth in human nature, just as is natural in mankind.

This voluntary abdication of the powers of speech and will was part of the 'emptying' of himself (Philippians 2. 7) which the Son readily accepted in becoming human. The only aspect of humanity which remained unassumed was its sinfulness. With the absence of this familiar feature he need not be thought inhuman if it is remembered that Christ is the one true human being, in whose humanity all participate. His natural development as a child contrasts with his fully-realized divinity:

> He weox and wæs gestrangod on þære menniscnysse, and he ne behofode nanes wæstmes ne nanre strangunge on þære godcundnysse. He æt, and dranc, and slep, and weox on gearum, and wæs þeah-hwæðere eal his lif butan synnum. (p. 150. lines 3-7)[87]

> He grew and was strengthened in the humanity and yet he needed no growth or strengthening in the divinity. He ate, and drank, and slept, and grew in years, and yet all through his life he was without sin.

Christ was protected by his divinity against sin when he was tempted, but his humanity was nevertheless subjected to temptation. He remained sinless, but in those trials he experienced and sanctified the struggle of every Christian. He was tempted to rely on himself rather than on God, and to glorify himself. This experience was possible only because of his true humanity. Ælfric observes that this human 'garment' made the devil suppose him to be susceptible to temptation like everyone else: it was a disguise which concealed his true identity. Other spiritual beings were not so deceived:

> Buton se deofol gesawe þæt Crist man wære, ne gecostnode he hine; and buton he soð God wære, noldon ða englas him ðenian. (Thorpe XI. p. 174. lines 20-22)

---

87. Compare Thorpe I. p. 26. 1-2; XI. p. 176. 3-9; XIII. p. 200. 4-9; Godden XIII. 260-61; Pope V. 234-39; XIa. 137; XX. 340.

Had the devil not seen that Christ was a man, he would not have tempted him, and had he not been true God, the angels would not have desired to serve him.

His true divinity was manifested by the service of angels, but this followed only after a manifestation of true humanity. Christ's experience in the wilderness describes the tension between the divine and the human in him. He did not work miracles upon his own person, to free himself of unnecessary danger or discomfort. Instead of exhibiting extraordinary strengths, he allowed himself to be afflicted, like everyone else, by hunger, thirst and weariness.[88] He shared joys and sorrows, taking delight in the company of the family at Bethany, and mourning for his friend Lazarus. Through these weaknesses he was able to reveal the nature of God. By a paradox, the divine is revealed by its union with the human:

Ne mihte ure mennisce gecynd Crist on ðære godcundlican acennednysse geseon; ac þæt ylce Word was geworden flæsc, and wunode on us, þæt we hine geseon mihton. (Thorpe II. p. 40. lines 15-18)[89]

Our human nature could not see Christ in (his) divine birth, but that same Word had become flesh, and was dwelling among us, so that we might see him.

The incarnation allowed more than simple revelation, however. Christ's weakness is the source of divine strength for the faithful. Augustine finds creative power in the weakness Christ accepted in humanity, which contrasts with his divine strength:

Fortitudo Christi te creauit, infirmitas Christi te recreauit. Fortitudo Christi fecit ut quod non erat esset: infirmitas Christi fecit ut quod erat non periret. Condidit nos fortitudine sua, quaesiuit nos infirmitate sua. (*In Ioannis Evangelium tractatus* XV.6. lines 19-23)

---

88. For example, Thorpe XI. p. 178. 8-10; Godden XXIX. 26-27; XXIII. 144; Pope V. 106-7 and 228-36.

89. The reference is to John 1. 14. Compare Augustine in *In Ioannis Evangelium tractatus* XXXVI.6.

The strength of Christ created you; the weakness of Christ recreated you. The strength of Christ caused what-was-not to be; the weakness of Christ caused what-was to perish not. He produced us in his strength; he sought us in his weakness.

Commenting on John 4. 6, Ælfric picks up Augustine's interpretation of the strong-weak Christ:

> . . . Crist wæs werig swaþeah
> on þære menniscnysse, æfter mannes gecynde,
> and his untrumnys is ure trumnys:
> his trumnys us gesceop, and his untrumnyss us alysde.
> On þære sixtan tide he sæt werig æt þam pytte,
> and on ðære syxtan ylde þysre worulde
> he com to middanearde mancynn to alysenne. (Pope V. lines 106-12)[90]

> Nevertheless, Christ was weary in his humanity, according to man's nature, and his weakness is our strength: his strength created us, and his weakness redeemed us. At the sixth hour he sat weary at the well, and in the sixth age of this world he came to the earth to redeem mankind.

The final expression of Christ's creative weakness was in his suffering and death: like the other human experiences of Christ this last pertained only to his human nature, for as God he is impassible. Ælfric is even willing to use the expression 'deadlic' ('mortal') of Christ:

> we gelyfan þæt he wæs deadlic on urum flæsce, seðe is unðrowigendlic on his godcundnysse. (Thorpe VII. p. 116. lines 26-27)[91]

> we believe that he was mortal in our flesh, who is impassible in his divinity.

---

90. The division of the world's history into six ages comes from Augustine, in *De civitate Dei* XXII.xxx. The sixth age is from Christ's birth to the end of the world. I return to the idea of the weakness of Christ on page 109.

91. Compare Thorpe VIII. p. 120. 18-20; Godden I. 33-35; IV. 170-72; Pope X. 157-58.

It is his mortality which most reveals his setting aside of the glory which is due to God alone (Pope X. 147-50).[92] As his mortality was due to his human nature, so also his death was the death of a man, not the death of God. Yet a firm conviction of the union of divine and human allows the paradoxes that Christ is life and has died, that his death destroyed death. No ordinary human death could have achieved this. In the perfect unity of the divine and human natures of Christ lies the salvific effect of his death, for although God by his nature cannot die, yet by a mystery he has undergone death in order to conquer death. The paradoxes of Christ's birth speak of how the omnipotent ruler of creation emptied himself and became weak for its redemption. The paradox of his death proclaims that in human weakness rests the intensity of divine power:

> Crist is lif. and swa ðeah he wæs on rode ahangen; He is soð lif. and swa ðeah he wæs dead on ðære menniscnysse. na on godcundnysse; On cristes deaðe wæs se deað adydd. for ðan þe þæt deade lif acwealde ðone deað. and he wæs fornumen on cristes lichaman. (Godden XIII. lines 272-76)[93]

> Christ is life, and yet he was hung upon the cross. He is true life, and yet he was dead in (his) humanity, not in (his) divinity. In Christ's death, death was destroyed, for that dead life killed death, which was annihilated in Christ's body.

In this triumphant paradox Ælfric draws on Augustine's exploration, in his commentary on John, of the prefiguring of Christ's death in the story of Moses and the brazen serpent (Numbers 21. 6-9). Following Augustine, Ælfric draws attention to the biting serpents which afflicted the Israelites: these are the sins deriving from mortality (257-58).[94] A sacramental understanding of signs finds salvation prefigured in the brazen serpent: as the Israelites looked upon it to render the real serpents harmless, so all may now look upon death in the person of Christ to render death harmless: 'Adtenditur mors, ut nihil ualeat mors' ('They set their

---

92. Compare Augustine in *In Ioannis Evangelium tractatus* XVIII.2.

93. Ælfric makes the same point when he says that it was the humanity of Christ that redeemed us (Pope XI. 88-89).

94. Compare Augustine in *In Ioannis Evangelium tractatus* XII.11. 19-20.

gaze upon death that death may have no power' *In Ioannis Evangelium tractatus* XII.11. line 24).[95] The paradox of Life accepting death is as great and as salutary as that of the Godhead accepting humanity:

> Nonne uita Christus? et tamen in cruce Christus. Nonne uita Christus? et tamen mortuus Christus. Sed in morte Christi mors mortua est; quia uita mortua occidit mortem, plenitudo uitae deglutiuit mortem: absorpta est mors in Christi corpore. (lines 28-32)

> Is not Christ life? And yet Christ (dying) on the cross. Is not Christ life? And yet Christ died. But in the death of Christ death died; for life, by having died, killed death; the fullness of life consumed death; death was swallowed up in the body of Christ.[96]

Christ's mortal body, the symbol and fact of his humanity, is the medium for the destruction of mortality. Here the metaphor of clothing or wrapping might be recalled to good effect, for the body hanging upon the cross conceals one who has the power to divest himself of that mortal covering. Ælfric derives this meaning from the stripping of Christ as the soldiers mock him at the trial:

> Hi hine unscryddon. and eft gescryddon. for ðan ðe he wolde. his lichaman forlætan. and siððan undeadlicne. eft aræran. (Godden XIV. lines 219-21)

> They stripped him and then dressed him again, for he wished to abandon his body, and afterwards, living, rise again.

This very action, in which the life-sustaining divinity is constantly present, is the work of recreation which changes the nature of humanity.

The triumphant conjunction of human and divine activity in Christ is the resurrection. Resurrection may seem to be a purely divine achievement, for it displays divine power at its

---

95. Compare Godden XIII. 266-67.

96. The opening phrases here might more literally be rendered, 'Is not Christ life? and yet Christ (is) on the cross. Is not Christ life? and yet Christ (is) dead.'

fullest. Yet since it presupposes death, it also presupposes humanity, and so Christ's resurrection is of his humanity as much as the rest of his life:

> be þam þe he mann wæs, he wæs of Marian acenned;
> be þam þe he lichama wæs, he læg bebyrged;
> on þam ðe he dead wæs, he aras of deaþe. (Pope X. lines 154-56)[97]

> in that he was man, he was born of Mary; in that he was body, he lay buried; in that he was dead, he arose from death.

Resurrection unites divine power and human life, so achieving the perfecting transformation of humanity, now elevated to the immortal nature of the Godhead. Augustine brings to a close his sermon on John 14. 27-28 with a summary of this recreating work of Christ in which his exalted humanity transforms the mortal into the immortal. His human life, raised to heavenly glory, raises all human life:

> Sed hoc erat ire ad eum et recedere a nobis, mutare atque immortale facere quod mortale suscepit ex nobis, et leuare in caelum per quod fuit in terra pro nobis. (*In Ioannis Evangelium tractatus* LXXVIII.3. lines 25-27)

> But His going unto Him and departing from us was were neither more nor less than His transforming and immortalizing that which He had taken upon Him from us in its mortal condition, and exalting that to heaven, by means of which He lived on earth in man's behalf.

The honour done to humanity is a source of rejoicing for all who can appropriate its effects:

> Quis non hinc gaudeat, qui sic diligit Christum, ut et suam naturam iam immortalem gratuletur in Christo, atque id se speret futurum esse per Christum? (lines 27-30)

---

97. Pope points to Augustine *In Ioannis Evangelium tractatus* LXXVIII.3 in connection with this passage. Ælfric almost certainly consulted the commentary on John, for the thought in these lines is much expanded beyond what is provided in Haymo (*Homilies*, p. 402).

And who would not draw rejoicing from such a source, who has such love to Christ that he can at once congratulate his own nature as already immortal in Christ, and cherish the hope that he himself will yet become so through Christ?

Picking up this theme, Ælfric finds it important to establish first of all that Christ's work of suffering is now complete. His resurrection means that the characteristics of his divinity are now extended to his humanity, and he is now 'eallswa ece on þære menniscnysse swa swa he is on þære godcundnysse' ('just as eternal in the humanity as he is in the divinity', Thorpe IX. p. 150. lines 24-25).[98] All mortal life is associated with this transformation by the incarnation of the Son, so that all who unite themselves with the eternal Man are carried through the barrier of death with the same transformed life. In Christ humanity is henceforward released from this most human of its chains:

Þæs Hælendes ærist is ure freols-tid and bliss, forðan ðe he gelædde us mid his æriste to ðære undeadlicnysse þe we to gesceapene wæron. (Thorpe XV. p. 222. lines 21-23)[99]

The Saviour's resurrection is our festival time and joy, for he led us by his resurrection to the immortality for which we were created.

The resurrection of the faithful thus brings to completion the plan of God in establishing creation. Immortality provides for the eternal praise and glorification of God: the perfection of the saints is the perfection of glory.

Ælfric's account of the person of the Son has at its centre the gracious and loving manifestation of sonship realized in the incarnation. The simultaneous expression of perfect obedience to the Father and of perfect love for the brothers and sisters he is to rescue makes

---

98. Compare Thorpe II. p. 28. 9-12; Godden XV. 143-44; XXII. 175-76 and 181-84; Pope VII. 143-44; VIII. 221-27; XI. 40-48 and 347-52; XIa. 143-45 and 162; XII. 190-92; XVIII. 213-15; and in Augustine, *In Ioannis Evangelium tractatus* XXXVI.12.

99. Compare Thorpe VII. p. 116. 27-30; XV. p. 224. 33-35; Godden XXII. 181-86; Pope VII. 158-61; XI. 46-53; XIa. 158-61; XII. 203-5.

the Son's humanity the object of wonder and devotion. Ælfric's account is particularly indebted to the devotion to Christ expressed in Augustine's commentary on John.

V. GOD THE HOLY SPIRIT

The third person of the trinity is the Holy Spirit. His special relation within the trinity differs from that of the Son, being procession rather than generation. The Spirit is neither the second son of the Father nor the second father of the Son, but he is the mysterious bond of love between the Father and the Son, the determining, effecting will which completes their creative activity:

> Nis he geworht, ne gesceapen, ne acenned, ac he is forðstæppende, þæt is ofgangende, of ðam Fæder and of ðam Suna, þam he is gelic and efen-ece. Nis se Halga Gast na Suna, forðan ðe he nis na acenned, ac he gæð of ðam Fæder and of ðam Suna gelice; forðan ðe he is heora beigra Willa and Lufu. (Thorpe XX. p. 280. lines 13-18)[100]

> He is not made, nor created, nor begotten, but he is proceeding, that is, going forth, from the Father and from the Son, with whom he is equal and co-eternal. The Holy Spirit is not a son, for he is not begotten, but he proceeds from the Father and from the Son equally, for he is the Will and Love of them both.

'Forðstæppende' normally translates 'procedens', and so it is found occasionally in Ælfric's homilies with a literal meaning.[101] 'Procedit' or 'procedens' may also be applied in a biblical text to the person of Christ, and Ælfric reproduces this in his own translation.[102] But his most distinctive use of the verb is in describing the Holy Spirit's procession from the

---

100. Compare Thorpe I. p. 10. 9-10; XX. p. 278. 12-13 and p. 280. 22-28; XXXIII. p. 498. 29-34 and p. 500. 9-11; *De penitentia* p. 604. 28-30; Pope VI. 240-41; VIII. 188-89; IX. 84-86 and 110-13; Skeat I. 76-77.

101. For example, Pope II. 209-10; VI. 99.

102. Thorpe XIII. p. 200. 17-22; Godden VI. 60-61; Pope IX. 7 and 86.

Father and Son, distinguishing the procession of the Spirit from the generation of the Son. In discussing the relations in the trinity, Ælfric regularly uses the verb 'forðstæppan' with special reference to the Spirit. Other Old English homilists, who do not attempt to explain the trinitarian relations, simply describe the Holy Spirit as 'of both Father and Son', indicating a general acceptance of this Augustinian formulation.[103] The use of 'forðstæppan' to denote the special place of the Spirit within the trinity, and in particular to distinguish the Spirit from the Son, is confined to Ælfric.[104]

As the Son gives expression to the Father's power, so the Spirit, their uniting love or will, brings creation to completion. Through the Holy Spirit all things are given life, without which they could not truly exist, nor offer rightful praise to their creator. The Spirit maintains life through his immanent presence in the whole of creation:

He is se Willa and seo soðe Lufu þæs Fæder and þæs Suna, ðurh ðone sind ealle ðing geliffæste and gehealdene, be ðam is þus gecweden, 'Godes Gast gefylð ealne ymbhwyrft middangeardes, and he hylt ealle ðing, and he hæfð ingehyd ælces gereordes.' (Thorpe XX. p. 280. lines 8-13)[105]

He is the will and the true love of the Father and the Son, and through him all things are quickened and preserved, of whom it is spoken thus, 'God's Spirit fills all the circumference of the earth, and he holds all things secure, and he has knowledge of every language.'

Through the Spirit's quickening the created world of the future is provided for and ordered. Ælfric points out that, according to the Bible, creation is truly complete, so far as God's

---

103. On the general adoption of the 'filioque', see Pelikan, *Tradition*, III, pp. 21-22.

104. *A Microfiche Concordance of Old English*, edited by Antonette diPaolo Healey and R.L. Venezky (Toronto, 1980) records no comparable use of the word.

105. Thorpe I. p. 10. 6-10; VIII. p. 134. 6; XIII. p. 192. 3-4; XV. p. 228. 23-25; XX. p. 282. 2-6; XXXIII. p. 498. 31-33; Godden III. 124-26; IV. 77-78; XXII. 71-73; *De penitentia* p. 604. 30-31; Pope VI. 234-35; VII. 210-11; X. 92-94; XIa. 11-16 and 210-15; XXI. 17-20; Skeat I. 37-38.

activity is concerned; and yet new creatures are apparently coming into being every day. This is through the disposition of the Spirit:

> and he hi ealle geliffæste þurh ðone halgan gast. and on ðam deopan dihte stodon ealle þa ðing ðe ða gyt næron; Witodlice we wæron on þam dihte. and eac ða ðe æfter us cumað. oð þyssere worulde geendunge. (Godden XII. lines 286-90)[106]

> and he gave them all life through the Holy Spirit, and in that profound disposition existed all those things which yet were not. Certainly we were in that disposition, and also those who will come after us, until the end of this world.

God's provision of life is through the Will of the trinity; it is the Will of the Godhead whose activity is preeminently expressed in the incarnation of the Son, for it was through the medium of the Spirit, that Jesus was conceived and born. Ælfric explains that this does not mean he is the father of Jesus:

> þæt cild nære of nanum men gestryned, ac wære of þam Halgan Gaste. Nis na hwæðere se Halga Gast Cristes Fæder, ac he is genemned to ðære fremminge Cristes mennisc-nysse; forðan ðe he is Willa and Lufu þæs Fæder and þæs Suna. (Thorpe XIII. p. 196. lines 20-24)[107]

> the child was not begotten from any man, but was from the Holy Spirit. Nevertheless, the Holy Spirit is not the father of Christ, but he is named as the instigation of Christ's humanity, for he is the will and love of the Father and of the Son.

Ælfric always refers to the Spirit as Will and Love: the means by which divine intention is accomplished. In his own basic explanation of why the Spirit is not the father of Jesus, Augustine concludes that when Jesus was born 'of the Spirit', grace joined together humanity and divinity, in such a way that grace became part of his nature:

---

106. Compare Pope II. 220-31.

107. Compare Thorpe XIII. p. 198. 30-33; XX. p. 284. 26-33; Godden III. 130-33; XV. 280-82; XXXV. 71-72.

Quae gratia propterea per spiritum sanctum fuerat significanda quia ipse proprie sic est deus ut dicatur etiam dei donum. (*Enchiridion* xii.40. lines 61-63)

And the reason why it was right that this grace be signified by the Holy Spirit was that He has proper attributes as God which make Him even called the 'gift of God'.

Ælfric speaks of a great outpouring of grace upon Jesus at his birth: the Spirit not only effected the birth of God as man; he also effected the sanctification of the man as God. This is the same grace, the same Spirit, as that at work in the sanctification of each Christian life:

Þurh ða gife þe se mennisca crist wearð godes bearn. þurh ða ylcan gife bið gehwilc cristenra manna gode gecoren. fram ðam anginne his geleafan; Ðurh ðone ylcan gast þe crist wæs acenned. ðurh þone ylcan his gecorenan beoð geedcennede. on ðam halgum fulluhte. (Godden XXXV. lines 68-72)[108]

Through that grace by which the human Christ became God's child, through that same grace every Christian is chosen by God, from the beginning of his belief. Through the same Spirit from which Christ was born, through the same his chosen are born again in holy baptism.

Augustine also describes exactly this continuity. The Spirit's gracious outpouring which effected the life of Christ is manifested in the life of all the saints:

Ea gratia fit ab initio fidei suæ homo quicumque christianus, qua gratia homo ille ab initio suo factus est Christus: de ipso Spiritu et hic renatus, de quo est ille natus; eodem Spiritu fit in nobis remissio peccatorum quo Spiritu factum est ut nullum haberet ille peccatum. (*De praedestinatione sanctorum* xv.31)

It is by that grace that every man from the beginning of his faith becomes a Christian, by which grace that one man from His beginning became Christ; the former also is born

---

108. Compare Thorpe IX. p. 150. 11-13.

again by the same Spirit of which the latter was born. By the same Spirit is effected in us the remission of sins, by which is was effected that He should have no sin.[109]

Both beginnings and developments are taken care of by the Spirit: birth and sanctification are his concern whether in the life of the Son or of the sons. This is not merely a satisfying parallel: the truth that the same spiritual energy as that poured out upon Christ is also available to all Christians is a profound inspiration to faith.

Augustine finds the Spirit's presence at the heart of the Christian response to God. he operates at every stage, initiating and energizing, supporting the converted will,

> ut divina gratia indeclinabiliter et inseparabiliter ageretur; et ideo, quamvis infirma, non tamen deficeret, neque adversitate aliqua vinceretur. (*De correptione et gratia* xii.38).[110]

with the result that it is unwaveringly and invincibly influenced by divine grace, and consequently, whatever its weakness, it does not fail, and is not overcome by any difficulty.

The Spirit gives all the things which are appropriate to the life of faith, and such gifts presuppose the indwelling of the Spirit himself (*Epistula* CXCIV.iv.18). Ælfric speaks of the same all-embracing influence of the Holy Spirit, the person of Grace, who informs and directs every stage of conversion and growth in the faith:

> Witodlice þa þe on God belyfað, hi sind þurh ðone Halgan Gast gewissode. Nis seo gecyrrednys to Gode of us sylfum, ac of Godes gife, swa swa se apostol cwyð, 'Þurh Godes gife ge sind gehealdene on geleafan.' (Thorpe VII. p. 114. lines 8-11)[111]

---

109. Quoted in the translation by Peter Holmes and Robert Ernest Wallis.

110. I refer to this passage again on page 134.

111. The reference is to Ephesians 2. 8. Compare Pope XII. 150-55. See also page 136 below, where I refer to these lines again.

Truly those who believe in God are directed by the Holy Spirit. Our turning to God is not of ourselves, but of God's grace, as the Apostle says, 'Through God's grace you are held fast in faith.'

The Holy Spirit's gift empowers the life of love, enabling the right response both to the love of God and to the needs of the neighbour whose features are discerned in all people. One of Augustine's favourite verses, Romans 5. 5, speaks of this infusion of love and identifies it with the indwelling of the Spirit:

Dilectio . . . dei diffusa est in cordibus nostris per spiritum sanctum qui datus est nobis. (*De trinitate* XV.xvii.31. lines 133-34)[112]

The charity of God is poured in our hearts by the Holy Spirit, who has been given to us.

The love which is given is the most excellent gift of God. The Christian who receives it is by this energizing grace enabled to give appropriately: his gifts are rendered acceptable by the presence of love. The corollary of this is that where love is absent all sacrifice is void (XV.xviii.32).

Further, Love in the person of the Spirit unites each faithful Christian with the trinity by his indwelling, just as within the trinity it unites Father and Son. The teaching of Scripture is that the Spirit is of both, and this double origin reveals the Spirit's nature: 'qua inuicem se diligunt pater et filius nobis insinuat caritatem' ('He insinuates to us the common love by which the Father and the Son mutually love each other', XV.xvii.27. lines 4-5). The presence of God is therefore readily identified with the active exercise of love in the heart.

---

112. In her article 'Le verset paulinien *Rom.*,v,5, dans l'oeuvre de saint Augustin', in *Augustinus Magister*, Congrès International Augustinien, 3 vols (Paris, 1954), I and II (Communications), pp. 657-58, A.-M. La Bonnardière notes that this text is cited at least 201 times by Augustine in the period 387-429, with very frequent citation in 411-421, corresponding to the period of his engagement with anti-Pelagian polemic. His use of the verse is essentially to support statements about the gift of the Holy Spirit.

For Augustine, the mutual relation between Father and Son is well expressed by the name 'gift', for a gift exists in a mysterious unity with its giver:

> 'Donum' ergo 'donatoris' et 'donator doni' cum dicimus relatiue utrumque ad inuicem dicimus. Ergo spiritus sanctus ineffabilis quaedam patris filiique communio. (V.xi.12. lines 27-30)

> When, therefore, we speak of the gift of a giver and the giver of a gift, we are clearly expressing their mutual relationship. Hence, the Holy Spirit is in a certain sense the ineffable communion of the Father and the Son.

Whether the Spirit is seen as Gift or Love, the union expressed defines the peculiar nature of the Spirit. As Love, the Spirit's nature is a manifestation of indissoluble unifying forces. As Gift, the Spirit's relation to Christians is also included, and the bond between giver and receiver finds expression in the person of the Spirit:

> Quod autem datum est, et ad eum qui dedit refertur, et ad eos quibus dedit; itaque spiritus sanctus, non tantum patris et filii qui dederunt sed etiam noster dicitur qui accepimus. (V.xiv.15. lines 14-17)

> But that which was given, bears a relation both to Him who gave, as well as to those to whom He was given. Therefore, the Holy Spirit is not only called the Spirit of the Father and the Son who gave Him, but ours as well, since we received Him.

This encounter with the Spirit, and through him with the trinity, operates entirely on the level of personal experience.

Ælfric's preferred name for the Holy Spirit is not 'gift', but 'love' or 'will'. Augustine finds that they are synonymous (*De trinitate* XV.xx.38. 36-39).[113] This suits Ælfric's view of the creating trinity very well, for it places the person of the Spirit in the context of the divine activity in bringing to completion the design of the Origin. As the mutual love of the

---

113. Compare Thorpe XX. p. 282. 4-6.

Father and Son he is the focus for the co-inherence of the trinity. This is dependent on the concept of the Spirit's double procession.

Like Augustine, Ælfric finds it difficult to explain how the procession of the Spirit differs from the generation of the Son. Augustine confesses to the inadequacy of human understanding in this matter even in the closing lines of *De trinitate*; here he concedes that only in the bliss of heaven, where all questions will be answered, will there be unclouded enjoyment of the truth about the Spirit's nature:

> Nec aliquid quaeremus mente ratiocinante, sed contemplante cernemus quare non sit filius spiritus sanctus, cum de patre procedat. In illa luce nulla erit quaestio. (XV. xxv.45. lines 18-21)

> Nor shall we seek anything by the reasoning of the mind, but by contemplating we shall perceive why the Holy Spirit is not the Son when He proceeds from the Father. In that light there shall no longer be any question.

The analogy of the sun, from Ælfric's sermon on the trinity, compares the Spirit's procession with the production of heat both from the sun itself and the light it generates:

> Ðære sunnan hætu gæð of hire and of hire leoman; and se Halga Gast gæð æfre of ðam Fæder and of þam Suna gelice; be ðam is þus awriten, 'Nis nan þe hine behydan mæge fram his hætan.' (Thorpe XX. p. 282. lines 15-18)[114]

> The heat of the sun proceeds from it and from its light; and the Holy Spirit proceeds eternally from the Father and from the Son equally, and of him it is written thus, 'There is none that may hide himself from his heat.'

---

114. These lines are referred to above (page 37) in the discussion of Ælfric's doctrine of the trinity, but are quoted here because of their particular relevance to his account of the person of the Holy Spirit. Compare *De penitentia* p. 606. 18-21; Skeat I. 73-77. The reference is to Psalm 18. 7.

This analogy is Ælfric's only attempt to clarify things; usually he merely repeats that the Holy Spirit is Love and Will, proceeding from both Father and Son. However, 'love' and 'will' are good expressions of the nature of the Spirit, free from any constraining corporality and allowing a perception of pure relation.

While the Father may be known through creation and through the Son, and the Son is revealed by means of his humanity, the Spirit has to be experienced directly, by the gracious gift of Father and Son. In a sense therefore, he is the most dynamic person of the trinity, but is, for the same reason, the most difficult to describe and define. Affirmations of the Spirit's place in the trinity occur repeatedly throughout Ælfric's work, but they are credal statements which are rarely enlarged. Also, especially in his sermons for the season of Pentecost, Ælfric explains the historical bestowal of the Holy Spirit. The Spirit is best understood, however, within the context of living the Christian life, where the indwelling of the Spirit is tested and proved: as the person of grace he is the stimulation and guide of Christians, providing the structure of life as Christ does its foundation.

The Gospel accounts of the bestowal of the Spirit may give an indication of that structure. The Spirit was first manifested at the baptism of Christ, when God also spoke to his Son (Mark 1. 10-11). This teaches that at every baptism the trinity is present and the Spirit is bestowed (Godden III. 108-21).[115] The Spirit appeared at the baptism of Jesus in the likeness of a dove: the dove, as Ælfric explains, is the symbol of innocence and love, and it points to the characteristics which should be found in all who imitate Christ (153-63). By contrast, the Spirit was bestowed on the apostles in the form of tongues of fire. The fire inflamed the disciples and empowered them for the work which Christ gave them:

> hi wurdon afyllede mid þære heofonlican lare, and cuðon ealle woruldlice gereord, and bodedon unforhtlice geleafan and fulluht ricum and reðum. (Thorpe XXI. p. 298. lines 6-9)[116]

> they were filled with heavenly knowledge, and they knew all earthly language, and fearlessly preached faith and baptism to the powerful and cruel.

---

115. Compare Augustine, *In Ioannis Evangelium tractatus* VI.5.

116. Compare Thorpe XXI. p. 324. 5-7; Godden III. 138-39 and 163-67; Pope VII. 196-202; IX. 135-38 and 152-57; X. 42-48; XI. 59-65; XIa. 176-82.

The Spirit empowered them to be obedient to the will of God, and to serve him with ardour. The two guises of dove and flame represent a potent association of loving innocence and fearless ardour, which should be found in all Christians:

> On culfran anlicnysse and on fyres hiwe wæs Godes Gast æteowod; forðan ðe he deð
> þæt ða beoð bilewite on unscæððignysse, and byrnende on Godes willan, þe he mid his
> gife gefylð. (Thorpe XXII. p. 320. lines 31-34)[117]

> In the likeness of a dove and in the semblance of fire the Spirit of God was manifested,
> for he causes to be meek in innocence and aflame with the will of God those whom he
> fills with his grace.

It is scarcely possible to decide whether in this passage 'Godes willan' and 'his gife' are different from 'Godes Gast': grace is the indwelling of the Spirit.

The Spirit is experienced by the Christian in the direct and transforming comfort of his presence. In place of the old characteristics of the sinful life, a new and positive guidance is bestowed:

> He is gehaten on Greciscum gereorde, Paraclitus, þæt is, Frofor-gast, forði ðe he frefrað
> þe dreorian, þe heora synna behreowsiað, and sylð him forgyfenysse hiht, and heora
> unrotan mod geliðegað. (p. 322. lines 20-23)[118]

> In the Greek tongue he is called 'Paraclitus', that is, Comforting Spirit, because he
> comforts the sorrowing who repent of their sins, and gives them the hope of
> forgiveness, and eases their troubled mind.

---

117. Compare Thorpe XXII. p. 322. 4-8; Godden III. 168-74; and in Augustine, *In Ioannis Evangelium tractatus* VI.3.

118. Compare Thorpe XXXVI. p. 550. 31-33; Pope VI. 252-53; IX. 84; X. 80-86; XIa. 7.

The special work of the Spirit is to be the medium of forgiveness (Pope VI. 250-53).[119] This again is part of the work of recreation, for the Spirit frees the mind from the slavery of sin and despair, replacing that imprisonment with a new liberty of love, service and hope. The Spirit's task is to equip the Christian with the qualities and energies which are pleasing to God, and these he bestows according to his grace. In each one the transforming touch is seen, even though its effects may vary from one person to another:

> He sylð his gife ðam ðe he wile . . . todælende æghwilcum be ðam ðe him gewyrð; forðam ðe he is Ælmihtig Wyrhta, and swa hraðe swa he þæs mannes mod onliht, he hit awent fram yfele to gode. (Thorpe XXII. p. 322. lines 24-32)[120]

> He gives his grace to whom he will . . . distributing to each as it seems fit to him; for he is the almighty creator, and as soon as he illumines the mind of man, he turns it from evil to good.

Enlightenment and transformation are followed by the gift of strength appropriate for service:

> Mid godum inngehyde he gladaþ ure mod,
> and þurh hine we oncnawað hwæt us to donne is,
> and he us gestrangað to þære fremminge,
> þæt we for earfoðnysse ure anginn ne forlæton. (Pope IX. lines 145-48)[121]

---

119. Compare Thorpe XXII. p. 322. 23-24; XXV. p. 352. 15; XXVII. p. 394. 31; XXXIII. p. 498. 27-28; XXXVI. p. 550. 30-31; Godden XVI. 190-92; XXXV. 74; Pope I. 96-97; VI. 242. Sometimes Ælfric says that the Spirit forgives, rather than that it is through the Spirit that God forgives; apparently the distinction is not important: Thorpe XXXVI. p. 370. 6-9; Pope VI. 250-55; VII. 57-60; X. 87-88; XIa. 9-10.

120. Compare Godden III. 112-14; XII. 247-50; Pope IX. 117-23; X. 116-19; XI. 70-71; XIa. 186-87; XII. 150-164.

121. Pope V. 131-34; X. 44-48 and 89-91.

With good understanding he gladdens our mind, and through him we know what we ought to do, and he strengthens us to enable us to do it, so that we do not abandon our beginning because of difficulty.

The gifts of the Spirit are in keeping with the needs of love and service. The ability to know and understand something of God is provided together with the means of transforming that knowledge into the practical and loving service of others:

he onbryrt ure mod mid seofonfealdre gife, þæt is, mid wisdome and andgyte, mid geðeahte and strencðe, mid ingehyde and arfæstnysse, and he us gefylð mid Godes ege. (Thorpe XXII. p. 326. lines 12-15)[122]

he stimulates our mind with sevenfold grace: that is with wisdom and understanding, with purpose and strength, with knowledge and piety, and he fills us with awe of God.

The last of these gifts emphasizes that the principal task of the Spirit is to direct the worshipping mind to God.

The Spirit's grace provides both receptivity and enlightenment in the hearts of those listening to the teacher. Without grace, all teaching is useless and unproductive. God's word cannot be understood by the intellect without the engagement of the heart, and the Spirit's influence is necessary for that involvement of the whole person (Pope X. 109-12).[123] Nevertheless, this grace is readily and freely available, and everyone who is responsive to it may receive its indwelling and illumination. Ælfric says that simply listening to the praise of God or the recital of his law opens the mind to such indwelling, for then the Holy Spirit is active and his voice is heard (Pope XII. 156). Indeed, whenever one thinks about God, the

---

122. Compare Thorpe VII. p. 110. 3-5; XXVI. p. 368. 5-11; XXXIII. p. 496. 30-32; Godden I. 167-69; XII. 13-16; XXV. 66-70; Pope IV. 160-62; V. 210-13; IX. 139-44; XIa. 8 and 185; XVII. 121-26.

123. Compare Thorpe XXII. p. 320. 25-27; Godden XXXVI. 30-32; Pope XIV. 123-25.

Spirit's grace is present ('þær man embe God smeað, þær bið þæs Gastes gifu', line 158).[124] This Spirit or grace works secretly within the mind, invisible yet with visible effect.

In baptism the recreative work of the Spirit is most clearly compared with his work in creation. It is the gift of the Spirit's grace which effects the rebirth into spiritual life. His life-giving role in this new creation was foreshadowed by the mysterious and dynamic movement of the Spirit over the waters (Genesis 1. 2). In each case the Spirit, present and active before creation, brings it to birth (Pope XII. 98-105).[125] He provides the conditions appropriate to the new beginning, and the resources which enable the Christian to follow the example of Christ.

Ælfric never underestimates the work of the Spirit in the Christian life: to him are to be attributed the rescue from sin by means of forgiveness, both at the outset of the Christian life and at every stage thereafter; the prompting and guidance in good works; the grace to complete the course defined for the elect.

---

124. Compare Augustine, *In Ioannis Evangelium tractatus* XX.5. 21-22 (Pope, *Homilies*, p. 478).

125. Compare Godden I. 108-14; III. 55-60 and 230-31; XV. 111-16; XXXV. 71-72; Pope XII. 135-38.

GRACE

Ælfric's understanding of the grace of God and the doctrine of predestination, and his belief in the necessity of the incarnation for salvation all indicate a profound affinity with the teaching of Augustine's later works. In these, Augustine examines the operation of grace in the soul's response to God, ascribing to grace every meritorious work. Especially against the Pelagians, he declares that mankind after the fall has no power to do good, relying completely upon God even for the initiation of faith. This is in contrast with his earlier defence of the freedom of the will, such as in *De libero arbitrio*, in which the Pelagians found a doctrine which agreed in many important respects with their own.[1] However, driven by his conflict with the Pelagians to an extreme position which upheld the perfect knowledge and freedom of God, Augustine effectively taught, in these last works, that God predestines some (the saints) to eternal life and others to eternal punishment.

It should be noted that for Augustine, the predestination of the saints in no way obviates the necessity of teaching and correction. Even though he conceives of the elect as a closed list of which every member will inevitably be saved, he still regards the preaching of the Gospel as one of his most important tasks. He sees that teaching the faith is useless without the operation of grace, but that if grace is present the teacher will find the listener receptive and capable of learning. For this reason he does not neglect the exhortation of the faithful to do good works and express their faith in practical ways. Good works cannot take the place of the gracious provisions of God, but they confirm and strengthen the chosen, and teach them to acknowledge their need of grace. Augustine regards the reward of eternal life as the bestowal of grace (the gift of life) upon grace (the gift of all things necessary for faith). Each gift, of which eternal life is the crown, is totally unmerited. God rewards virtues and strengths, certainly, but these are present only because of the prior working of grace. It is this 'closed circuit' of grace which effectively shuts out the non-elect. According to Augustine's understanding, anyone not provided with the necessary gift is necessarily excluded from the reward.

---

1. G.R. Evans, *Augustine on Evil* (Cambridge, 1982), p. 113.

Augustine's teaching on grace was formally adopted as Catholic doctrine by the Council of Orange (529). At this Council some of the precepts of the 'Semi-Pelagians' (chiefly of Gaul) were addressed and the supremacy of Augustine affirmed. Orange placed its emphasis very heavily upon Augustine's doctrine of grace but avoided as far as possible his related teaching on predestination, finding its occasionally harsh rigidity virtually blasphemous.[2]

Ælfric acknowledges that God's grace is necessary for every stage of the Christian's conversion and development. Within the boundless sphere of grace, Ælfric gladly accepts the idea of election, and his sermons demonstrate that the concept of the predestination of the saints has not merely intellectual force but practical reality for him. The very harshest of Augustine's ideas, expressed only rarely, that the logical corollary of predestination to eternal life for the elect was a predestination to eternal punishment for the non-elect, appears only once in Ælfric. Otherwise, he prefers to appeal to God's mercy, which may be believed to be a greater force than any predetermination of human history.

Linked to this recognition of divine mercy, apparently, is Ælfric's approval of the value of faith in action. He exhorts Christians to do good that they may win through to the reward of eternal life; without belittling the role of grace he also recognizes the importance of the active response of the soul and its effort to do God's will. For him, the appropriation of grace is manifested in good works. He seems also to believe that the exercise of these gracious gifts is a pleasing offering to God. In particular, he finds special value in the actions of penance and almsgiving, the outward signs of inward conversion.

When Ælfric's teaching on grace is compared with Augustine's it is seen that some subjects extensively treated by Augustine are given only passing attention, and some are not addressed at all. Ælfric apparently feels that he is in a position to make assumptions about some elements of doctrine, and to feel released from the obligation to support every statement with lengthy and detailed argument. Thus, for example, whilst Augustine devotes much attention to the interpretation of Romans 5. 12, reaching the conclusion that all have sinned in Adam, Ælfric never discusses this verse or even refers to it. However, the premise that all have sinned in Adam is accepted without debate and is the necessary starting-point for Ælfric's teaching on mankind's present condition and the need for salutary grace.

---

2. For an account of the Council's response to this Augustinian doctrine, see Pelikan, *Tradition*, I, pp. 327-29.

Ælfric considers each stage of Christian development, with special emphasis on the present needs of the people and on their encouragement in the faith. His account of grace begins with the creation of the angels and Adam, assessing Adam's original state of grace and the effect of sin upon him and his descendants. Human experience declares that the will is enslaved to sin, no longer at liberty to choose the right. To recover this liberty, it needs the grace of God. God in his mercy gives grace to some, but in his justice leaves the rest of mankind to suffer the punishment due to all. His mercy includes the provision of the means of redemption in the person of Jesus Christ. The Son of God became incarnate in order to be the mediator of God's grace, and his death made possible the relationship with God which he intends for the elect. Finally, Ælfric affirms the pre-eminence of grace in the life of faith: grace is present at every stage and is responsible for all good works. Yet these good works are counted worthy of reward and upon the faithful God bestows the grace of eternal life to crown all his other gifts.

I. CREATION AND FALL

Ælfric speaks of the creation always in the context of the history of redemption. The events described in the first chapters of Genesis are for him of unquestionable historicity and veracity. The creation story becomes the story of how sin came into the world, how it became the dominant and destructive force in human experience, and how this force was challenged and eradicated by the greater force of grace in Christ's incarnation and redeeming work. Mankind occupies Ælfric's attention: the creation and fall of the angels are of interest primarily to provide a context for the human creation. God created mankind to make up the loss after the fall of the sinful angels, and he has chosen sufficient numbers to complete the population of heaven (Thorpe I. p. 12. 23-28). The door, indeed, is flung still wider:

> Na þæt an þæt he ðone lyre anfealdlice gefylde, ac eac swylce micclum geihte. Soðlice swa micel getel mancynnes becymð þurh Cristes menniscnysse to engla werodum, swa

micel swa on heofonum belaf haligra engla æfter ðæs deofles hryre. (Thorpe II. p. 32. 24-28)[3]

Not only did he simply supply the loss, but also greatly added (to it). Truly, as great a number of mankind will come to the hosts of angels through Christ's incarnation as the number of holy angels which were left in heaven after the devil's fall.

This idea is familiar from Augustine's *Enchiridion*. Luke 20. 36 promises that those who are resurrected 'are equal to the angels', and this is the basis for Augustine's argument that a part of mankind will be promoted to the place formerly occupied by the angels (*Enchiridion* ix.29 and xvi.62).

The angels who fell from heaven abused the freedom of choice offered to them:

God hi geworhte to wlitegum engla gecynde, and let hi habban agenne cyre, and hi næfre ne gebigde ne ne nydde mid nanum þingum to þam yfelan ræde; ne næfre se yfela ræd ne com of Godes geþance, ac com of þæs deofles. (Thorpe I. p. 12. lines 13-17)[4]

God created them in the beautiful nature of angels and allowed them to have their own choice, and never compelled them or forced them by any means to that evil decision; nor did the evil decision ever come from God's deliberation, but it came from the devil's.

The choice of obedience was the prerequisite of happiness. In his gift of this freedom God was both just and righteous: had he subjected the angels to his service by force, or in some way required them to follow the evil instigation of Lucifer, then it could not now be true to attribute justice and righteousness to God (Thorpe VII. p. 112. 4-7). Ælfric stresses that this

---

3. Compare Thorpe XIII. p. 192. 9-13; XIV. p. 214. 21-26; XV. p. 222. 24-25; XXIV. p. 342. 24-25; Godden V. 188-91.

4. Compare Thorpe I. p. 10. 18-20; Skeat XVII. 242-45; and in Augustine, *De civitate Dei* XII.ix, where two alternative interpretations are offered as to how it came about that the angels fell, of which Ælfric's teaching follows the second.

choice was free of any obligation that derived from predestination: if the angels lost their happiness it was 'na for gewyrde, ac for ungehyrsumnysse' ('not because of destiny, but through disobedience', lines 2-3).

Ælfric does not explain how it was possible for evil to develop in the perfect nature of angels. He does not ask the terrible question: the 'yfela ræd' came not from God's thoughts but the devil's, yet the origin of the devil's 'yfela ræd' is not examined. That it is related to the free will of the angels is certain, and also that free will is to be regarded as part of original angelic perfection.[5] But that a further degree of perfection was possible is suggested by the subsequent confirmation of the remaining angels, now unable to sin:

> Þa sona þa nigon werod, þe ðær to lafe wæron, bugon to heora Scyppende mid ealre eaðmodnesse, and betæhton heora ræd to his willan. Þa getrymde se Ælmihtiga God þa nigon engla werod, and gestaþelfæste swa þæt hi næfre ne mihton ne noldon syððan fram his willan gebugan; ne hi ne magon nu, ne hi nellað nane synne gewyrcan. (Thorpe I. p. 12. lines 5-11)[6]

> Then immediately the nine hosts which were remaining submitted to their Creator with all humility and dedicated their intentions to his will. Then the Almighty God strengthened and confirmed the nine hosts of angels, so that never afterwards would they be able to or wish to depart from his will, and nor can they now, nor do they desire to do anything sinful.

---

5. R.F. Evans, in his description of Augustine's own statement (in *De civitate Dei* XII.ix) concerning the greater or lesser grace given to persevering or rebel angels, makes a radical connection between evil and the absence of grace: 'The electing grace of God discriminates among rational creatures without basis in any merit that might attach to them, and the will of men to cleave to the good is wholly dependent upon the sustaining divine grace. Without the divine grace the will of the rational creature becomes a bad will' (R.F. Evans, *One and Holy: The Church in Latin Patristic Thought*, Church Historical Series, 92 (London, 1972), p. 116).

6. Compare Augustine, *De civitate Dei* XXII.i. 43-46.

The angels who remain in heaven, loyal and obedient, are now secure in the perfect harmony of their wills with God's: it is a harmony that was apparently not possible before the angelic revolt. Ælfric never admits the possibility that there might have been any kind of fault in the creation of the angels which could have given them a tendency to sin. But clearly the angels were not infallible until they had undergone a period of testing, and those who passed the test were freed of any possibility of sin in confirmation of their status.

Augustine's account recognizes that God in his justice gave his creation the free choice of abandoning him. The angels, if they so wished, could desert God, although misery would follow if they did. He emphasizes that because it was just, this gift of freedom was also good, even with the possibility that evil might come of it. God's justice and righteousness were thus better served by this gift of freedom than if his creation were held in bondage to goodness:

> non eis ademit hanc potestatem, potentius et melius esse iudicans etiam de malis bene facere quam mala esse non sinere. (*De civitate Dei* XXII.i. lines 27-29)

> yet he did not deprive them of this power, judging it an act of greater power and greater goodness to bring good even out of evil than to exclude the existence of evil.[7]

The same principle applied to the creation of man. He was given the same freedom, and, in dependence on God, had the capacity to merit heaven, 'caelo dignum si suo cohaereret auctori' ('worthy of heaven if he adhered to the author of his being', lines 47-48). As with the angels, desertion would lead to misery. God allowed sin to happen with prescient certainty that it would, but also planned from the first the gracious transformation of its effects, 'simul praeuidens, quid boni de malo eius esset ipse facturus' ('foreseeing, at the same time, the good that he was to bring out of man's evil', lines 51-52). Freedom was therefore a gift of justice and goodness and, though it provided opportunity for revolt and rejection, God knew how he would use these creatively.

Ælfric also describes how Adam, like the angels, was endowed with the freedom to choose. God did not oblige him to obey, nor, perhaps more importantly, to disobey:

---

7. Quoted in the translation by Henry Bettenson.

þa forgeaf he Adame and Euan agenne cyre, swa hi, ðurh gehyrsumnysse, a on ecnysse, butan deaðe, on gesælðe wunodon, mid eallum heora ofspringe, swa hi, ðurh ungehyrsumnysse, deadlice wurdon. (Thorpe VII. p. 112. lines 11-14)[8]

Then he gave Adam and Eve their own choice, whether, through obedience, they might live in happiness forever, without death, with all their offspring, or whether, through disobedience, they might become mortal.

Ælfric is in no doubt that Adam was created with the capacity to respond in obedience to God's direction and that his obedience would be rewarded with the crowns of sinlessness and immortality (Pope XI. 95-97). He was provided with the necessary grace both to will the good and to perform it. His goodness was natural to him, created in him ('þa gecyndelican good þe him God on gesceop', Pope XXI. line 52). This goodness was to be exercised in obedience.

Augustine asks how humanity was to remain in this state of goodness and obedience. Though free, it was nevertheless dependent upon the grace of God to give that freedom its widest dimension. He concludes that God's intention in creating Adam was never to make an entirely independent being who could cut himself loose from God's care and protection. Adam was to be free to choose his destiny, but with every good choice provided for and assisted by grace, 'sine qua etiam cum libero arbitrio bonus esse non posset' ('without it he could not be good, even with all his freedom', *De correptione et gratia* xi.31).[9] Adam did not need grace to recover goodness, as mankind does now, but needed it purely for perseverance in the good he already possessed.

Using the gift of free will with the assistance of grace, Adam could easily have maintained his innocence before God. Ælfric points out that the command which Adam broke was a very small one, which it was perfectly in his power to obey (he describes it as 'þæt lytle bebod' 'that little command', Pope XXI. line 44).[10] Augustine makes the same point

---

8. Compare Thorpe I. p. 18. 21-31 and p. 20. 1-2; Pope XI. 97-99; XXI. 31-35; Skeat I. 150-51.

9. Quoted in the translation by John Courtney Murray.

10. Compare Thorpe I. p. 18. 21-23.

in *De civitate Dei* (XIV.xii. 16-22). The fact that obedience was so easy, and the consequences of disobedience so terrible, made the crime so much more devastating:

> quisnam satis explicet, quantum malum sit non oboedire in re facili et tantae potestatis
> imperio et tanto terrente supplicio? (XIV.xv. lines 28-30)

> who can adequately describe the enormity of the evil in a refusal to obey in a matter
> so easy, when the command comes from so great a power, and the punishment that
> threatens is so grave?

Both Augustine and Ælfric seem acutely and painfully aware of the folly and shame of man's wilful disobedience to such an easy command.

The problem of the emergence of evil in a good world prompts Ælfric to look at each stage in the process of the fall, seeking a moment when evil might be said to begin. He identifies that moment, but remains unable to explain why evil should gain entrance to the human mind then or at any other time. In a description of Adam's first sin, he shows that the devil's instigation found its response in the human mind. Ælfric says that Adam and Eve were tempted to greed, covetousness, and pride: greed prompted them to eat the apple, covetousness made them want the knowledge of good and evil; pride made them desire to be better than they were created (Thorpe XI. p. 176. lines 21-23). Where did this proud desire come from? Ælfric cannot explain: it seems that the vices sprang up in the mind in order to respond to the temptation offered. This does not mean that man was created with sinful tendencies which were awakened and exploited by the devil, but that at the critical moment of choice he rejected the good, the fatal turning away. In Augustine's terms, it was the moment when Adam failed to avail himself of the provision of grace intended to help him use his free will to good effect.

Ælfric is clear that whatever the influence of the devil, the responsibility for the turning away from obedience rests with free will:

> Seo sawul is gesceadwis gast. æfre cucu and mæg underfon ge godne wyllan. and
> yfelne. æfter agenum cyre. Se welwillende scyppend læt hi habben agenes cyres

geweald. þa wearð heo be agenum wyllan gewæmmed þurh þæs deofles lare. (Skeat I. lines 171-74)[11]

> The soul is rational spirit, immortal, and can assume both good will and evil, according to its own choice. The benevolent creator allowed it to have the power of its own choice: then by its own free will it became stained through the devil's teaching.

Why did God give his human creation freedom if he knew that such freedom would be abused? Ælfric concludes that he must ascribe God's choice for mankind, as he did for the angels, to the perfection and justice of his creation. For just as service freely given to an earthly king is of a higher order than slavery, the service offered by humanity to God should also be free:

> Swa eac ne gedafnode þam ælmihtigan drihtne
> þæt on eallum his rice nære ænig gesceaft
> þe nære on ðeowte þearle genyrwed. (Skeat XVII. lines 263-65)[12]

> In the same way it did not befit the almighty Lord that there should be in all his kingdom any creature that was cruelly constrained in bondage.

Free to choose, Adam broke the 'little command', and brought upon himself a punishment similar to that invoked upon the rebel angels:

---

11. Compare Thorpe I. p. 18. 28-31; Skeat I. 153-55; XVII. 245-50.

12. The same point is found in Augustine, for example in *De vera religione* xiv.27, or in *De gratia Christi* xiii.14. p. 137. 14-22. That the abuse of such freedom would ultimately result in the perfect manifestation of God's glorious goodness, justice and mercy is the view he takes in *De catechizandis rudibus* xviii.30. 34-37.

Þa wearð eac se mann mid deofles lotwrencum bepæht, swa þæt he tobræc his Scyppendes bebod, and wearð deofle betæht, and eal his ofspring into helle-wite. (Thorpe XIII. p. 192. lines 6-9)[13]

Then man was also deceived by the devil's deception, so that he broke his creator's command, and was delivered to the devil, and all his progeny into hell-torment.

Not only Adam, but all who come after him, are to bear this punishment.

Ælfric's sense of the extent of this disaster is derived from Augustine's doctrine of original sin, in which the introduction of sin by one man into human nature results in the condemnation of the entire race. Augustine speaks of ruin so extreme that escape from condemnation is impossible without the intervention of God:

profecto uniuersa massa perditionis facta est possessio perditoris. nemo itaque, nemo prorsus inde liberatus est, aut liberatur, aut liberabitur nisi gratia redemptoris. (*De peccato originali* xxix.34. p. 194. lines 2-4)

the entire mass of our nature was ruined beyond doubt, and fell into the possession of its destroyer. And from him no one — no, not one — has been delivered, or is being delivered, or ever will be delivered, except by the grace of the Redeemer.[14]

The experience of the human condition after the fall is that sin and evil are limiting, imprisoning powers which have impoverished every aspect of life. Augustine specifically locates the transmission of sin in the sexual act, and for him 'concupiscence', sexual pleasure, is implicated.[15] Whatever the means of transmission it is clear that Augustine understands a kind of spiritual solidarity of each person with Adam: carnal generation involves each person in an unbroken continuity of association with that first sin. Each new-born baby is inevitably part of the condemned mass, 'in qua stirpe damnata tenet hominem generatio

---

13. Compare Thorpe I. p. 18. 31-33; VII. p. 114. 4-5; Godden I. 15-17.

14. Quoted in the translation by Peter Holmes.

15. For example, *De peccato originali* xxxvii.42; *De nuptiis et concupiscentia* II.v.15.

carnalis' ('in this radical ruin carnal generation involves every man' *De peccato originali* xxxviii.43. p. 201. lines 3-4).

This belief was so clearly and strongly held by Augustine that he was not even prepared to make an exception in the case of Mary, the Mother of Jesus. He was forced to consider whether Mary might be said to be free of original sin (the later doctrine of the Immaculate Conception) by Julian of Eclanum's accusation that his teaching on original sin implied the condition of sin even for Mary, simply because she had been born. His response indicates that Mary, just like everyone else, required the liberating grace which was brought by her Son's incarnation:

> Non transcribimus diabolo Mariam conditione nascendi; sed ideo, quia ipsa conditio solvitur gratia renascendi. (*Contra Iulianum opus imperfectum* IV.cxxii)

> We do not free Mary from the devil because of the condition in which she was born, but on this account, that she was set free from that condition, reborn in grace.

According to Augustine's view of the condition of man only Christ was free of original sin. Natural birth, to which all but Christ are subjected, affects everyone with the stain of sin carried by concupiscence. Augustine excepts no-one, in order to emphasize the unique nature of the one who was born without sin:

> quaecumque nascitur proles originali est obligata peccato, nisi in illo renascatur, quem sine ista concupiscentia uirgo concepit, propterea, quando nasci est in carne dignatus, sine peccato solus est natus. (*De nuptiis et concupiscentia* I.xxiv.27. p. 240. lines 6-10)

> Whatever comes into being by natural birth is tied and bound by original sin, unless, indeed, it be born again in Him whom the Virgin conceived without this concupiscence. When He vouchsafed to become incarnate, He, and He alone, was born without sin.[16]

Augustine accordingly insists that Mary's faith, not her human desire, was the context of conception. The nature of Christ's conception sets him apart from all other men, and at the

---

16. Quoted in the translation by Peter Holmes.

same time separates his mother from all other women; she conceived her son in faith, not in desire (*Sermo* LXIX.iii.4). Again, Mary is described as ardent in faith, not in passion, in contrast with the sinful context of all other conceptions (*Sermo* CLIII.xi.14). The remark is not so much about Mary as about her Son.

That Ælfric also believed Mary to be subject to original sin can be inferred only from his own assertion of the unique sinlessness of Christ. In his commentary on the annunciation Ælfric describes Mary's 'overshadowing' by the Holy Spirit: she is freed from sin by divine grace. The child to be born will be the Son of God. Here Ælfric comments that all are conceived with unrighteousness and born with sins ('mid unrihtwisnysse geeacnode, and mid synnum acennede', Thorpe XIII. p. 200. lines 5-6) with the single exception of Christ. No further qualification of the rule is made for Mary. That she is ordinarily human (if extraordinarily endowed with grace) is confirmed by her implicit inclusion in the third of four types of human creation: Adam and Eve, types one and two, were each created in unique ways; type three accommodates all those generated by their parents; type four is again unique, that of the birth of Christ (Godden I. 59-69).

The birth of the uniquely sinless one therefore confirms both for Augustine and for Ælfric the condition of all other births since the fall. Guilt, according to Augustine, is transmitted like an ineradicable impression, so heavily stamped on each soul that even the children of the baptised (who have been washed clean of original sin) are affected. Individual cleansing is necessary (*De peccato originali* xxxviii.44). The Church is precise and urgent about the need for baptism: for Augustine this is proof that each new-born child inherits Adam's guilt. He cites Ambrose and Cyprian as saints who have required the baptism of infants in order to cleanse them from original sin. Cyprian, for example, insisted upon early baptism (within eight days of birth), in case the child should die and perish (*De nuptiis et concupiscentia* II.xxix. 51. p. 307, line 23-p. 308 line 9).[17] Because baptism is necessary for all children, even for those who have no sins of their own, it follows that it is original sin which must be dealt with in this regenerative washing:

---

17. This was not the only conclusion to be drawn from the Church's long-established insistence on the necessity of infant baptism: Pelagius considered infant baptism to be 'not remission of sins but a higher sanctification through union with Christ' (John Ferguson, *Pelagius: a historical and theological study* (Cambridge, 1965), p. 50). This, for Pelagius, was the meaning of the words 'the kingdom of heaven' (p. 178).

97

remanet igitur originale peccatum, per quod sub diaboli potestate captiui sunt, nisi inde lauacro regenerationis et Christi sanguine redimantur' (I.xx.22. p. 236. lines 3-5)

Only original sin, therefore, remains, whereby they are made captive under the devil's power, until they are redeemed therefrom by the laver of regeneration and the blood of Christ.

The necessity of baptism supports Augustine's interpretation of Romans 5. 12: here he reads that the whole of humanity is involved in Adam's sin. His Latin Bible spoke of Adam 'in quo omnes peccaverunt' ('in whom all have sinned'), which had earlier been interpreted by Ambrosiaster as an indictment of the human race.[18] 'In quo' confirms that all are born in sin, having been present in Adam whose seed carried the curse. This validating text is cited many times. When, for example, Augustine is discussing how it is that the devil has gained his power over men, he cites this verse, and explains:

per unius illius uoluntatem malam omnes in eo peccauerunt, quando omnes ille unus fuerunt, de quo propterea singuli peccatum originali traxerunt' (II.v.15. p. 266. line 24-p. 267. line 2)

By the depraved will of that one man all sinned in him since all were (in) that one man, from whom, therefore, they individually derived original sin.

Ælfric also teaches that from the moment of birth each life is tainted: sin is the inheritance of all Adam's descendants (Thorpe XI. p. 176. lines 1-3). So even babies are sinful 'through Adam's transgression' ('þurh Adames forgægednesse', Pope XII. lines 134-35), and need the cleansing power of baptism.[19] That simple preposition 'þurh' is the closest Ælfric comes to explaining Romans 5. 12. Birth implies the transmission of original

---

18. For a fuller discussion, see Pelikan, *Tradition*, I, pp. 299-300.

19. Compare Godden I. 110-14; XIII. 126-27; XIV. 321-23; Pope XI. 498-500. These passages state that baptism is necessary for the cleansing specifically of inherited sin (on many more occasions original sin is not specified and baptism is described as the means of the forgiveness of all sins).

sin, but Ælfric does not explain how. Although Augustine's interpretation of the verse is the basis of Ælfric's teaching that all are 'born with sins' ('mid synnum acennede'), it is not discussed in the homilies: apparently the doctrine no longer requires proof or justification. With Augustine Ælfric affirms that the creation of mankind is good, because it is of God (Godden XIII. 66). But it has been corrupted by evil and its allegiance turned from God to the devil; sin distorts the family likeness between God and mankind to the point where the resemblance is almost completely lost. In sinning, people emulate the devil and grow instead more like him. Just as the good may be called 'children of God' because they imitate God in his goodness, the sinful are children of the devil, not because God made them evil, but because they have in them an imitation of the evil nature of the devil. An adoption process is at work:

> Gif he geeuenlæcð deofle on manlicum dædum. he bið ðonne deofles bearn þurh his yfelan geeuenlæcunga. na gecyndelice. (lines 72-74)

> If he emulates the devil in sinful deeds, then he is the child of the devil, not according to nature but through evil emulation of him.

This 'emulation' therefore, is sin, the turning away from the good, just as being restored to harmony with the good results in an 'emulation' of God. But the emulation of the devil is the only course of action open to the will unliberated by grace, and emulation of God is possible only with the infusion of grace offered in Christ. Ælfric seems to mean that this evil emulation is contrary to the nature which God intends for humankind, but that it is part of being human now: no-one is free from the devil's distorting influence.

Ælfric expresses that distortion by sin in the image of exile, 'wræcsiðe' (Pope I. line 219).[20] In his sinful, graceless state, man is exiled from his true relationship with God. Adam and Eve were created in paradise, to live there in perfect harmony with God, with each other, and with the rest of creation. But sin destroyed that harmony and mankind was banished from paradise. Therefore, Ælfric says, each man now wanders as an exile, deprived of the country for which he was created. Nor can he retrace his steps and return by that same route by which

---

20. Compare Thorpe X. p. 162. 16-17; Godden XXXVII. 62. The same thought is found in Augustine, for example in *Enchiridion* viii.26.

his ancestors left paradise: he needs 'another route', his salvation in Christ. In his exegesis of the Gospel for Epiphany the return of the three kings by another route (Matthew 2. 12) is thus interpreted:

> Ure eard soðlice is neorxna-wang, to ðam we ne magon gecyrran þæs wæges ðe we comon. Se frumsceapena man and eall his ofspring wearð adræfed of neorxena-wanges myrhðe . . . Ac us is micel neod þæt we ðurh oðerne weg þone swicolan deofol forbugan, þæt we moton gesæliglice to urum eðele becuman, þe we to gesceapene wæron. (Thorpe VII. p. 118. lines 21-30)[21]

> Truly our country is paradise, to which we cannot return by the way we came. The first created man and all his descendants were driven out of the joy of paradise . . . But for us it is very necessary to evade the deceitful devil by another route, so that we may happily reach our homeland for which we were created.

Sin exiles humanity from the rest of creation. All God's creatures obey him and live within his laws; only mankind persists in proud insularity and fatal disobedience with the encouragement of the deceitful devil. Consequently, instead of serving God with the rest of creation, human beings are the devil's slaves (Thorpe XI. p. 172. lines 20-21), despising the one who created them. The willing slaves of sin are a grotesque distortion of humanity's true nature, the noble image transformed into something unworthy and degrading, even disgusting:

> Ælc þara manna þe his andgit awent
> to yfelum weorcum fram rihtwisnysse,
> and nele understandan his agenne wurðmynt,
> þæt he is sylf geworht to Godes anlicnysse,
> and mid gewitleaste unwurðað hine sylfne

---

21. The idea is found in Augustine, in *De trinitate* IV.xv. 11-13. Ælfric's source here is a sermon of Gregory the Great, *Homeliae in Evangelia* I.X.7. In Ælfric, see also Thorpe X. p. 162. 15-20; Pope XVII. 144-45.

fram þam micclan wurðmynte, þæt he on meoxe licge
on þam fulum leahtrum. (Pope XVI. lines 62-68)[22]

Every person who turns his mind from righteousness to evil deeds, and refuses to
acknowledge his own value, that he is himself made in the image of God, and, in his
folly, degrades himself from that great value, that he will lie in filth, in foul sins.

Ælfric emphasizes here the perversity of choice involved: instead of delighting in the honour
of being God's image, people choose sin, the foulest thing imaginable. In this they are worse
than animals, 'fulre þonne nyten' (Pope XVI. line 68).[23] Ælfric insists that God cannot be
blamed for this, and nor can Adam; certainly, the legacy of original sin plays a large part in
the sinfulness of human nature, but the burden of responsibility lies solidly upon each
individual:

Ne talige nan man his yfelan dæda to Gode, ac talige ærest to þam deofle, þe mancym
beswac, and to Adames forgægednysse; ac ðeah swiðost to him sylfum, þæt him yfel
gelicað, and ne licað god. (Thorpe VII. p. 114. lines 18-21)[24]

Let no man impute his evil deeds to God, but impute them first to the devil who
deceived mankind, and to Adam's transgression; and yet most strongly to himself,
because evil pleases him and good does not.

Because birth is outside the individual's control, and because the result of birth is that free
will is constrained to do evil rather than good, this may seem harsh and unjust. But with
Augustine Ælfric sees that the inclusion of each person in the sin of Adam is no denial of
individual responsibility. Augustine is completely uncompromising: 'Tuum quippe vitium est
quod malus es' ('It is your own fault that you are bad', *De correptione et gratia* v.7).

---

22. Compare Skeat I. 153-54.

23. Augustine speaks of this perversity in *De diversis quaestionibus ad Simplicianum* I.2.18.

24. Compare Thorpe XIV. p. 212. 10-12; Augustine says the same in *De correptione et gratia* vi.9.

Ælfric is persuaded that man's condition would be completely hopeless without the aid of God's grace. On his own, he can only fight a losing battle against sin. Grace alone provides the right weapons and the skill to use them, restoring the efficacy of God-given freedom:

> Nu behofað ure freo-dom æfre godes fultumes.
> forþan ðe we ne doð nan god butan godes fultume. (Skeat XVII. lines 266-67)

> Now our freedom always requires God's help, because we do not do any good without God's help.

To be free for anything other than sin human nature requires the grace of God. Without grace, free will is virtually a self-contradiction: only with grace may the will be regarded as truly free, once again possessed of the lost liberty of doing the right. The first man was to have merited freedom from sin by obedience, just as the obedient angels, remaining in heaven after the fall of the rebels, were confirmed in their sinless service of God. Now that disobedience has removed the possibility of such merit, grace must substitute for merit:

> Nunc autem per peccatum perdito bono merito, in his qui liberantur factum est donum gratiæ, quæ merces meriti futura erat. (*De correptione et gratia* xi.32)

> however, now that our merit is all lost through sin, those who are freed receive as the gift of grace that which was to have been the reward of merit.

Ælfric's teaching on the creation, the beginning of sin and its effects on man's nature follows Augustine closely, failing to discuss two points only which are of central importance to Augustine: he makes no attempt to define how sin is transmitted from generation to generation, and he includes no exegesis of the text which for Augustine was so pertinent, Romans 5. 12. Ælfric does not, however, deviate from the basic principles established by Augustine, and the omission of these details has no distorting effect on the doctrine expounded as a whole. For Ælfric, human freedom is circumscribed, but nevertheless valid, because of the potential of grace. If humanity chooses to pursue evil, it may do so; yet grace can enable the choice of good. This grace is offered as the result of the restoration of humanity to God, achieved through the incarnation.

II. THE INCARNATION OF THE SON: THE MEANS OF REDEMPTION

The incarnation was the culmination in time of God's redemptive plan, initiated at the beginning of creation. In completing this plan, the incarnation introduced radical new elements into mankind's relationship with God. First it halted the disastrous progression from sin to death established by the fall. Secondly, it restored the possibility of a proper response to God in love and obedience. The indwelling of humanity by divine grace achieved first humanity's transformation and, finally, its glorification. In the Son's incarnation God acted in time decisively, in a moment revealing his eternal activity to recreate in mankind the image of the divine.

The place of the incarnation in the plan of redemption was established outside time from the beginning of the world. But Ælfric locates God's response to the phenomenon of sin in time. His narrative describes the creation of mankind, the deception and the fall, and humanity's subjection to the devil. Then, Ælfric says, God had pity on his deceived creation, and considered how mercy might nullify the consequences of disobedience:

> Đa ðeah-hwæðere ofðuhte ðam Ælmihtigum Gode ealles mancynnes yrmða, and smeade hu he mihte his hand-geweorc of deofles anwealde alysan; forði him ofhreow þæs mannes, forðon ðe he wæs bepæht mid þæs deofles scearocræftum. (Thorpe XIII. p. 192. lines 9-13)[25]

> Then, however, the almighty God regretted all mankind's miseries, and meditated how he might redeem his handiwork from the devil's power; for he took pity on man, because he had been deceived by the devil's wiles.

Mercy had not characterized God's response to the sin of the angels: their condemnation was born of justice alone. But because Adam was deceived by the devil, he was not held wholly

---

25. Compare Thorpe I. p. 18. 34-35; Godden I. 18-19.

responsible for his sin, and thus benefitted from God's pity. Mercy, here apparently a response in time to events in time, is nevertheless conceived as eternal (Thorpe XIII. p. 192, lines 18-21). Augustine's account shows that God prepared his response to man's sin in advance of sin, accommodating evil within the accomplishment of the divine purpose. His eternal knowledge took account of all future events in predetermining the working of good (*Enchiridion* xxviii.104).

God's merciful response to the problem of sin is to send his Son, the medium of creation, to redeem that creation:

> Ac se mildheorta Fæder, ðe us to mannum gesceop
> þurh his ancennedan Suna, wolde eft alysan
> ðurh ðone ylcan Suna eall manncynn
> of deofle and fram ðam ecan deaðe. (Pope XIa. lines 53-56)[26]

> But the merciful Father, who created us as men through his only-begotten Son, afterwards desired through that same Son to redeem all mankind from the devil and from the eternal death.

The Son's humility in descending from the height of his divine glory shows the extent of God's love: God came down to creation's level to raise it to his. The incarnation offers an alternative to solidarity with Adam: instead of an association which is sinful and condemning, humanity is offered a brotherhood which is liberating and elevating, in a new and transforming recreation through the Son. Christ's acceptance of humanity raises God's chosen to the status of sons. His Sonship, though uniquely given to him who is coequal and coeternal with the Father, is a gift now extended to all mankind through the Son's incarnation. Augustine makes the point in his sermons on John that, far from narrowing the inheritance due to one heir, God's gift when infinitely divided among many heirs loses nothing of its value, but is the same salvation to all (*In Ioannis Evangelium tractatus* II.13). In his sermon *De falsis diis*, Ælfric finds this inheritance described in Psalm 81. 6, dismissing the legions

---

26. Compare Thorpe I. p. 24. 31-33; II. p. 32. 5-9; XIII. p. 192. 18-21; XIX. p. 260. 1-2; Godden I. 12-14; Pope XI. 146-52.

of false gods and finally acclaiming the new gods brought into the family of God by the power of their creator:

> Ic cwæð þæt ge synd godas, and ealle suna þæs Hehstan.
>
> Swa micelne wurðmynt forgeaf se mildheorta Drihten
>
> his halgum þegnum, þæt he het hi godas;
>
> ac nan mann næfð swaþeah nane mihte þurh hine sylfne,
>
> buton of þam anum Gode þe ealle þing gesceop. (Pope XXI. lines 671-75)[27]

'I said that you are gods and all sons of the Highest'. The merciful Lord gave such honour to his holy servants that he called them gods; nevertheless, no-one has this power through himself, but through the one God who created all things.

This is the recreative work of God through the Son. The first creation did not make men gods, even though Adam and his descendants were to have lived a life of blessedness untroubled by sickness and death. Merely to have restored this life would have been a gracious gift, but in his second creation God achieves more than the simple rebuilding of the old Adam. He works a transformation of nature by grace. Now no longer restricted to natural humanity, human beings participate in humanity made divine by Christ. The difference is grace.

By his advent, Ælfric says, Christ offered the means of regaining the lost relationship with God, and by his death he removed all obstacles to the enjoyment of that relationship, ensuring that justice as well as mercy had nullified the devil's usurpation of power. Redemption, as Ælfric seeks to show, was not a gratuitous display of might, but a just response to the crisis. This justice is visible first in the sacrifice of Christ, and secondly in the rescue of souls from hell.

God's justice required the sacrifice of one who was sinless to atone for the sins of all humanity. The Son of God accepted the task in the knowledge that only the incarnate Son could be that sacrifice:

---

27. Compare Thorpe II. p. 34. 25-28; IX. p. 140. 7-12; XXII. p. 324. 11-16; Pope I. 352-63 and 386-90; in Augustine, *Enchiridion* x.33. 22-25.

(He) geðafode swiðe geðyldelice þæt he wære geoffrod for ealles middaneardes synnum; For ði buton he ðrowode for us. ne mihte ure nan cuman to godes rice. (Godden III. lines 87-90)

(He) gave his assent to it very patiently that he should be offered for the sins of all the world; because unless he suffered for us, none of us might come to God's kingdom.

He countered the effects of sin both in the purity of his sacrifice and the humility of his response to God. Though his claims to glory infinitely exceeded those of the proud Adam, he emptied himself of the Son's privileges and opposed the sin of wilful pride with perfect humility and obedience:

he ne wiðerode na ongean, ac wæs gehyrsum hys Fæder,
for ðære micclan lufe þe he to mancynne hæfð,
þæt he sylfwilles sealde hys lif for us. (Pope III. lines 130-32)[28]

he offered no resistance, but was obedient to his Father because of the great love which he has for mankind, such that he gave his life voluntarily for us.

As well as an act of obedience, this was an act of love. The Son's gift of his life was an offering in power; yet it involved a complete loss of power, corresponding to the human state. In embracing human weakness the Son proved his obedience and love. For Augustine too, the Son of God was the supreme example of humility and obedience. It was necessary, he says, that the Mediator be born, live and die without sin,

ut humana superbia per humilitatem dei argueretur ac sanaretur, et demonstraretur homini quam longe a deo recesserat, cum per incarnatum deum reuocaretur, et

---

28. Compare Thorpe X. p. 162. 10-16; XI. p. 168. 1-6 and p. 174. 22-29; XIV. p. 214. 17-19 and 33-35; XV. p. 224. 22-25 and p. 226. 10-13; XVI. p. 232. 1-3; Godden I. 24-29; III. 86-90; IV. 168; XIV. 30-37; Skeat XII. 284-88; XVI. 117-28.

exemplum oboedientiae per hominem deum contumaci homini praeberetur. (*Enchiridion* xxviii.108. lines 72-76)

in order that human pride might be convicted and healed through the humility of God, and that man might be shown how far he had departed from God, when it was through God made flesh that he was being called back. And this was done also in order that an example of obedience in the person of the God-man might be given to man's stubbornness.

The necessity of sacrifice for redemption derived from the distance of man's separation from God. A mediator between man and God was essential, one who was both man and God. Ælfric once or twice chooses to stress that Christ's death was necessary only in the sense that it was the will of God that his Son should take the place of sinners: there was no constraint on the free will of God that this should be the means of redemption. Here, then, the emphasis is upon the omnipotence of God rather than the necessity of the suffering and death of Christ:

> . . . se Hælend sealde hine sylfne for us,
> þeah þe he mihte eall mancynn ahreddan
> butan his agenum deaðe, and of ðam deofle geniman
> his agen handgeweorc, gif he swa don wolde. (Pope IX. lines 60-63)[29]

the Saviour gave himself for us although he could have rescued all mankind without his own death, and snatched his own handiwork from the devil, if he had wished to do so.

However, the implication is that no other means of rescuing mankind would have been perfectly just. Augustine is also careful to point out that God's will, rather than necessity, defined redemption. Just as Christ received baptism, needing no cleansing but desiring to show his humility, so he suffered death, guiltless of the sin for which it was the punishment, that his unjust death might result in the just liberation of sinners. These were acts of compassion, not necessity (*Enchiridion* xiv.49).

---

29. Compare Thorpe X. p. 164. 14-16.

Ælfric teaches that the sacrifice of Christ was adumbrated by Jewish sacrifices which were offered in propitiation for sin. His death was the culmination and fulfilment of these offerings (Godden XII. 344-47).[30] The sacrifices of the old law are now no longer necessary because of the new relationship with God. Ælfric explains how each Old Testament sacrifice prefigured an aspect of Christ's own death: for example, the lamb symbolized his innocence, the goat, his human nature (347-56). The unique offering of Christ was best prefigured in that offered by Abraham, who was found ready to make the supreme sacrifice of his son in obedience to God's will. Although in the event Abraham sacrificed not his son but the ram provided by God, by his obedience to God's command the spiritual sacrifice had already been made. Here Ælfric finds a sign of human and divine co-operation in the crucifixion:

> Næs ðeah isaac ofslegen, ac se ramm hine spelode. for ðan ðe crist wæs unðrowigendlic on þære godcundnysse. and seo menniscnys ana deað and sar for us ðrowade; Swilce se sunu wære geoffrod. and se ramm ofsniden. (Godden IV. lines 169-72)[31]

> Yet Isaac was not killed, but the ram took his place, because Christ was impassible in his divinity and his humanity alone suffered death and pain for us; it was as if the son was offered and the ram killed.

The mystery of Christ is at the heart of the mystery of the atonement. Ælfric shows that it is impossible to separate what was human from what was divine about Christ's sacrifice. It is true that Christ's humanity was capable of suffering, while his divinity was not. But the suffering and unsuffering in Christ were united indivisibly according to the unity of the God-man: this unity allowed the mystery that his humanity and divinity somehow suffered both together, and somehow triumphed both together. While the man in Christ was killed, his humanity was not eternally destroyed but rose again, and in this human death, the divine itself was offered, as Isaac was offered, in free obedience, and was thus eternally modified by its assumption of humanity.

---

30. Compare Thorpe XXXVIII. p. 590. 26-30; Godden III. 78-79; XV. 45-49.

31. This pleasing exegesis is from Bede, *Homeliarum Evangelii* I.14. 178-79.

The death of Christ cancels the death which is humanity's inheritance; mankind is thus cleansed of sin and released from automatic condemnation. By a mysterious paradox, the Son's death has destroyed death:

> On cristes deaðe wæs se deað adydd. for ðan þe þæt deade lif acwealde ðone deað. and he wæs fornumen on cristes lichaman. (Godden XIII. lines 274-76)[32]

> By Christ's death, death itself was destroyed. For that dead life killed death, and it was annihilated in Christ's body.

The paradox displays again Christ's unity of purpose, divine and human co-operating. His mortality achieved the death of death, yet it possessed such power only through his divine immortality. From a human point of view this death appears to be the epitome of weakness, yet paradoxically it has become the source of strength. Comparing the divine power displayed by the creating Son with his human weakness on the cross, Ælfric comments:

> . . . his untrumnys is ure trumnys:
> his trumnys us gesceop, and his untrumnyss us alysde. (Pope V. lines 108-9)[33]

> his weakness is our strength: his strength created us, and his weakness redeemed us.

For Ælfric, the most dramatic achievement of Christ's suffering is that his voluntary death, innocent of sin and its effects, redeemed humanity from a captivity enforced by both ancient and personal sins. Hell, its torments and the rescue of souls from the devil's clutches are vividly evoked. Through Christ's death the faithful are redeemed from the torments of hell (Thorpe I. p. 26. line 29),[34] which are eternal (Pope VI. line 158); they are rescued from the

---

32. Compare Godden XIII. 266-72; Pope VII. 111-12; XII. 233-38; XX. 347-50.

33. From an exegesis of John 4. 1-42 (the Samaritan woman) drawn from Augustine, *In Ioannis Evangelium tractatus* XV.6.

34. Compare Thorpe XIX. p. 264. 11; XX. p. 292. 3; Godden I. 17; Pope XIa. 85.

devil's slavery (Thorpe XXII. p. 324. line 22),[35] released from the darkness of separation from God, the devil's darkness (Thorpe XXXIX. p. 604. lines 3-4), and from eternal death (Godden XV. line 47).[36]

This rescue may be vividly described in terms of a battle fought between Christ and the devil, a trial of strength in which Christ fights like a warrior for mankind and is proved to be the decisive victor. The Devil is the 'strong man' of Luke 11. 21, in possession of all mankind,

> . . . ac Godes Sunu com,
>
> strengra þonne he, and hine gewylde,
>
> and his wepna him ætbræd and tobræc his searocræftas,
>
> and his herereaf todælde þe he mid his deaðe alysde. (Pope IV. lines 190-93)[37]

> but God's Son came, stronger than he, and subjected him to his control, and took away his weapons from him and destroyed his wiles, and divided his spoils which He redeemed with His death.

In *De trinitate* Augustine describes the just redemption of those justly held in the devil's power. Sin gave the devil justified power over mankind, but the devil could have no power over Christ, whose nature was without sin. His unjust punishment of Christ by death cancelled the just imprisonment of others:

> ut quia eos diabolus merito tenebat quos peccati reos conditione mortis obstrinxit, hos per eum merito demitteret quem nullius peccati reum immerito poena mortis affecit. (*De trinitate* XIII.xv.19. lines 7-9)

---

35. Compare Thorpe XXXI. p. 464. 33; XXXIII. p. 494. 33; XXXVI. p. 546. 34-35; Godden XV. 47; Pope VII. 126 and 170; X. 191; XIa. 84.

36. Compare Pope VI. 342; VII. 126; XIa. 56.

37. Compare Pope VII. 124; X. 201-3; XIa. 146.

that because the devil deservedly held those whom he had bound by the condition of death as guilty of sin, he might deservedly loose them through Him who was guilty of no sin, and whom he had undeservedly struck with the punishment of death.

Thus justice was maintained. Ælfric says that Christ refused to take men forcibly from the devil, but his own innocence broke the devil's grasp on them:

> He hit forwyrhte ðaða he tihte þæt folc to Cristes cwale, þæs Ælmihtigan Godes; and ða þurh his unscæððigan deað wurdon we alysede fram ðam ecan deaðe, gif we us sylfe ne forpæra. (Thorpe XIV. p. 216. lines 6-9)[38]

> He forfeited it when he incited the people to the killing of Christ, the almighty God; and then through his innocent death we were redeemed from eternal death, if we do not destroy ourselves.

This is the 'ransom' theory of redemption, which is pervasive in Augustine's teaching. He developed it from Ambrosiaster's study of Colossians 2. 13-15, describing the cancellation of the sentence against man and the triumph of Christ over the forces of evil. Ambrosiaster found that the accuser was guilty of false accusation (TeSelle, *Augustine*, p. 166). In the *Enchiridion*, Augustine observes that the sinless Christ bore the punishment of death unjustly, and in so doing he destroyed the power of death:

> mors nihil quod puniret, inuenit, ut diabolus ueritate iustitiae, non uiolentia potestatis, oppressus et uictus, quoniam ipsum sine ullo peccati merito iniquissime occiderat, per ipsum iustissime amitteret quos peccati merito detinebat. (*Enchiridion* xiv.49. lines 22-25)

> death found (in Him) nothing to punish. In strict justice, then, not through violence of power, was the Devil overwhelmed and conquered. Since he had most wickedly slain Him who was without sin, through that same Person he most justly deserved to lose mastery of those whom he held in the bondage of sin.

---

38. Compare Thorpe I. p. 26. 31-32; XX. p. 292. 5-8.

Augustine gives dramatic expression to the idea of cancelled debt and the freedom obtained by redemption in a passage in *Confessiones*, where he imagines his mother entering heaven; she will claim her exemption from debt because Christ has already paid everything she owes:

> neque enim respondebit illa nihil se debere, ne conuincatur et obtineatur ab accusatore callido, sed respondebit dimissa debita sua ab eo, cui nemo reddet, quod pro nobis non debens reddidit. (IX.xiii.36. lines 41-44)[39]

> nor will she answer that she owes nothing, lest she be convicted and seized by the crafty complainant; rather will she answer that her debts are forgiven by Him to whom no one can make restitution of what He, who is not a debtor, paid for us.[40]

To the idea of ransom, Ælfric adds the traditional teaching that the devil was deceived like a fish which takes the bait and only then feels the fatal hook. To the devil, Christ's humanity was the bait which tricked him in his greed:

> Swa wæs þam deofle: he geseh ða menniscnysse on Criste, and na ða godcundnysse: ða sprytte he þæt Iudeisce folc to his slege, and gefredde ða þone angel Cristes godcundnysse, þurh ða he wæs deaðe aceocod, and benæmed ealles mancynnes þara ðe on God belyfað. (Thorpe XIV. p. 216. lines 13-17)

> So it was with the devil: he saw the humanity in Christ, and not the divinity; then he instigated the Jewish people to his slaying, and felt then the hook of Christ's divinity, by which he was choked to death, and was deprived of those of all mankind who believe in God.

According to this model, Christ deceived the devil by using his humanity to disguise his divinity. Ælfric seems undisturbed by this, emphasizing not the deception but the triumph of

---

39. TeSelle, *Augustine*, p. 174.

40. Quoted in the translation by Vernon J. Bourke.

Christ in this symbolic struggle. Gregory of Nyssa was the first to formulate this vivid image.[41] As in the 'ransom' theory, the devil is imagined expecting his usual spoils. In attempting to 'devour' Jesus on the cross the devil mistakenly assumed that this human being was like any other, held by the power of death. Switching metaphors to that of the triumph of light over darkness, Gregory explains that in swallowing the 'bait' of divinity the devil took light into his dark self, life into death. With the unconquerable presence of light and life, darkness and destruction were annihilated (Aulén, *Christus*, p. 68). This clearly explains how the devil's hold over human lives was eliminated for all time. Ælfric's version says the same thing but remains in the world of the original metaphor. The devil himself was 'choked to death', which expresses the conquering ascendancy of Gregory's Life and Light in a more concrete way: the adversary is dead.

Ælfric is part of an illustrious company in his use of this metaphor for the atoning action of God. Gregory's idea was picked up eagerly by later teachers. Gregory the Great used it often (for example in *Moralia in Iob* XXXIII.vii.14), exploiting its potential for dramatic effect. Augustine has a similar idea when he imagines the cross to be the mousetrap of the devil, with the death of Christ serving as the bait (*Sermo* CCLXIII.i.1). The image is picturesque, perhaps even grotesque, but it does address the reality of evil, which is recognized as a force to be reckoned with not just mentally and spiritually but physically as well. Finally, as Aulén comments, 'the power of evil ultimately overreaches itself when it comes in conflict with the power of good, with God himself' (*Christus*, p. 71).

Because the devil expected sin in Christ and failed to find it, he forfeited his power over the chosen whom Christ was able to abduct from hell, leading them in victory to heaven (Pope X. 192-203). This triumphant return is a victory for all to share. Not only does the death of Christ make atonement for sin and annul the condemnation into which humanity is born, but it also restores to man the delight of God's presence, raising him to the privilege of a better paradise than the lost one:

On his acennednysse wæs geðuht swilce seo Godcundnys wære geeadmet, and on his upstige wæs seo menniscnys ahafen and gemærsod. Mid his upstige is adylegod þæt

---

41. G. Aulén, *Christus Victor: an historical study of the three main types of the idea of atonement*, translated by A.G. Hebert (London, 1931), p. 71.

cyrographum ure geniðerunge, and se cwyde ure brosnunge is awend. (Thorpe XXI. p. 300. lines 2-6)[42]

At his birth it seemed as though his divinity was humbled and at his ascension his humanity was exalted and glorified. With his ascension the writ of our condemnation is annulled, and the sentence of our destruction is turned aside.

For Ælfric, God's response to the spoiling of creation in providing a new creation, effected like the first by his Son, is the dynamic mystery of the history of grace. Like Augustine he teaches that through Christ's death reconciliation with God is brought about by grace under conditions transformed by grace from judgement to love. The alienation experienced by humanity after the expulsion from paradise, whether physical or spiritual, is eliminated in the self-giving love of the Son's death. The two metaphors of redemption found in Augustine, those of ransom and sacrifice, are both used by Ælfric as dramatic expressions of Christ's victory.

Ælfric's particular emphasis is that the incarnation was God's response to the fact of sin. He does not suggest that God was taken by surprise when humanity failed: on the contrary, the incarnation was planned before the world began. Thus the events and effects of Christ's life and death were necessarily always known to God. In Ælfric's teaching this assertion of God's eternal omniscience, which is a necessary attribute of one to whom the past and future are eternally present, is combined with the happy image of God's 'meditation' about the redemption of his handiwork. Ælfric vividly evokes God's mercy as a response to the crisis: the perfect love of God is placed in context when he is seen responding to the sin abhorrent to him. This emphasis makes the cross central to the relationship of God with mankind, locating here the moment of transformation, bringing to an end the old dispensation in which the usurping devil held power, and initiating the new life of liberty and obedience. The incarnation is thus in Ælfric's view both the culmination of God's plan for mankind which was preordained from the beginning, and a loving impetus manifested in the beginning of a new creation. This new creation is realized in the life of the elect.

---

42. Compare Augustine, for example *Sermo* CXCII.i.1.

Grace

III. PREDESTINATION AND GRACE

Predestination may readily be defined, from Ælfric's sermons, as God's plan for mankind, prepared right from the beginning of creation. He stresses the way in which this plan affects each individual, for predestination also implies the necessity of election. All aspects of this important issue are treated in considerable detail by Ælfric and his teaching is closely related to that of Augustine.

Ælfric states that no-one may be saved except by grace, which has been established from eternity:

> forðan þe nan man ne bið gehealden buton þurh gife Hælendes Cristes: þa gife he gearcode and forestihte on ecum ræde ær middangeardes gesetnysse. (Thorpe VII. p. 114. lines 29-32)[43]

> for no man will be saved, except through the grace of Christ the saviour: that grace he prepared and preordained in eternal decision before the establishment of the world.

No-one can learn how to save himself, or acquire salvation through the effort of will, or through the exercise of reason. Intellectual understanding can never substitute for the gift of illumination by grace, an enlightenment which surpasses, and yet completes, human endeavour. Except grace illuminate a man's heart, no amount of teaching will suffice for salvation. Ælfric explains Psalm 126. 1 in such terms:

> Buton Drihten sylf þæt hus getimbrige
> on idel hy swincað, þa ðe hit wyrcað.
> Butan God sylf onlihte þara manna heortan
> þe his lare gehyrað mid his halgan gife,
> on idel swincð se lareow mid his lare wiðutan. (Pope XIV. lines 121-25)

---

43. The same point is made by Augustine, for example in *De dono perseverantiae* xiii.33 and xviii.47, or in *De praedestinatione sanctorum* xvii.34.

Unless the Lord himself build the house, those who build it labour in vain. Unless God himself, with his holy grace, illuminate the hearts of the men who hear his teaching, the teacher labours in vain with his teaching from outside.

Inevitably the teacher must fail to penetrate the heart that lacks the illumination of grace. Exactly the same idea is to be found in Augustine's late works on predestination and grace:

non lege atque doctrina insonante forinsecus, sed interna et occulta, mirabili ac ineffabili potestate operari deum in cordibus hominum non solum ueras reuelationes, sed bonas etiam uoluntates. (*De gratia Christi* xxiv.25. p. 145. lines 22-25)

it is not by law and doctrine uttering their lessons from without, but by a secret, wonderful and ineffable power operating within, that God works in men's hearts not only revelations of the truth, but also good dispositions of the will.[44]

Grace is the prerequisite even for the beginning of faith.

Those who are to receive this grace are chosen from the beginning of creation and they are drawn from all ages of the world (Godden V. 48-50).[45] God knows the numbers of the elect and will continue to gather them until the desired total is reached:

Þa geceas he us of eallum leodscipum
and he swa gefylð þæt fulle getel
þe he habban wyle to his ecan wuldre. (Pope XIV. lines 185-87)

Then he chose us from all peoples, and in this way he fills up that total number which he desires to have for his eternal glory.

For Augustine, the precise number of the elect is unalterable:

---

44. Quoted in the translation by Peter Holmes.

45. Compare Godden VII. 145-46; XXII. 116-17; XXXVII. 203-5; Pope XI. 259-60 and 409-11.

Haec de his loquor, qui praedestinati sunt in regnum Dei, quorum ita certus est numerus, ut nec addatur eis quisquam, nec minuatur ex eis. (*De correptione et gratia* xiii.39)

I have said all this about those who have been predestined to the kingdom of God, whose number is so fixed that not one can be added to it, or taken from it.

This belief leads him to interpret the text 'God our Saviour, who will have all men to be saved, and to come to the knowledge of the truth' (I Timothy 2. 3-4) in a variety of ways: only the obvious meaning of the words is rejected. Finding it impossible to read the verse literally, he strives to harmonize it with his belief in God's predestination of a fixed number. His overriding concern is that no interpretation of the verse should suggest that God's will might be influenced or altered. In one of many discussions of this important verse, he offers a selection of possible readings, any of which may be regarded as a proper interpretation. He concludes that in fact it does not matter what interpretation is chosen. Any is to be accepted, provided it maintains God's supreme freedom:

Et quocumque alio modo intellegi potest, dum tamen credere non cogamur aliquid omnipotentem deum uoluisse fieri, factumque non esse. (*Enchiridion* xxvii.103. lines 45-47)[46]

or we may understand it in any other way possible. It must only be assured that we be not compelled to believe that the Almighty willed that something be done and it was not done.

Ælfric's attitude, by contrast, suggests a rather more universal interpretation of the text. He avoids the question to a certain extent in that he does not attempt any exegesis of this

---

46. Augustine's interpretation of this verse was rejected by the 'Semi-Pelagians', who considered it to be blasphemous. 'In sum, Augustine's doctrine of the will of God appeared to overlook the revealed will of God, which desired all men to be saved, and to have constant recourse to the hidden will of God, into which it was illegitimate to inquire', Pelikan, *Tradition*, I, p. 323.

problematical verse. But his sermons quite clearly indicate that he does disagree with Augustine on this point. He is careful not to draw too much attention to this divergence, and he does insist on God's perfect knowledge of the number of the elect. However, he prefers to emphasize the unknown quantity of mercy, written into the provision of the closed list but inaccessible to limited human understanding. Ælfric's teaching is based on the belief that God offers salvation with joy to all who ask in faith and penitence. Interpreting Jesus' words in John 4. 34 that doing the Father's will is his sustenance, Ælfric shows that mankind's redemption is desired with urgency:

> Hys gastlica mete ys mancynnes alysednyss,
> and him þyrste on þam wife hyre geleafan,
> and he symble gewilnað urre sawla hælu. (Pope V. lines 242-44)

> His spiritual food is mankind's redemption, and he thirsted for the woman's faith, and he always desires our souls' healing.

In his humanity God the Son hungered for the salvation of others, and he continues to do so with the same intensity, having ascended to heaven bearing his human form. The salvation of mankind continues to give him joy. Ælfric's exegesis of the parable of the lost sheep illustrates this. He desires the listener to notice that heaven rejoices with the Shepherd rather than with the sheep:

> Ne cwæð he, 'Blissiað mid þam sceape', ac 'mid me', forðan ðe ure alysednys soðlice is his bliss; and ðonne we beoð to ðære heofonlican eardung-stowe gelædde, þonne gefylle we ða micclan mærsunge his gefean. (Thorpe XXIV. p. 340. lines 13-17)[47]

> He did not say, 'Rejoice with the sheep', but 'with me', for truly our redemption is his joy; and when we are led to that heavenly dwelling-place then we shall complete the great glorification of his joy.

---

47. Compare Thorpe XXIV. p. 342. 13-15.

This rejoicing is confirmation that God does indeed desire all men to be saved and come to a knowledge of the truth. It seems that Ælfric would willingly believe the one interpretation of this verse which Augustine was unable to accept:

> Ælc ðæra ðe geornlice bitt, and þære bene ne geswicð, þam getiðað God þæs ecan lifes. (Thorpe XVIII. p. 250. lines 4-6)[48]

> To each one who fervently prays and does not desist from the praying, God grants him eternal life.

Ælfric's understanding of the limits of election may be correspondingly flexible. He suggests that people without Christian virtues should pray to receive those virtues and to be included among the elect (Thorpe XXIV. p. 346. 27-29). Similarly this prayer, at the end of a sermon, appeals to that unknown quantity of mercy:

> Læd us, Ælmihtig God, to getele ðinra gecorenra halgena, inn to þære ecan blisse ðines rices, þe þu gearcodest fram frymðe middangeardes þe lufigendum, þu ðe leofast and rixast mid þam Ecan Fæder and Halgum Gaste on ealre worulda woruld. Amen. (Thorpe XXXV. p. 538. lines 1-5)

> Lead us, almighty God, to the number of your chosen saints, into the eternal bliss of your kingdom, which you have prepared from the beginning of the world for those who love you, who live and reign with the eternal Father and Holy Spirit for ever and ever, Amen.

Ælfric's belief in the extent of mercy allows this view of the community of the elect. Sharing Augustine's conviction that God is in complete control, however, he finds this flexibility to be encompassed by God's gracious predestination. The dimension of mercy always gives hope because God is love, but the final account must lie with him in timeless knowledge. So although it is not improper to pray for inclusion in the number of the elect, indubitably God already knows that prescribed number in immutable certainty. That certainty is the 'book' in

---

48. Compare Thorpe IV. p. 64. 30-33; XXV. p. 350. 16-19; Pope XV. 50-54.

which the names of the elect are recorded. The people whose names are missing from the register will be missing from the kingdom:

> Ælc ðæra manna wæs aworpen into ðam widgillan mere
> ðæs bradan fyres, ðe on ðære liflican bec
> æror næs awriten on þam ecan gemynde,
> swa swa ðæra halgena naman ðe mid þam Hælende wuniað
> syndon awritene on ðære wuldorfullan bec,
> þæt is seo forestihting fram frymðe mid Gode.' (Pope XI. lines 467-72)

Each one of those people was thrown into the wide sea of the broad fire, who earlier was not written in the book of life in the eternal remembrance, just as the names of the saints who dwell with the saviour are written in the glorious book: that is the predestination from the beginning with God.

Ælfric combines Augustine's teaching with his own conviction that God is above the inflexibility which human understanding infers of predestination. Clearly implied in the certainty of election even before birth is the fact that election to grace takes place before the will desires God. This was the important development in Augustine's thought when he decided that divine election must precede any human decision.[49] God provides both the capacity to believe and the impetus to turn towards him: 'whether a man believes or does not is decided by God' (TeSelle, *Augustine*, p. 178). The mystery of God's election is beyond human comprehension: it cannot be known to whom he may grant repentance. Ælfric illustrates this point with a debate between an angel and the devils, in which one of the devils claims the soul of a sinner because in his judgement there remain uncleansed sins in the soul. The angel counters each accusation by the devil with the response that God's mercy is unknowable:

---

49. TeSelle identifies the moment of this realization when Augustine was writing the *De diversis quaestionibus ad Simplicianum*: question 2 reveals this new understanding of the priority of grace; *Augustine*, p. 178.

Ne tæle ge to dyrstelice. for ðan ðe ge nyton godes digelan domas . . . Æfre bið godes mildheortnys mid þam men. þa hwile ðe ðær bið gewened ænig behreowsung . . . Nyte ge ða micclan deopnysse godes gerynu. weald þeah him beo alyfed gyt behreowsung. (Godden XX. lines 127-33)[50]

Do not make your accusations too presumptuously, for you do not know God's secret judgements . . . God's mercy is always upon the man while repentance may still be looked for . . . You do not know the great profundity of God's mysteries: perhaps repentance will yet be granted to him.

The angel's determination to beat down the presumption of the devil encourages a glad optimism about the breadth of God's mercy. It affirms God's desire for the salvation of sinners. Yet sometimes the devil is right: sometimes the sinner does not repent. If, as the angel says, repentance may be granted even at the last moment, are there cases where repentance is not granted, even actively withheld?

According to Augustine's teaching, the mystery of mercy allows some to be called to repentance, yet others not. This is a mystery which cannot be understood:

Certe hic judicia Dei, quoniam justa et alta sunt, nec vituperari possunt, nec penetrari. (*De correptione et gratia* viii.18)

Assuredly, since the judgments of God in these matters are just, they cannot be criticized; and since they are deep, their reasons cannot be reached.

These puzzling judgements, in the words of Romans 11. 33, are simply to be accepted:

De utrisque ergo exclamemus, O altitudo divitiarum sapientiæ et scientiæ Dei! quam inscrutabilia sunt judicia ejus! (viii.18)

---

50. I refer to this passage again on pages 238 and 270.

Confronted with them, let us exclaim, 'O the depth of the riches of the wisdom and of the knowledge of God! How incomprehensible are his judgments, and how unsearchable his ways!'

Either God makes merciful provision for the good response of the will or he allows the fallible will to choose evil; whichever is the case he acts justly, however hard this is to accept. Augustine advises that the believer must cling to the conviction that God is always just:

> Fixum enim debet esse et immobile in corde vestro, quia non est iniquitas apud Deum. (*De gratia et libero arbitrio* xxi.43)

> You must keep this conviction firm and unshaken in your heart that in God there is no injustice.[51]

Ælfric accepts that some are chosen, others not. There are two distinct groups:

> Of þam woruldmannum witodlice beoð
> on twa wisan gemodode and mislice gelogode;
> sume beoð gecorene, sume wiðercorene. (Pope XVIII. lines 130-32)

> Certainly the men living in this world are disposed in two ways and variously ordered. Some are chosen, some rejected.

The former are actively chosen by God for life, while the others are abandoned. It should be noted that the latter are not specifically chosen for perdition:

> þonne genimð se Hælend to hys heofonlican rice
> on þam micclan dæge of þam woruldmannum
> þa ðe mid goodum willan and weorcum æfre
> hym ær gecwemdan oð heora lifes ende,

---

51. Quoted in the translation by Robert P. Russell.

and þa wiðercorenan beoð wiðutan belocene;

þonne bið seo an genumen, and seo oðer forlæten. (lines 135-40)[52]

then the saviour will take to his heavenly kingdom on that great day those of the people
of the world who were always pleasing to him by their good will and their good deeds
up until the end of their life; and the non-elect will be locked out; then shall the one
be taken, and the other left.

Those who have pleased God are the elect; the non-elect are allowed to follow their own
inclinations and suffer the punishments required by justice.

But it is clear that one who may appear to the observer to be counted among the elect
may actually be excluded. This is the meaning of the story of the draught of fish (Luke 5. 6),
where fish lost from the net symbolize Christians who will not persevere:

and þes fixnoð getacnað þa halgan Gelaðunge,

þæt is eall Cristen folc þe on God nu gelyfað,

on ðam syndon ægðer ge yfele ge gode,

and hy sume misfarað. (Pope XIV. lines 154-57)

and this draught of fish symbolizes the holy church, which is all Christian people who
now believe in God, among whom are both good and bad, and some of them go astray.

Belief is apparently not enough. It is a disturbing fact that many enter the community of the
church without necessarily entering the community of the elect. Many are called, Jesus said,
but few are chosen (Matthew 20. 16; 22. 14). Ælfric comments that this is 'swiðe
ondrædendlic' ('very much to be feared', Godden V. line 183). Uncharacteristically, however,
he fails to address the fear, for the exegesis he adopts from Gregory is one which uses
semantic quibbles to avoid the otherwise ineluctable and harsh condemnation of many who
believe.[53] According to this the 'many/few' antithesis is easily explained:

---

52. Compare Pope II. 174-76; XI. 343-46; XXI. 66-71.

53. In Gregory, *Homiliae in Evangelia* I.xix.5.

Þeah ða gecorenan godes cempan sind feawa geðuhte on andweardum life betwux flæsclicum mannum ðe heora lustum gehyrsumiað. ac hi ne beoð feawa ðonne hi gegaderode beoð. (lines 191-94)[54]

God's chosen warriors, however, seem few in this present life among carnal men who are obedient to their desires, but they will not be few when they are gathered together.

Thus although Ælfric admits that some people who are apparently elect (those who are 'called') will fail to find a place in the kingdom (with the 'chosen'), he is here unable to explain this verse which is so much to be dreaded.

Augustine does make a serious attempt to interpret the verse. He explains why some people answer God's call in faith but others reject it: the response of faith depends on the provision of grace. If the person is made 'congruent' ('congruenter') by grace, the calling is effective (*De diversis quaestionibus* I.2.13). To put it another way, these are called 'secundum propositum' ('according to the purpose', *De correptione et gratia* vii.14).[55] Only the congruent, those called to the purpose, are given the grace of perseverance: those who do not persevere fail with God's knowledge, just as he knows who will persevere to the end. Although some may be are considered 'elect' by those who do not know their true condition, God knows that condition with certainty (vii.16). But Augustine admits that it is a mystery why one person but not another should be given the grace to persevere. The fact is that the omnipotent God is free to give or withhold mercy as he chooses (viii.17).

Augustine's approach to the predestination of the elect involves two affirmations: one is that all are guilty and deserve punishment, but only some have this guilt remitted; the second is that God actively bestows on his chosen the gifts appropriate to their liberation. Thus both elimination of guilt and the giving of gifts are necessary for restoration in the sight of God. The one manifests God's righteousness, the other his mercy. Augustine insists that complete justice characterizes God's dealing with sinners, whether he remits the debt or not (*Contra duas epistolas Pelagianorum* II.vii.13). Having cancelled the debts of some in his mercy, God then endows them with the means by which they will be liberated from that slavery to sin.

---

54. Compare Augustine, *De correptione et gratia* x.28, which emphasizes the great company of the elect, even though they are few in comparison with the lost.

55. The reference is to Romans 9. 28.

Grace

Both the redeemed debtors and the loving-kindness which prompts mercy are eternally known to God:

> Haec est praedestinatio sanctorum, nihil aliud: praescientia scilicet et praeparatio beneficiorum Dei, quibus certissime liberantur, quicumque liberantur. (*De dono perseverantiae* xiv.35. lines 5-7)

> This is the predestination of the saints, nothing else: that is, the prescience and the preparation of God's kindnesses, whereby they are most certainly delivered whoever they are that are delivered.[56]

'Certissime' emphasizes both the security of that deliverance and the immutable prescience of God. The remainder are abandoned, 'in massa perditionis iusto divino iudicio relinquuntur' ('in the mass of perdition, abandoned by the just judgement of God' lines 7-8).

Augustine's conclusion that God merely abandons the non-elect to their proper punishment is his judgement in most of the discussions of this matter. But occasionally he ascribes to God's predestination an active condemnation of the non-elect, as he does here in defending the inexorable progress of God's will and its incontrovertible effect:

> bene utens et malis tanquam summe bonus, ad eorum damnationem quos iuste praedestinauit ad poenam, et ad eorum salutem quos benigne praedestinauit ad gratiam. (*Enchiridion* xxvi.100. lines 6-8)

> Supremely good Himself, He made good use also of evils, for the damnation of those whom He had justly predestined to punishment, and for the salvation of those whom He had mercifully predestined to grace.

The possibility of predestination to punishment or to evil is found again in a remark made by Augustine in which he suggests that Judas was chosen for his role as betrayer according to judgement rather than mercy. Mercy provides that the other disciples will achieve the kingdom, but judgement condemns Judas:

---

56. Quoted in the translation by Sister M.A. Lesousky.

illos debemus intelligere electos per misericordiam, illum per judicium; illos ad obtinendum regnum suum, illum ad fundendum sanguinem suum. (*De correptione et gratia* vii.14)

we must understand that the one was chosen in judgment, the rest in mercy; the others were chosen to possess His kingdom, the one was chosen to shed His blood.

If some sinners are abandoned to the punishment which all deserve, from which others are graciously released, then they may be understood to be predestined to death, since they were not predestined to mercy. In this case, punishment is justly imposed:

qui est et illis quos praedestinauit ad aeternam mortem iustissimus supplicii retributor. (*De anima et ejus origine* IV.xi.16 p. 396 lines 8-9)

whilst to those whom He has predestinated to eternal death, He is also the most righteous awarder of punishment.[57]

Augustine admits this is a harsh truth, but he can see no other way to describe these mysteries of God ('occulta opera Dei', 'hidden things of God' xi.16). Although it is logically unavoidable, the conclusion that God predestines some to punishment is, however, rarely given prominence.

Ælfric refers to this predestination only once. Speaking of the spiritual death of the wicked, he says that the Jews who condemned Christ (Matthew 27. 25) were spiritually dead already, 'ða giu hi wæron deade' ('they were long dead', Godden XIII. line 163); then he comments:

Se bið dead ecum deaðe. se ðe is forestiht to ðam ecum deaðe; He leofað on lichaman. and is swa ðeah soðlice dead. (lines 164-66)

he is dead in eternal death, who is predestined to eternal death. He lives in body, yet is truly dead.

---

57. Quoted in the translation by Peter Holmes.

Ælfric may mean merely that people who live such wicked lives have ensured their own damnation, and in their wickedness they cannot be said to be living, even before they experience bodily death. But here he might intend to affirm a predestination to death: the Jews' collusion with the devil in crucifying Jesus is the one act of sin which fills him with irrepressible horror. As the devil's servants *par excellence*, the Jews might, in his view, deserve such condemnation.

In the centuries between Augustine and Ælfric, others had to struggle with Augustine's uncompromising doctrine of predestination. Its harshness led the Council of Orange to reject it. They upheld his teaching on grace, against the 'Semi-Pelagians', who thought that a portion of man's noble and creative free will still operated after the fall, permitting him to initiate his own conversion to God. But the Council ignored as far as possible Augustine's clear, although partly distasteful, doctrine of predestination. The twenty-five canons of the Council affirm the necessity of grace for all things and insist that fallen man owes everything good in himself to God. But these canons do not mention predestination at all. The Council summarized its understanding of grace in the form of a creed, which included a complete rejection of the idea that God might predestine anyone to evil, declaring any who believed this doctrine to be anathema.[58] As the only mention of predestination in the record of the Council's proceedings, it is hardly an adequate response to the difficulty posed by Augustine's teaching. Pelikan points out that all other elements of Augustine's doctrine of grace continued to be repeated, in spite of its apparently inescapable conclusion of double predestination. This point alone was determinedly rejected, but no alternative solution to the problem was proposed (*Tradition*, I, p. 328). The debate seems less to have been concluded than allowed to quiesce.

For Ælfric, Augustine's double predestination is no longer a prominent difficulty. Apart from the one instance where he refers to a predestination to death, apparently prompted by the recognition of an unique class of sinners, Ælfric takes a view which emphasizes God's predestination of the elect to eternal life and his prescience of those who will be condemned to punishment. Here, for example, Ælfric repudiates the idea that God might predestine a soul to perdition, suggesting that this contradicts the very nature of God:

---

58. C.J. von Hefele, *History of the Christian Councils, from the Original Documents*, 5 vols, translated and edited by W.R. Clark and H.N. Oxenham (Edinburgh, 1871-96), IV, edited by H.N. Oxenham (1895), p. 164.

ac he ne forestihte nænne to yfelnysse, forðan þe he sylf is eall godnyss; ne he nænne to forwyrde ne gestihte, forðan þe he is soð lif. (Thorpe VII. p. 112. lines 28-30)

but he predestined no-one to wickedness, for he himself is all goodness; nor did he predestine anyone to perdition, for he is true life.

Instead, God's prescience distinguishes between the obedient, whom he graciously chooses, and the wicked, whom he does not choose:

He forestihte ða gecorenan to ðam ecan life, forðan ðe he wiste hi swilce towearde, þurh his gife and agene gehyrsumnysse. He nolde forestihtan þa arleasan to his rice, forðan ðe he wiste hi swilce towearde, þurh heora agene forgægednysse and ðwyrnysse. (lines 30-35)[59]

He predestined the elect to the eternal life, because he knew they would be so in the future, by his grace and own obedience. He would not predestine the wicked to his kingdom, for he knew that they would be so in the future, through their own transgression and perversity.

Ælfric does not say in these lines that God knows, in his eternal present, whether people will be good or bad. He knows whether they will be chosen or wicked. Associated with the chosen are grace and obedience, while associated with the wicked are transgression and perversity. The obedience which is involved here may seem to be ambiguous, for Ælfric supplies no pronoun to supplant that which clearly belongs with grace: 'his gife and agene gehyrsum-nysse'. That it is the obedience of the chosen (rather than that of Christ on the cross), is made clear by Ælfric's remark a few lines earlier, that the incarnation of the Son is redeeming for those who are obedient:

Ac eft seo miccle mildheortnys ures Drihtnes us alysde þurh his menniscnysse, gif we his bebodum mid ealre heortan gehyrsumiað. (lines 19-21)

---

59. I refer to these lines again below on page 140.

But again the great mercy of our Lord has redeemed us through his incarnation, if we obey his commands with all our heart.

These lines illustrate a tension in Ælfric's concept of obedience: it is within obedience that the harmony of divine grace and human response is found, and it may not be possible to say where one ends and the other begins. Zealous obedience is rewarded by salvation within the context of grace: the obedience of God's chosen is preceded and followed by grace even when it is most their own.[60] Obedience combined with grace is the mark of the chosen. Those who are not chosen are not marked by God in a negative way, but by their own disobedience and perversity: this clearly ascribes the responsibility for sin and the rejection of God to the wicked.

The existence of punishment and reward, under the control of a just God, are for Ælfric clear indicators that each individual has the capacity of choice. Justice demands that there be a free decision: a command to turn from sin and do good is useless if there are some people who are predestined to disobey it. If this is the case then both punishment and reward are arbitrary and unjust:

> Gif ælces mannes lif æfre sceola swa gan.
> þæt he ne mæge forbugan bysmorlice dæda.
> þonne bið unrihtlice þæt ða unrihtwisan onfon
> ænigne witnunge for heora wohnysse.
> Eac ða arfæstan beoð wolice gearwurðode.
> gif þæt soð beon mæg þæt him swa gesceapen wæs. (Skeat XVII. lines 229-34)[61]

If every man's life must always proceed in such a way that he cannot turn aside from disgraceful deeds, then it is unjust that the unrighteous should receive any punishment for their wickedness. Also the righteous are perversely honoured, if it can be true that it was ordained that they should be so.

---

60. I return to this point below, on pages 140-43.

61. Compare Pope XXI. 667-68; Skeat XVII. 251-56.

Similar words, from Jerome, were triumphantly cited by Pelagius in the belief that they argued against Augustine's constriction of the will's freedom to do good. In his rejoinder, Augustine agrees that necessity makes a mockery of reward, as Jerome rightly says:

> quis non agnoscat, quis non toto corde suscipiat, quis aliter conditam humanam neget esse naturam? sed in recte faciendo ideo nullum est uinculum necessitatis, quia libertas est caritatis. (*De natura et gratia* lxv.78. p. 293. lines 3-6)

> Who would deny that human nature was so created? The reason, however, why in doing a right action there is no bondage of necessity, is that liberty is the essence of charity.[62]

Pelagius must understand that the liberty under discussion is that born of love. Just as those enslaved by the devil cheerfully do evil, offering willing service, so also the servitude of God's chosen is one of joy, offered in love. Their liberty is love. The righteous free will is made free to do the right by the indwelling of grace.

Ælfric follows the main trend of Augustine's treatment of this question in embracing the merciful predestination of the elect, whilst leaving the painful mystery of the fate of the non-elect to the trustworthy provisions of God's justice. Neither Augustine nor Ælfric is quite happy to say that the non-elect are predestined to evil, at least in the sense of being made capable of sin but incapable of redemption. This may be seen in the sensitivity with which each deals with the idea (in Romans 9. 18) that God hardens some hearts, which might seem to offer evidence to counterbalance the text from I Timothy. Ælfric does not teach that God hardens the hearts of those who will not be among the elect; however, in several sermons those who do not believe in Christ are described as hardhearted:

> Se mann þe ortruwað, and endeleaslice syngað,
> and on his heardheortnysse his lif geendað,
> se byð gewislice dead þam wyrstan deaðe. (Pope VI. lines 313-15)[63]

---

62. Quoted in the translation by Peter Holmes.

63. Compare Pope III. 168-69; IV. 31; Skeat XXV. 528-29.

The man who loses faith and sins endlessly, and ends his life in his hardheartedness, he is certainly dead in the worst death.

Here, hardheartedness derives from a lack of faith: it is the condition of one who has excluded God. It comes from within him, and is not imposed by God. Sometimes, indeed, Ælfric suggests that hardness is the normal condition of the heart, for it is impervious to the word unless the Holy Spirit bestow his enlightenment:

Buton se Halga Gast nu eowre heortan onlihte
mid his gastlican gife, ne gað ure word aht
innto eowre heortan, eow to onbryrdnysse,
ne to nanre beterunge butan his gife. (Pope X. lines 109-12)[64]

Unless the Holy Spirit enlighten now your heart with his spiritual grace, our words will not enter into your heart by any means as compunction for you, nor as any improvement without his grace.

Grace inspires compunction as well as transformation, rendering the hard heart vulnerable to its softening illumination.

Augustine says that God gives his grace to those who will respond to it, and withholds it from any who will live wicked lives; even a baptised person may be abandoned for this reason. Commenting upon Romans 9. 18, Augustine insists that a hardened heart is the result of an evil life, foreknown by God (*De gratia et libero arbitrio* xxiii.45). One whose heart is not hardened is the recipient of grace. The gift of grace is present in the case of Jacob, whom God loved, but absent in Esau, whose heart was hardened. What God loved in Jacob was not the merit of works or even faith, but simply grace (Romans 9. 13-16).

Ælfric also refers to the example of Jacob and Esau, offering Augustine's explanation. He says that Esau was not predestined to be unpleasing to God, but suggests that God's attitude to the brothers was determined by his foreknowledge of the life each would lead:

---

64. Compare Thorpe XXII. p. 320. 25-27 and p. 322. 4-8.

Witodlice þæt halige gewrit cwyð þæt God lufode Iacob, and hatode Esau; na for gewyrde, ac for mislicum geearnungum. (Thorpe VII. p. 110. lines 24-26)

Certainly holy Scripture says certainly that God loved Jacob and hated Esau; not according to destiny but according to their disparate merits.

God's prescience of the lives of the non-elect is the reason for their abandonment. He knows those who will sin before they do, for to him all time is present, all knowledge present:

se Ælmihtiga and se Rihtwisa God nænne mann ne neadað to syngigenne, ac he wat swa-ðeah on ær hwilce þurh agenne willan syngian willað. Hwi ne sceal he ðonne rihtlice wrecan þæt yfel þæt he onscunað? (p.114. lines 1-5)[65]

The almighty and righteous God does not compel anyone to sin, but nevertheless he knows beforehand who will wish to sin through their own will. Why, is he not then to avenge justly that evil which he abhors?

Knowing now the future sins of men, God, in his justice, has made provision of appropriate punishment.

Ælfric concludes that it is free will, not predestination, which directs the choice of evil. Such a choice implies the rejection of God, but he insists that the possibility of turning to God is always open. God abandons only those who have rejected him:

God sylf afandað ælces mannes heortan,
hwæðer se mann wylle his wununge habban,
oþþe leahtras lufian, þe Gode misliciað;
and nan mann ne bið fram Gode forlæten,
buton he sylf forlæte his lufe him ær fram. (Pope X. lines 49-54)

---

65. Compare Skeat XVII. 248-50.

God himself examines every man's heart, to see if a man desire to have his continued presence or to love sins, which displeases God; and no-one is abandoned by God unless he first deprive himself of God's love.

Those who never turn to God are justly given over to the devil's power (Pope XIII. 52-53). Rejection of God is the free act of mankind, compounding the effect of original sin, the first rejection. The incarnation of Christ was a second creation, offering a second chance of obedience in faith. Where this is rejected, a second fall renders mankind doubly guilty:

> Anfealdlice hi sind scyldige ðurh Adames synne, and twyfealdlice hi beoð fordemde, þonne hi wiðsacað Cristes to-cymes, and nellað gelyfan on ðone soðan Hælend. (Thorpe IX. p. 144. lines 22-24)[66]

> They are singly guilty through Adam's sin, and they are doubly condemned because they deny Christ's coming and are not willing to believe in the true saviour.

God's eternal and timeless knowledge observed the angelic and human history even before creation (Thorpe VII. p. 112. lines 24-28). Ælfric finds an important distinction between God's attitude to fallen humanity, whom he pities, and the fallen angels, who are lost forever, without hope of mercy. The hopeless nature of the fallen angels' state is implied by the fact that no-one, whether angel or human, could expect mercy, because it is not a prerequisite of God's righteousness. Ælfric comments that if God had shown no more mercy to mankind than to the devils, there would still be no ground for disputing God's righteousness: still it would be infinite ('untæle', Thorpe VII. p. 112. line 19). This is consistent with Augustine's teaching that all deserve punishment. God cannot be accused of injustice if only some are saved. God's justice demands punishment; if he remits it, God shows his goodness. In either case, his righteousness is unchanged:

> Si in remittendo debito bonitas, in exigendo aequitas intelligitur, numquam esse apud Deum iniquitas invenitur. (*De dono perseverantiae* viii.16. lines 12-14)

---

66. Compare Pope VII. 90-91; and in Augustine, *Enchiridion* x.33.

If generosity is seen in canceling a debt, justice in exacting it, iniquity is never found in God.

In the incarnation God's mercy has already been poured out. Redemption has already been achieved. All that is necessary is that redemption should be appropriated through obedience:

> Ac eft seo miccle mildheortnys ures Drihtnes us alysde þurh his menniscnysse, gif we his bebodum mid ealre heortan gehyrsumiað. (Thorpe VII. p. 112. lines 19-21)[67]

> But again the great mercy of our Lord has redeemed us through his incarnation, if we obey his commands with all our heart.

This obedience, according to Augustine, is preceded by grace, as is the love which enables obedience to be offered with joy: 'et haec omnia gratia in eo cui datur et cuius haec omnia praevenit, operatur' ('Grace effects all these things in him to whom it is given and in whom it anticipates all these things', *De dono perseverantiae* xvi.41. lines 20-21). The prevenience of grace is truly the actuality of predestination. Indeed, Augustine's belief in the provision of grace is sometimes carried to the point where grace appears irresistible. This may lead him to a virtual denial of the liberty of the human response, as in these lines which describe a will wholly controlled by grace, wholly incapable of failure:

> Subventum est igitur infirmitati voluntatis humanæ, ut divina gratia indeclinabiliter et inseparabiliter ageretur; et ideo, quamvis infirma, non tamen deficeret, neque adversitate aliqua vinceretur. (*De correptione et gratia* xii.38)

> Consequently, an aid was given to the weakness of the human will, with the result that it is unwaveringly and invincibly influenced by divine grace, and consequently, whatever its weakness, it does not fail, and is not overcome by any difficulty.

---

67. Compare Thorpe XIII. p. 192. 4-6.

Portalié notes that even this apparently incontrovertible grace is guided by God's timeless knowledge that his grace will be accepted by those on whom he chooses to bestow it. God can always find the appropriate gifts: human freedom of choice cannot hinder God from choosing among his graces that one which will in fact meet with acceptance.[68]

Thus grace ensures that every response is the right one. Augustine's point is clear, but so too is the tension involved in choosing exactly the right words. He says that grace and the will co-operate, but that this is possible because mercy provides the context: 'quia misericordia eius praeuenit nos' ('because his mercy prevents us', *De natura et gratia* xxxi.35. p. 259. lines 1-2). In fact in every action of the obedient will, grace surrounds and protects it:

> praeuenit, ut pie uiuamus, subsequetur ut cum illo semper uiuamus, quia sine illo nihil facere possumus. (lines 4-6)[69]

> He prevents us that we may lead godly lives; He will follow us that we may always live with Him, because without Him we can do nothing.

On turning to Ælfric, a similar affirmation of the prevenience of grace is found. Grace is the enlightenment of the understanding, which enables a return to God from the control of the devil:

> Gif he ðonne eft þone deofol anrædlice forlæt, ðonne gemet he eft þæs halgan Gastes gife, þe his heortan onliht, and to Crist gelæt. (Thorpe VII. p. 110. lines 3-5)[70]

---

68. E. Portalié, *A Guide to the Thought of St Augustine*, translated by R.J. Bastian (Chicago, London, 1960), p. 227.

69. The reference is to John 15. 5.

70. Compare Thorpe X. p. 154. 20-24 and 32-34, p. 156. 25-28; XXV. p. 356. 16-18; Pope VIII. 233-35; XIV. 123-25; and in Augustine, for example, *Sermo* CXLIII.v.5 and *Sermo* CXLIV.i.1.

If then he resolutely forsakes the devil, then he will again encounter the grace of the Holy Spirit, who illumines and leads his heart to Christ.

Here, although the will clearly offers its own energy in turning from sin, the provision of grace exactly corresponds to that energy, confirming and rewarding it. Later in this sermon he proves that man's first conversion is through grace by appealing to a verse which actually states that God maintains faith through grace; clearly the grace is the same in both cases:

> Witodlice þa þe on God belyfað, hi sind þurh ðone Halgan Gast gewissode. Nis seo gecyrrednys to Gode of us sylfum, ac of Godes gife, swa swa se apostol cwyð, 'Þurh Godes gife ge sind gehealdene on geleafan.' (Thorpe VII. p. 114. lines 8-11)[71]

> Truly those who believe in God are directed by the Holy Spirit. Our turning to God is not of ourselves, but of God's grace: as the Apostle says, 'Through God's grace you are held fast in faith.'

Yet Ælfric also preserves a tension, already noted, between free action and obedience: no coercion is involved. This is the meaning, he explains, of the untying of the colt (Matthew 21. 2-3) in the Gospel for Palm Sunday. Here he balances the ideas of free choice and necessary obedience to the Lord's command:

> Hi cwædon, 'He sent hi eft ongean.' We sind gemanode and geladode to Godes rice, ac we ne sind na genedde. Þonne we sind geladode, þonne sind we untigede; and þonne we beoð forlætene to urum agenum cyre, þonne bið hit swilce we beon ongean asende. (Thorpe XIV. p. 210. lines 5-8)[72]

---

71. The reference is to Ephesians 2. 8.

72. In Matthew 21. 3, Jesus assures the disciples that the keeper of the asses will readily let them go: 'et confestim dimittet eos'; Ælfric gives these words to the disciples, which distorts their meaning.

They said, 'He will send them back again.' We are invited and summoned to God's kingdom, but we are not forced. When we are summoned, then we are untied; whenever we are left to our own choice, then it is as if we may be sent back again.

Ælfric's point seems to be that freedom and obedience are somehow combined: the liberated colt gives its service freely though under the constraining hands of the disciples, and the loving service freely given by the elect is a similar tension of liberation and constraint, made possible by God's call: 'we sind gelaðode'. By contrast, human choice unaided (or uncompelled) by grace is brought up sharply against its own limitations. The meaning of 'we beon ongean asende', at first rather indistinct, is made clear by Ælfric's final remarks in this section of the sermon, where the necessity of grace is emphasized. The Christian's 'untying', or liberation, is the product of mercy, whilst glad obedience is a conjunction of grace and will. Of the two, the former is of preeminent importance, and where it is lacking, free choice is fruitless:

> Godes mildheortnys is þæt we untigede syndon; ac gif we rihtlice lybbað, þæt bið ægðer ge Godes gifu ge eac ure agen geornfulnys. We sceolon symle biddan Drihtnes fultum, forðan ðe ure agen cyre næfð nænne forðgang, buton he beo gefyrðrod þurh þone Ælmihtigan. (lines 9-13)

> It is God's mercy that we are untied; but if we live rightly, that is both God's grace and our own zeal. We must always pray for the Lord's assistance, because our own choice has no success unless it is furthered by the Almighty.

Liberation allows the possibility of zealous obedience on the part of the chosen. Those who are left to their own choice cannot obey. Ælfric's use of 'forlæten' (line 7) is instructive: it is the word he uses elsewhere of the abandoned, the non-elect: 'þonne bið seo an genumen, and seo oðer forlæten' ('then shall the one be taken, and the other left', Pope XVIII. lines 135-40). The necessity of 'being untied' is therefore emphasized. For the abandoned, their own choice has no 'forðgang': it cannot further them in the service of God. Unlike the liberated colt, they cannot go anywhere.

After the initial conversion the Spirit's indwelling is found to be both the source of guidance in the will of God, and the ground on which all good works rest:

Godes gyfu is se Halga Gast;

soðlice þone Gast forgyfð God hys gecorenum,

swa þæt he him on wunað and gewissað hi symble

to Godes willan and to godum weorcum. (Pope V. lines 131-34)[73]

God's grace is the Holy Spirit; truly, God gives the Spirit to his chosen, so that he dwells in them and guides them always to God's will and to good works.

These good works are the manifestation of the Spirit's presence, his gifts. They are the special characteristics of the Christian life, a life effectively made pleasing to God, and they are clear indicators of the elect:

An is se halga gast þe sylð gecorenum mannum ða seofonfealdan gife. þæt is wisdom. and andgit. ræd. and strengð. ingehyd. and arfæstnys. godes ege is seo seofoðe; Se ðe þissera gifa orhlyte eallunge bið. næfð he gemanan mid godes gecorenan. (Godden XXV. lines 68-71)[74]

It is the Holy Spirit alone who gives the chosen the sevenfold grace, which is wisdom and understanding, counsel and strength, knowledge and piety; fear of God is the seventh. He who has no share at all in these gifts has no communion with God's chosen.

The sevenfold grace (or gift) given by the Spirit is an expression of the participation of the chosen in the grace of the Son's incarnation. Ælfric makes the link. As man, Christ was 'mihtiglice gesmyrod/mid seofonfealdre gyfe', ('powerfully anointed with sevenfold grace', Pope V. lines 211-12).[75] Now, he says, the sevenfold grace of the Spirit may be given to all.

---

73. Compare Thorpe XXVII. p. 388. 20-22; Godden XXXII. 42; Pope IX. 145-48; X. 44-48; XV. 224-25; XVI. 239.

74. Compare Thorpe XVIII. p. 250. 12-14; Pope IX. 139-49; XI. 66-70; XIa. 183-85; XVI. 44-46.

75. Ælfric follows Augustine here in interpreting the word 'Messiah' as 'anointed',

On the faithful are bestowed the gifts which manifest the continuity of grace poured out for salvation (Godden XXXV. 68-72).[76] They are given according to the Spirit's pleasure ('be ðam ðe him gewyrð', Thorpe XXII. p. 322. line 30). Different graces are bestowed, resulting in a variety of Christian qualities. Ælfric is careful to choose the right expression. Grace is found to co-operate with human endeavour, continually providing virtues and glorifying them in the recipient:

> Nabbað ealle menn gelice gife æt Gode, forðan ðe he forgifð ða gastlican geðincðu ælcum be his gecneordnyssum. (Thorpe XXIV. p. 346. lines 29-31)[77]

> Men do not all have the same gifts from God, for he gives spiritual dignity to each according to his diligence.

The grace of God supplies everything necessary to live a life of obedience. His mercy both prevents and follows; he directs the will towards the good and enables its fulfilment. Here Ælfric again insists on the prevenient and subsequent nurture of grace whilst subtly asserting that the will thus guided is free to obey:

> Godes mildheortnys us forestæpð. and his mildheortnys us fyligð; Þa ða we wel noldon. ða forhradode godes mildheortnys us þæt we wel woldon; Nu we wel willað. us fyligð godes mildheortnys þæt ure willa ydel ne sy; He gearcað urne godan willan to fultumigenne. and he fylst ðam willan gegearcodne. (Godden V. lines 227-32)[78]

---

elaborating on the nature of that anointing with the idea of sevenfold grace; see for example Augustine, *In Ioannis Evangelium tractatus* XV.27. 11-13. In Ælfric, compare Thorpe IX. p. 150. 9-13; XIII. p. 198. 1-2.

76. Compare Pope I. 393-402; IX. lines 116-21.

77. Compare Thorpe XXIV. p. 346. 8-11; Godden XX. 252-54; XXVII. 136-38; Pope XIX. 105.

78. Compare Thorpe XXII. p. 312. 33-35, p. 320. 31-34 and p. 322. 12-16; XXXVIII. p. 586. 24-27; Godden XXIV. 200-4; Skeat XVII. 266-70; Pope V. 133-34; IX. 135-38 and 145-48; XI. 150-52; XII. 163-64; XV. 119.

God's mercy goes before us and his mercy follows us. When we had no wish to act aright, God's mercy preceded us so that we were willing. Now we wish to act aright, God's mercy follows us that our will may not be in vain. He prepares our good will to help it, and he supports the prepared will.

This is the work of the grace of perseverance, which ensures that the chosen live in a way which is pleasing to God. With such support, the will is ready and able to do good, and the Christian excels in the works of mercy which characterize the servant of Christ. Grace works in coherent and forceful combination with the free response of the will. Predestination is the formal expression of God's prescience of this partnership:

He forestihte ða gecorenan to ðam ecan life, forðan ðe he wiste hi swylce towearde, þurh his gife and agene gehyrsumnysse. (Thorpe VII. p. 112. lines 30-32)

He predestined the elect to the eternal life, because he knew they would be so in the future, by his grace and own obedience.

Grace and obedience are closely associated again by Ælfric when he explains the 'three ages' of man's relationship with God.[79] The third age, after the incarnation, is called 'under grace' because during this period God's elect are specially guided:

his gifu gewissað ða gecorenan symle to soðfæstnysse and to lifes bebodum þæt hi ða ðing gastlice gehealdon ðe seo ealde æ. lichamlice bebead. (Godden XII. lines 13-16)

his grace always directs the elect towards the truth and to the commandments pertaining to life so that they obey in a spiritual way those things which the old law commanded in a physical way.

---

79. Thorpe XXII. p. 312. 29-35; Pope XV. 31. Augustine classifies these three ages in *Sermo* CX.i.1 but usually prefers a division into four, described, for example, in *Enchiridion* xxxi.118, which includes the fourth age of the blessed in heaven.

New laws, spiritual rather than physical, characterize the new chosen people, and a new obedience is made possible by grace. If every stage of the Christian's conversion towards God is due to grace, it is certain that even this obedience is another gift. Ælfric shows that the elect have made this gift part of themselves: obedience now characterizes their response just as disobedience characterizes that of the non-elect. The tension is maintained here as in every aspect of the mutual compatibility of grace and free will.

Even in his late works, in which he marvels at the way in which grace is necessary for the very impetus of the soul's movement towards God, Augustine still finds a need for the human response to the provisions of grace. In brief, grace alone does not give a complete account of man's relationship with God, for something of the trinitarian image remains, even after the fall. Augustine's work *De gratia et libero arbitrio* is especially concerned with the way grace and the human will co-operate: TeSelle summarizes thus: 'everything is the result of grace — but . . . it must also become human actuality' (*Augustine*, p. 327). Augustine describes the working of the will within the context of gracious provision by God:

> Certum est nos facere, cum facimus: sed ille facit ut faciamus, præbendo vires eficacissimas voluntati. (*De gratia et libero arbitrio* xvi.32)

> In doing anything it is certainly we who act, but it is God's act that enables us to act by His bestowal of efficacious power upon our will.[80]

Augustine is prepared to acknowledge that mankind is not without merit in the sight of God. All may be worthy of the reward of eternal life, with the assistance of grace. However, this assistance is so fundamental that 'merit' becomes merely another word for 'grace'. Moreover, eternal life, given in reward for grace-merit, is also grace:

> gratia est pro gratia, tanquam merces pro justitia; ut verum sit, quoniam verum est, quia reddet unicuique Deus secundum opera ejus. (viii.20)

---

80. Quoted in the translation by Robert P. Russell.

(it) is a grace given for a grace, a kind of remuneration, as it were, in accordance with justice. Hence the truth, as it is indeed a truth, that God 'will render to everyone according to his works.'

Augustine finds that reward for works is taught by the Scriptures (as in Matthew 16. 27; Romans 2. 6): for this to make sense, both works and reward must be grace.

In his own approach to the question of merit, Ælfric sees that free will is constrained by original and individual sin; but the grace of God liberates the will to respond obediently to God's commands. The soul corrupted by sin is offered restoration by grace: the disobedience which first rejected grace is overcome by a greater grace to which a new obedience responds. Ælfric does not diminish the value of this response, conceiving an active role for the will: the soul will be saved by grace if it obeys God ('gif heo gode gehyrsumað', Skeat I. line 175). Now, obedience counts as merit before God. Ælfric brings together the responsibility mankind must take for its predicament and the generous effects of mercy:

Þonne gif he mid deofles weorcum hine sylfne bebint, ðonne ne mæg he mid his agenre mihte hine unbindan, buton se Ælmihtiga God mid strangre handa his mildheortnysse hine unbinde. Agenes willan and agenre gymeleaste he bið gebunden, ac þurh Godes mildheortnysse he bið unbunden, gif he ða alysednysse eft æt Gode geearnað. (Thorpe XIV. p. 212. lines 12-18)

Then if he bind himself with the works of the devil, he cannot free himself by his own power, unless Almighty God unbind him with the strong hand of his mercy. Of his own will and negligence he is bound, but he will be freed by God's mercy, if he has merited that redemption by God.

Ælfric preserves both the idea of dependence upon God's loving-kindness and that of human merit: they have a mysterious symbiosis. The priority of grace is accepted, but after that initial gift of God Ælfric is able to see that the best response of the will is to take that grace to itself. Good is latent in the human creation, and grace vivifies it:

We sceolon on urum weldædum blissian mid soðre eadmodnysse. and urum drihtne geornlice ðancian his gife. þæt he us geuðe þæt we moston his willan gewyrcan. ðurh sume weldæde; Ne mæg nan man naht to gode gedon buton godes gife. swa swa se apostol paulus cwæð; Þu mann, hwæt hæfst ðu þæs þe ðu fram gode ne underfenge? (Godden XXVIII. lines 83-88)[81]

We must rejoice in our good deeds with true humility and thank our Lord earnestly for his grace, which he has given us that we may do his will through some good deed. No man may do anything good without God's grace: as the apostle Paul said, 'Man, what do you have which you have not received from God?'

Here Ælfric echoes the words of I Corinthians 4. 7 which Augustine quotes repeatedly: 'Quid enim habebunt, quod non accepturi sunt? aut quid habent, quod non acceperunt?' ('For what will they have, except what they shall receive? And what have they, except what they have received?', *De correptione et gratia* ii.4). Ælfric's conclusion that all the good man can do must be ascribed to God's grace is exactly Augustine's understanding at the close of this work. Grace indwells the will, perpetually strengthening and energizing it. It might be said that grace becomes the very fabric of the will.

This coinherence of grace and obedience is expressed in love. Love is the presence of God, an indwelling which is manifested in obedience:

God wunað on us, gif we us betwynan lufiað. and his soðe lufu. bið swa on us gefylled. and we magon his .æ. mid ðam anum gefyllan. (Godden XIX. lines 61-63)[82]

God dwells in us, if we love one another, and his true love is thus fulfilled in us, and we are able to fulfil his law by that one means.

The giving and receiving of love and the confirmation of both in action are all inextricably bound up: they precede and follow each other in natural sequence and form a self-contained source of power. Indeed there is little difference here between the shared love and the co-

---

81. I refer to this passage again below on page 211. Compare Thorpe IX. p. 144. 28-33; X. p. 160. 12-13; XXI. p. 310. 16-18; Pope I. 335.

82. Compare Thorpe XXXVIII. p. 586. 24-27; Godden XXVI. 90-95; Pope X. 36-38; XXX. 50-51.

operating grace and obedience. In practice, they are identical. Once the Christian returns God's love, he is held within a self-perpetuating system of loving. Grace ensures that it is so. According to Augustine too it is the indwelling presence of God which generates the quickening power of love (*Sermo* CXXVIII.v.5). Further, this binding relationship of love effects the performance of good works precisely because it is the characteristic of the grace of perseverance. God bestows this grace to enable a joyful response to his law and to empower the obedience of the elect (*De nuptiis et concupiscentia* I.xxx.33. p. 245. line 8). Perseverance is strength and delight in obedience; it is a freedom to obey:

> Voluntas quippe humana non libertate consequitur gratiam, sed gratia potius libertatem, et ut perseveret delectabilem perpetuitatem, et insuperabilem fortitudinem. (*De correptione et gratia* viii.17)

> The fact is that the human will does not achieve grace through freedom, but rather freedom through grace, and through grace, too, joyous consistency, and invincible strength to persevere.

Ælfric seems scarcely to question the inclusion of his listeners among the elect. References to the rewards awaiting the good have an exhortatory effect; there appears to be little point in drawing attention to the possibility of not meriting the reward. Ælfric seems to assume that all of the people can, and indeed will, be among the elect. For by their very presence, listening to the sermon, they demonstrate God's care of them: he has brought them there to listen. The community of God is provided with everything necessary to enable it to attain perfection in heaven, including salutary teaching which is valuable for guiding and correcting the will. This is how 'irresistible' grace operates, by ensuring that the gift is received in ideal conditions. So for Augustine, the elect are continually moulded by their experience within God's providence. The opportunity to hear the Gospel and the means to act upon its precepts in love are always appropriately provided:

non est dubium quod et procuratur eis audiendum Evangelium et cum audiunt, credunt; et in fide quæ per dilectionem operatur, usque in finem perseverant. (*De correptione et gratia* vii.13)[83]

there is no doubt that the opportunity to hear the Gospel is arranged for them; and, when they hear, they believe, and persevere unto the end in the faith which worketh by charity.

Perseverance is assured by correction, so that the elect are constantly confirmed in their daily lives. The medium of correction may be personal rebuke, or they may be guided back to the true path without the intervention of another:

et si quando exorbitant, correpti emendantur, et quidem eorum etsi ab hominibus con corripiantur, in viam reliquerant redeunt. (vii.13)

and if ever they deviate from the track, they are chastised by admonitions; and some of them, even though they are not admonished by men, return to the path they had abandoned.

For Ælfric, teachers have a responsibility both to preach the Gospel so that all have the opportunity to hear and respond (Thorpe XXI. p. 302. 8-11) and to correct the wayward, turning them from their folly (Thorpe XIX. p. 268. 1-4). Preaching opens the way for the operation of grace within the hearer. It is a means of communication between God and the individual:

Godes gifu us gewissað to his willan, gif we gemyndige beoð Cristes bebodum and ðæra apostola lare. (Thorpe XXII. p. 312. lines 33-35)

God's grace directs us to his will if we are mindful of Christ's commandments and the teachings of the apostles.

---

83. The reference is to Galatians 5. 6.

This is essentially where Ælfric's optimism lies: he believes that communication can and will take place, that Augustine's 'congruence' will occur, where the provision of instruction has been made. From this belief stems his sense of responsibility and urgency in preaching the Gospel. It rests on the conviction that God truly desires all men to be saved. This is the one point where Ælfric is prepared to hope for more than Augustine can. He agrees that God knows the total number of the elect with immutable, eternal knowledge. Equally, he is sure that this total is defined by the parameters of grace. Grace promises the kingdom to the new chosen: the Jews were promised earthly blessings in return for their obedience, but for the elect the blessings are eternal. Recalling the words of II Corinthians 2. 9, Ælfric says that Christ now

> behet þæt ece lif þam þe his word healdað,
> þæt þe mannes eage ne mihte geseon,
> ne eare gehyran, ne heorte asmeagan,
> þa micclan mærðe þe se mildheorta Crist
> þam eallum behet þe hine lufiað;
> and þærtoeacan he forgifð us ure neode. (Pope XV. lines 114-19)[84]

promises eternal life to those who keep his commandments, such that the eye of man may not see, nor ear hear, nor heart imagine, the great glory which the merciful Christ promises to all those who love him; and in addition to that he gives us what we need.

Ælfric's doctrine of grace is complete, even thought it lacks discussion of certain theoretical questions which particularly interested and challenged Augustine or which Augustine was obliged to discuss in response to the teachings of an opponent. Ælfric has no such obligations. Hence, for example, he does not examine seriously the painful experience of fruitless striving in the Christian life by those who will at the end prove to have been non-elect and unendowed with the appropriate grace for their needs. To do so could only inspire unnecessary fear and despair. Such questions, which are purely intellectual and beyond solution, are consistently avoided. So are the questions raised by heresy and refuted by

---

84. I cite this passage again on page 265. Compare Pope XVI. 44-45.

Augustine: Ælfric finds it entirely possible to present the doctrine of grace without entering into an analysis of Pelagianism.

For Ælfric, as for Augustine, the will is initiated, formed and constantly nourished by grace, and having made grace part of its own life, it responds in obedience to God. God sees this and accommodates his grace to the individual's needs, preparing also the appropriate reward. Ælfric's teaching about predestination is also close to Augustine's. He acknowledges God's predestination of the elect from the very beginning of creation, and teaches God's preparation and provision of the means of grace sufficient for their salvation. By making a conscious distinction between God's predestination and his prescience he normally avoids the idea that God might predestine anyone to punishment. There is only the one exception to the rule, and it refers to the sin of the Jews which Ælfric particularly despised.[85] The fixed number of the elect apparently requires that many will indeed be lost, and Ælfric locates the reason for their perdition in the perfect justice and knowledge of God. Evil is abhorrent to God: he is both entirely just in his condemnation of it, and entirely gracious to those whom he chooses to rescue from the consequences of sin. The emphasis, however, is on salvation rather than condemnation. Everything necessary for salvation is provided. The reward of grace is promised, and the means of attaining to that reward provided at every stage, grace always sufficient to precede, enable and follow obedience.

---

85. See above, pages 126-27.

3

THE CHURCH AND SACRAMENTS

That the church was 'one, holy, catholic and apostolic' had been an article of faith from the earliest formulations (Pelikan, *Tradition*, I, p. 156), but in Augustine's writings against the Donatists these characteristics of the church were more clearly defined than had previously been possible or necessary. The conflict with Donatism forced Augustine to reconsider Cyprian's teaching concerning schismatics. With a careful emphasis of framework rather than content, he gladly echoed the great African saint's desire for unity, which Cyprian had valued more highly than the assertion of dogma.[1] Thus he was able to place himself within the Cyprianic tradition, even when holding differing views on the treatment of schismatics. R.F. Evans has shown that Augustine's use of Cyprian was selective and subjective, but Augustine appears to have believed that he was within the spirit of Cyprianic teaching on baptism and the church.[2]

The debate with Donatism not only clarified the concepts of unity and catholicity, but it also prompted an analysis of the two principal sacraments of the church, baptism and the eucharist. In considering the re-entry of reformed Donatists into the church and the question of rebaptism, Augustine identified the source of the baptismal rite's spiritual force and incidentally produced a rationale for the established practice of infant baptism. Further, his thinking about the unity of the church found its fullest expression in the image of the church as the body of Christ, which brought with it a particularly radical and inspired insight into the mystery of the eucharist. As well as clarifying the church's understanding of individual sacraments, Augustine also explored the nature of the sacramental sign itself, and his discoveries shaped the understanding of successive generations.

Like Augustine, Ælfric confidently identifies the Catholic church, flawed as it is, with the body of Christ. Augustine's doctrine of baptism is received as orthodox, and presented

---

1. G.G. Willis, *St Augustine and the Donatist Controversy* (London, 1950), p. 122.

2. R.F. Evans, *One and Holy: the Church in Latin Patristic thought*, Church Historical Series, 92 (London, 1972), pp. 76-77.

without discussion. Only the end result of the debate with Donatism is offered, and none of the debate itself.

Ælfric's treatment of the sacrament of the eucharist is more profound. The strength of his teaching lies in its adoption of Augustine's readiness to seek out the spiritual force of sacraments: as a result, his account avoids a materialistic identification of the Lord's physical body with his eucharistic body. Ælfric explains how it is that the sacrament can properly be said to be the body of Christ, asserting that two different levels of reality are present and discernible. A clear affirmation of the unity of the church and Christ is the fruit of his enquiry.

Associated with baptism and the eucharist in Ælfric's account of the sacramental framework of the Christian life is the mystery of penance. Penance continually renews the purification effected by baptism, and, like the spiritual food of the eucharist, it is necessary for the healthy development of the Christian. For Augustine, penance was a public exercise, and he did not recognize it as a sacrament. However, his teaching about sacramental signs has some bearing on penance, which he sees as conveying an inner cleansing by means of an outward sign. Ælfric has a similar view of penance, even though he is the inheritor of the Celtic as well as the Latin tradition. On the matter of penance, the Celtic church maintained a tradition of individual confession and absolution, a practice which developed in the devotional climate of the early monastic communities and continued to be the medium of penance in the Anglo-Saxon church. Although his approach to the ritual of penance is different from Augustine's, Ælfric's insistence on the need for genuine conversion is the same. Penance without true repentance is irrelevant and worthless: without the spiritual dimension, actions which merely subject the body to meaningless labour are empty gestures which do not speak of spiritual improvement. They have to be the manifestation of inner transformation. God looks for the spiritual conversion, not the outward demonstration of piety, however impressive such a demonstration may be to human eyes. Such conversion, always impelled and supported by the grace of God, is nevertheless made visible in the loving works of almsgiving and of mercy, which may be called spiritual almsgiving: these are the truest manifestations of penitential discipline. This is at the heart of Ælfric's piety. Rather than a squaring of accounts with God, penance is actually the means by which the grace of perseverance is seen. It is the context in which Christians achieve a conscious growth in their devotional life, with those who fall away always welcomed back into the living fellowship of the church, their sin put behind them and no longer a bar to their spiritual development.

I. THE CHURCH IN EARTH AND HEAVEN

Ælfric locates the beginning of the universal church in Christ's commissioning of his disciples to be his witnesses and preach the gospel to all nations. This worldwide task of teaching the faith began with the apostles' missionary journeys, and continued long after their years of preaching through the medium of their writings:

> Þa apostoli wæron gewitan Cristes weorca, forðan ðe hi bodedon his ðrowunge, and his ærist, and upstige, ærst Iudeiscre ðeode, and syððan becom heora stemn to ælcum lande, and heora word to gemærum ealles ymbhwyrftes. (Thorpe XXI. p. 298. lines 18-21)[3]

> The apostles were witnesses to Christ's works, because they preached his suffering, his resurrection and ascension, first to the Jewish people, and afterwards their voice reached every land and their words the boundaries of the whole earth.

Here Ælfric points out not only the extent of the church's early missionary teaching but also its essential content. The apostles preached on the three key events in Christ's redemptive work: his humanity, his divinity, and finally his ascension in which all mankind is raised with him. In this missionary endeavour of the witnesses Ælfric says that the power of God accompanied them and ensured their success:

> and Godes miht him wæs mid, to gefremminge heora bodunga and ungerimra tacna; forðan ðe Crist cwæð, 'Ne mage ge nan ðing don butan me.' (p. 310. lines 16-18)[4]

> and God's power was with them, as confirmation of their preaching and of numberless signs; because Christ said, 'You can do nothing without me.'

This verse explains how each individual needs the support of God's grace to achieve anything in his service. As the apostles were given grace, so the church grew, dependent as a

---

3. Compare Thorpe XV. p. 220. 20-22; XVI. p. 232. 5-7; XXI. p. 294. 15-18; XXI. p. 300. 27-29; Godden XXIII. 24-27; Pope XIV. 220-33.

4. The reference is to John 15. 5. Compare Thorpe XIV. p. 208. 7-11.

community on the grace appropriated by its ministers. Ælfric's 'forðan ðe' suggests that the verse is not merely an explanation of why God's help was provided, but that it also contains the promise that the apostles' labour would be thus sustained.

It is important, too, that the apostles' teaching has reached every land, even to the ends of the earth. This universality is a guarantor of the true church. As a result of the joint work of apostles and grace, the church is spread over the whole earth, represented by innumerable small communities. Nevertheless, it may truly be called one church because of the unity of faith professed. Regional variations in languages and customs cannot obscure the unity of faith and the worship of the one true God which continue to distinguish the true church:

> Fela sind nu godes hus. ac swa ðeah an. for ðære annysse þæs soðan geleafan. þe hi
> ealle andettað; Fela ðeoda sind þe mid mislicum gereordum god heriað. ac swa ðeah
> hi habbað ealle ænne geleafan. and ænne soðne god wurðiað. þeah ðe heora gereord and
> gebedhus manega sind. (Godden XL. lines 110-15).[5]

Many are now God's houses, and yet one, because of the unity of the true faith, which they all confess. Many peoples there are, who worship God with various voices, nevertheless they all have one faith, and worship one true God, though their voices and their houses of prayer are many.

This unity is the church's most important quality: because it is the sign of God's presence, it is essential for salvation. Ælfric remarks that the sacraments of baptism and the eucharist are efficacious only within the unity of the church, and the common bond of the united church is itself a required characteristic of the saved. For him, Christ's gift of the key of heaven to Peter symbolizes this unity:

> Ac forði is seo cæig Petre sinderlice betæht, þæt eal ðeodscipe gleawlice tocnawe, þæt
> swa hwa swa oðscyt from annysse ðæs geleafan ðe Petrus ða andette Criste, þæt him
> ne bið getiðod naðor ne synna forgyfenys ne infær þæs heofenlican rices. (Thorpe
> XXVI. p. 370. lines 15-19)

---

5. Compare Thorpe XIV. p. 214. 9-10; Godden I. 98-100; Pope II. 131-33; XXI. 8.

For this reason the key is especially committed to Peter, that every nation may know with certainty that whoever cuts himself off from the unity of the faith which Peter then confessed to Christ, to him will be given neither the forgiveness of sins nor entry into the kingdom of heaven.

If unity is an entry qualification for the kingdom of heaven, it is also a delight: when Christians cherish their common faith and express it in active love, they offer a sacrifice of unity to God which is the spiritual equivalent of the Jewish offering of doves (Thorpe IX. p. 142. lines 10-12).[6]

Unity is Augustine's theme against the Donatists' claim to be the true church. In their insistence on the sinlessness of the Donatist church, exemplified by priests who had not handed over the Scriptures to escape persecution, they claimed a perfection which Augustine found himself obliged to challenge. As he considered the Donatist definition of purity, he concluded that it is impossible for anyone, save God alone, to estimate the guilt or innocence of another. The pure church, so often spoken of in the Bible, is the church in heaven: risen, perfected, sanctified. The present task of the church is to maintain its unity, not to guess the relative merits of its members.

In his teaching about the church and its sacraments Augustine responds to the various charges of the Donatists, at each point being challenged to think anew about the evidence of Scripture and the authority of the church's history. For him the most obvious proof that the Donatists are wrong lies in the assurance that the church is spread throughout the world and is found among all peoples. The Donatists are confined to North Africa: how then can they claim that essential ubiquity and catholicity? The church is that community prophesied by the Lord (Acts 1. 8):

nos quippe in ecclesia sumus, quae ipsius testimonio praenuntiata est et ubi suis testibus attestatus est dicens: eritis mihi testes in Hierusalem, et in totam Iudaeam et Samariam et usque in totam terram. (*Contra litteras Petiliani* II.lviii.132. p. 93. lines 18-21)

---

6. Compare Thorpe III. p. 52. 23-25; XIX. p. 260. 9-11 and p. 274. 12-14; XXXIX. p. 606. 15-18; Godden XV. 237-40.

For we are in the Church which was foretold by his own testimony, and where He bore witness to his witnesses, saying, 'Ye shall be witnesses unto me both in Jerusalem, and in all Judea, and in Samaria, and unto the uttermost part of the earth.'[7]

The church's distribution over the whole earth is also prophesied in the Old Testament. It is to the church, for example, that the blessing pronounced upon Abraham's line refers (Genesis 22. 17-18). This blessing, in the person of Jesus Christ, cannot possibly be confined to one small community but is promised to all the world:

unde apparet in Christo non solum Afros aut Africam, sed omnes gentes habituras benedictionem, per quas catholica dilatatur ecclesia, tanto ante promissum. (III.1.62. p. 214. lines 22-25)

Whence it is evident that in Christ not only Africans or Africa but all the nations through which the Catholic Church is spread abroad, should receive the blessing which was promised so long before.

Although the church is widely disseminated, Augustine believes that its unity is indispensable. It is the one quality which must be guarded above all others and without which all others are rendered void. Without unity, even miracles are meaningless (*In Ioannis Evangelium tractatus* XIII.17. lines 14-15).

According to Augustine, the principal effect of disunity for any group in schism is to make sterile the special benefits offered by the church. In his exploration of the efficacy of the sacraments when they are administered outside the community of the true church, Augustine clarifies and defines the very nature of sacraments, finding that for their fruitful operation they require the activating presence of God. He declares that this may be found only in the church. The sacraments themselves are unaltered when they are found outside the church: indeed, disagreeing with Cyprian, Augustine affirms that schismatics do have valid sacraments. However, their separation from the church removes them from the sphere of grace. Separated from the bond of peace, schismatics are not therefore in a position to receive

---

7. Quoted in the translation by J.R. King.

the mysteries beneficially. Furthermore, the sacraments become directly harmful outside the proper context:

> Qui accipit mysterium unitatis, et non tenet vinculum pacis, non mysterium accipit pro se, sed testimonium contra se. (*Sermo* CCLXXII)

> He who receives the mystery of unity, and does not hold the bond of peace, does not receive the mystery for himself, but as testimony against him.

For Ælfric, one of the most important symbols of church unity is that of the body of Christ, a symbol familiar from the earliest Christian writings. Commenting upon the fact that the Lord's Prayer invokes 'Our Father', not 'My Father', Ælfric points out that this daily prayer, the pattern for all prayers, requires an acknowledgement that all Christians share the same relationship with the Father. In prayer, Christians are united with each other and with the church. All the petitions of the prayer are applicable to the whole community. That Jesus taught his followers to pray in this way shows that God loves unity and fellowship in his people.[8] The image of unity is one all can recognize:

> Æfter Godes gesetnysse ealle cristene men sceoldon beon swa geðwære swilce hit an man wære: forði wa ðam men þe ða annysse tobrycð. (Thorpe XIX. p. 272. lines 23-25)

> According to God's law all Christian people must be as united as if it were one man; woe therefore to anyone who breaks this unity.

The image of the human body is a helpful one, for it emphasizes not only the interaction of the various members, but also makes clear their necessary subjection to the head. It means, too, that no group can claim to be the body of Christ simply because it can demonstrate internal unity. The body cannot function without the guiding power of the head, and only that body which has Christ as its head may claim his power. As the limbs of the human body obey the brain in co-operation, so must the church obey Christ in unity, 'forðon þe he is ure

---

8.   Compare Augustine in *Epistula* CLXXXVII.viii.28.

heafod, and we synd his lima' ('for he is our head, and we are his limbs', lines 28-29).[9]
Because the ascended Christ continues to experience the world through his body, he is
directly touched by the persecution of his limbs. So Christ challenged Saul (Acts 9. 4):

He cwæð, 'Hwi ehtst ðu min?' forðan ðe he is cristenra manna heafod, and besargað
swa hwæt swa his lima on eorðan ðrowiað. (Thorpe XXVII. p. 390. lines 11-14)[10]

He said, 'Why do you persecute me?' because he is the head of Christian people, and
sorrows for whatever his limbs on earth suffer.

Here Ælfric gains a rare insight into what it means for Christ to be united with the church.
The unity of the limbs and head is more often seen from the other perspective.

The church as the body of Christ is one of the most powerful and pervasive images in
Augustine's work, expressing the single inseparable nature of the church and Christ. In the
church many members unite in a common life, just as in the human body; the life of the
Spirit suffuses it just as the soul pervades the body:

Quod autem est anima corpori hominis, hoc est Spiritus sanctus corpori Christi, quod
est Ecclesia: hoc agit Spiritus sanctus in tota Ecclesia, quod agit anima in omnibus
membris unius corporis. (*Sermo* CCLXVII.iv.4)

What the soul is to a man's body, so is the Holy Spirit to the body of Christ, which is
the church: the Spirit dwells in the whole church, as the soul dwells in all members of
one body.

Schism means cutting off the life-giving force, for the vivifying flow stops completely when
a member is removed from the body: 'membrum amputatum non sequitur spiritus' ('the soul
does not follow the amputated limb', iv.4).

---

9. Compare Thorpe XVII. p. 238. 19-20; XXVI. p. 368. 23-24; XXXII. p. 482. 10-13;
   Godden XV. 251-54.

10. Compare Pope XXV(c). 4-7; and in Augustine, *Enarrationes in Psalmos* CXXX.6. 55-58.

Augustine goes yet further: the importance of unity within the body of Christ is so strong that he is sure that schismatics do not simply harm themselves by separating from the church (as Cyprian had suggested), but they actually rend the body of Christ: 'diuidunt membra Christi et exsufflant sacramenta Christi' ('they bring division among the members of Christ and pour scorn upon the sacraments of Christ', *Epistula* CLXXXV.ii.8. p. 8. line 6). For Cyprian, the body of Christ could not be rent: its unity defined the nature of the church, for all those who separated themselves from the true church were necessarily excluded from the body.[11] By contrast, Augustine's belief that schismatics possess the sacraments means that they are included within the bounds of the church, but their inefficacious use of them abuses the unity of the body and is therefore a destructive force. All members of the body suffer the pain of disunity, and should seek the restoration of health to the whole body. Only as members of the body of Christ can Christians be redeemed and admitted to the community of the blessed, for it is only his body that Christ justifies,

> sic homo, qui praeciditur de Christi iusti corpore, nullo modo potest spiritum tenere iustitiae. (ix.42. p. 37. lines 1-2)

> so a man cannot possibly retain the spirit of justice if he is cut off from the body of the just Christ.

It is this belief which leads Augustine to insist that the Donatists must return to the church (ix.43. p. 38. lines 5-6).

Resurrection transforms the earthly body of Christ into the heavenly community, and, again, this is possible only for those who are united with Christ. The Scriptures state that only the one who descends from heaven may return there:

> Non ergo ascendit, nisi Christus. Si vis ascendere, esto in corpore Christi: si vis ascendere, esto membrum Christi. (*Sermo* CCXCIV.x.10)

---

11. H. Cunliffe-Jones, editor, *A History of Christian Doctrine* (Edinburgh, 1978), p. 171.

None but Christ ascended, therefore. If you desire to ascend, be in the body of Christ; if you desire to ascend, be a limb of Christ.

The full restoration of salvation is open only to those whose association with Christ is so intimate that his ascension, in which humanity is raised with divinity, raises them too.

This image of the body of Christ is not simply a happy choice of metaphor. For Augustine the church is one complete manifestation of the body of Christ, who exists as the Word, eternal and universal; as the Mediator in the likeness of man, incarnate at an unique moment in history; and finally as the church, the living body of Christ on earth, his contemporary form, also sacramentally represented by the eucharist. The clear implication is that each of these manifestations is true, real, divine. The body of Christ in the church is 'an organic unity in which all have their several functions, and which is figuratively represented in the one bread of the eucharist' (Kelly, *Doctrines*, pp. 413-14). The importance of this vision in Augustine's work is very great: none of his successors appreciates it so deeply. Ælfric's treatment of the idea recognizes its importance, but it lacks Augustine's strongly sensed 'organic unity' of the body. Nevertheless, his perception that the risen Christ experiences persecution through his church rises above this limitation. So does his account of the communion experienced in the eucharist.

The experience of the eucharist provides the most mysterious and yet the most audacious expression of Christian unity. 'Quoniam unus panis, unum corpus multi sumus' ('We, being many, are one bread, one body', I Corinthians 10. 17); St Paul's words, at once astonishing and domestically ordinary, unite the Christian, the community and the head:

Understandað nu. and blissiað. fela sind an hlaf. and an lichama on criste; He is ure heafod. and we sind his lima. (Godden XV. lines 233-36)

Understand now and rejoice: many are one bread and one body in Christ. He is our head, and we are his limbs.

The mystery contained by the 'one bread' can properly be received only within the bond of unity: only to the faithful within the church is the eucharist profitable. As Augustine taught, to anyone outside that unity, partaking of the sacrament is actually dangerous. In place of the benefit which is the property of the eucharist in the right setting, anyone outside the 'bond of peace' receives condemnation:

> Crist gehalgode on his beode þa gerynu ure sibbe. and ure annysse. se ðe underfehð þære annysse gerynu. and ne hylt ðone bend þære soðan sibbe. ne underfehð he na gerynu for him sylfum. ac gecyðnysse togeanes him sylfum. (lines 241-44)[12]

> Christ sanctified on his table the mystery of our peace and our unity; anyone who receives the mystery of unity and does not hold the bond of true peace does not receive the mystery for himself but testimony against himself.

Within the unity of the church, however, the eucharist presents and contains the reality of a communion between God and his people on a most intimate level. The sacrament is both a giving and a receiving between Christ and his body:

> Ge soðlice sindon cristes lichama. and leomu; Nu is eower gerynu geled on godes mysan. and ge underfoð eower gerynu. to ðan þe ge sylfe sind. (lines 229-31)[13]

> Truly you are Christ's body and limbs. Now your mystery is laid on God's table, and you receive your mystery, which you yourselves are.

Here Ælfric clearly perceives Augustine's 'organic unity': 'mysterium vestrum in mensa Dominica positum est: mysterium vestrum accepitis' ('your mystery is placed on the Lord's table: receive your mystery', *Sermo* CCLXXII). The body of Christ is the community of the saints, offered in the sacrament of the eucharist. In these lines from *De civitate Dei*, Augustine combines the idea of Christ's emptying himself with the glorification of the whole body:

> tota ipsa redempta ciuitas, hoc est congregatio societasque sanctorum, uniuersale sacrificium offeratur Deo per sacerdotem magnum, qui etiam se ipsum obtulit in

---

12. Compare Augustine, *Sermo* CCLXXII.

13. Cited again, with the comment from Augustine which follows, on pages 193-94.

passione pro nobis, ut tanti capitis corpus essemus, secundum formam serui. (X.vi. lines 33-37)

the whole redeemed community, that is to say, the congregation and fellowship of the saints, is offered to God as a universal sacrifice, through the great Priest who offered himself in his suffering for us — so that we might be the body of so great a head — under 'the form of a servant'.

For Ælfric, too, the union of Christ and his body permits the Christian to participate in Christ's heavenly reign:

Se Hælend soðlice is his halgena heafod,
and hi mid him rixiað, his englum gelice,
and hi God geseoð, swa swutellice swa swa englas. (Pope XI. lines 533-37)[14]

The saviour truly is the head of his saints, and they reign with him, like his angels, and they see God, as clearly as the angels.

This is the perfect unity of the body of Christ in bliss.

A quite separate vision of the church's relationship with Christ is to be found in the traditional symbol of the bride of Christ, who remains a virgin while bringing forth offspring in fecundity. For Augustine, God and the church may be regarded as the spiritual parents of all Christians (*Sermo* XXII.xxii.9. 259-64). A very clear distinction is made between spiritual and earthly birth. The children of earthly parents inherit death from them; the children of God and the church are assured of a spiritual inheritance:

Generant autem ad uitam aeternam, quia et ipsi aeterni sunt. Et habemus hereditatem promissam a Christo uitam aeternam. (xxii.10. lines 276-78)

---

14. Compare Pope XII. 206-11.

They gave birth to us for eternal life, for they are themselves eternal. Thus we have eternal life, our inheritance promised to us by Christ.[15]

The church is the Christian's 'uera mater' ('true mother', *Epistula* CLXXXV.vii.30. p. 28. line 1); those who return to her are welcomed as an earthly mother gathers her children, offering a liberating security, 'pio matris catholicae gremio collecti, ita liberantur' ('they are gathered into the loving bosom of our Catholic mother, and delivered', iii.12. p. 12. lines 4-5).

Ælfric finds this traditional image of the church as bride and mother very pleasing. It corresponds to his own delight in the miraculous ordinariness of the Blessed Virgin. This young woman, excellent in the purity of her devotion to God and in her loving obedience, was nevertheless merely human. As her own person inspires an individual response to God, so her symbolic representation in the church lends it beauty. In its ordinariness it is also found to be miraculous, like the Virgin.

The image of bride and mother appears in Ælfric's exegesis of Matthew 22. 1-14, the story of a royal wedding celebration. Here, the church is first of all seen in the person of the bride, and the fruitful motherhood of the bride is immediately perceived:

> Se cyning ðe worhte his suna gifta is God Fæder, þe ða halgan gelaðunge geðeodde his Bearne þurh geryno his flæsclicnysse. Seo halige gelaðung is Cristes bryd, þurh ða he gestrynð dæghwomlice gastlice bearn, and heo is ealra cristenra manna modor, and ðeah-hwæðere ungewemmed mæden. (Thorpe XXXV. p. 520. lines 24-28)[16]

> The king who arranged his son's marriage is God the Father, who united the holy church to his Son through the mystery of his incarnation. The holy church is Christ's bride, through whom he begets spiritual children daily, and she is the mother of all Christian people and yet an immaculate virgin.

---

15. Quoted in the translation by Quincy Howe, Jr.

16. The exegesis is Gregory's, from *Homeliae in Evangelia* II.XXXVIII.3. Compare Thorpe XXXIII. p. 492. 4-8; Godden I. 91-102 and 115-17; IV. 33-36 and 102-4; VIII. 34-36; Pope IV. 282-84; XII. 123-24.

The model for this fertile mother yet immaculate virgin is Mary. Ælfric points to this correspondence even in his account of the annunciation, where Mary is found to be aware of her role in the economy of salvation and in the initiation of the church. Ælfric portrays her as an ordinary woman, but one possessed of perfect humility, who is given the grace to understand that the birth of her child will also be the birth of a new people. His amplification of her response to the angel's greeting shows that the beginning of salvation lay in the humble obedience of the virgin, and also suggests that she understood this:

> Heo cwæð to ðam engle, 'Getimige me æfter ðinum worde:' þæt is, Gewurðe hit swa ðu segst, þæt ðæs Ælmihtigan Godes Sunu become on minne innoð, and mennisce edwiste of me genime, and to alysednysse middangeardes forðstæppe of me, swa swa brydguma of his brydbedde. (Thorpe XIII. p. 200. lines 17-22)

> She said to the angel, 'May it happen to me according to your word,' that is, Let it be as you say, that the Son of Almighty God might come into my womb, and receive human substance from me, and proceed from me as the redemption of the world, like a bridegroom from his bridal bed.

Augustine also puts into Mary's mouth an exegetical commentary on her own humble response to the angel's announcement, giving her a prophetic understanding of her physical and spiritual conception of the incarnate Son, which is also the moment of birth for the church:

> Fiat, inquit, sine virili semine conceptus in virgine; nascatur de Spiritu sancto et integra femina, in quo renascatur de Spiritu sancto integra Ecclesia. (*Sermo* CCXV.4)

> 'Be it done,' she said, 'Let Him, conceived in a virgin without man's co-operation, be born of the Holy Spirit and of an inviolate woman, and in Him let an unspotted Church be born of the Holy Spirit.[17]

---

17. Quoted in the translation of Sister Mary Sarah Muldowney. 'Sine virili semine' might more literally be translated 'without man's seed'.

In his homily provided for the Nativity of the Virgin, Ælfric says that it was in redeeming mankind that the Son chose his bride:

> Ac us alysde se hælend mid his halgum blode
>
> of þam ecan þeowte þæs ealdan deofles.
>
> He geceas þa him sylfum, swa swa us secgað bec,
>
> þa halgan gelaðunge him sylfum to bryde
>
> þæt is eall godes folc, þe on god nu gelyfð. (Assmann III. lines 67-71)

But the saviour redeemed us with his holy blood from the eternal slavery of the old devil. Then he chose for himself, as the Scriptures tell us, the holy church as a bride for himself, that is, all God's people, who now believe in God.

The church is like Mary, both in is its perfect devotion to God, which is the devotion of a bride, and in its fruitful virginity. This bride retains her virgin purity, yet brings to birth new children of God (Godden I. 100-2)[18] The marriage of the bridegroom and bride is pure yet fruitful. The spiritual birth of these children links them with the Son of Mary, for although Mary gave birth to Jesus bodily, she did so by means of grace, and the church daily brings forth the members of Christ's body by grace. Here Mary and the church are one, because as the mother of Christ's limbs, the church may truly be said to be Christ's mother:

> Eall Cristes gelaðung is Cristes modor,
>
> forðan ðe heo acenð Cristes sylfes limu
>
> þurh ða halgan gife on ðam halgan fulluhte. (Assmann III. lines 216-18)[19]

The whole of Christ's church is Christ's mother, for she gives birth to the limbs of Christ himself, through holy grace in holy baptism.

The identification of Mary and the church means that the latter may properly be described in terms which deliberately refer to the tenets of faith concerning the person of Mary:

---

18. Compare Godden I. 115-17; Assmann III. 87-92, 110-14 and 159-64.

19. Compare Augustine, *De sancta virginitate* v.5.

Ðurh þone halgan geleafan heo is him beweddod
ure ealra modor, and heo is mæden swa þeah,
æfre ungewemmed, þonne heo æfre þurhwunað
on godes geleafan and nele abugan
to nanum hæðenscipe fram þæs hælendes geleafan,
fram hyre brydguman to bysmorfullum deofolgylde,
ne to wiccecræfte, ne to wiglungum,
mid nanum gedwylde fram hyre drihtne ahwar. (Assmann III. lines 93-100)

Through holy faith she is married to him, the mother of us all, and she is nevertheless
a virgin, eternally spotless, when she dwells eternally in the faith of God and will not
bend from the Saviour's faith to any heathenism, from her bridegroom to shameful
devil-worship, nor to witchcraft, nor to auguries, nor from her Lord with any error in
any way.

Just as Mary maintained her virginal purity within her marriage, so the virginal purity of the
church is seen in its refusal to admit any other suitor: both heresy and heathenism are rejected
as the church sustains a steadfast devotion to the bridegroom and Lord. Mary's role as type
of the church therefore insists upon a doctrine of perpetual virginity, for only as a model of
pure, unsullied faith does she properly delineate the church's ideal. Mary's preeminence in
virginity is a sign and model both for the whole church and for its individual members. As
it is for the church, whose pure faith is found to be typified by the Virgin, so for the
individual it is essential that Mary remained a virgin at every stage of her life. Each is called
to a purity of faith which contributes to the purity of the whole body, and additionally, each
may adopt Mary's standard as one to strive for. Ælfric finds that this standard applies not
only to the physical life of the faithful, but also to the spiritual.

Mary's perfect virginity is attested by Scripture. Ælfric discusses the frequent prophecies
of the manner of Jesus' birth which are to be found in the Old Testament, among them those
which contain particular reference, according to exegesis, to the Virgin Mary. Of these the
most important is Ezechiel's prophecy (44. 1-2) which described the gate closed to all except
the Lord:

Þæt beclysede geat on Godes huse getacnode þone halgan mæigðhad þære eadigan Marian. Se Hlaford, ealra hlaforda Hlaford, þæt is Crist, becom on hire innoð, and ðurh hi on menniscnysse wearð acenned, and þæt geat bið belocen on ecnysse; þæt is, þæt Maria wæs mæden ær ðære cenninge, and mæden on ðære cenninge, and mæden æfter þære cenninge. (Thorpe XIII. p. 194. lines 5-11)[20]

The closed gate in the house of God betokened the holy virginity of the blessed Mary. The Lord, the Lord of all lords, that is Christ, came into her womb, and through her was born in human nature, and that gate is locked for eternity; that is, Mary was virgin before the birth, a virgin at the birth, and a virgin after the birth.

Ælfric's conclusion here may be compared with Augustine's 'Illa enim virgo concepit, virgo peperit, virgo permansit' ('For as a virgin she conceived Him, as a virgin brought Him forth, and a virgin she continued', *Sermo* LI.18).[21] Ælfric, like Augustine, observes that no other virgin can also choose to be a mother as well: that privilege was uniquely Mary's. She alone is blessed with the most perfect expression of both motherhood and virginity:

Nis on nanum oðrum men mægðhad, gif þær bið wæstmbærnys; ne wæstmbærnys, gif þær bið ansund mægðhad. Nu is forði gehalgod ægðer ge Marian mægðhad ge hyre wæstmbærnys þurh þa godcundlican acennednysse; and heo ealle oðre oferstihð on mægðhade and on wæstmbærnysse. (Thorpe XXX. p. 438. lines 26-31)[22]

In no other person is there virginity if there is fruitfulness, nor is there fruitfulness if there is unbroken virginity. Now for this reason both Mary's virginity and her fruitfulness are sanctified through the divine birth; and she surpasses all others in virginity and in fruitfulness.

---

20. Compare Thorpe I. p. 24. 26-27; XIII. p. 198. 10-11; Godden I. 74-79; Pope I. 414-26. Ælfric's translation of the verses from Ezekiel is in Thorpe XIII. p. 194. 3-5.

21. Quoted in the translation by R.G. Macmullen.

22. Compare Godden I. 54-58; Pope XI. 11; XIa. 80; Assmann III. 207-11; in Augustine, *De sancta virginitate* vii.7.

Pre-eminent in virginity, Mary is glorious in motherhood.

Mary's excellence, both in virginity and in motherhood, undoubtedly exalts her above all those who seek to emulate her. Yet, Ælfric suggests, the humble obedience which she offered to God is something attainable by each Christian. He says that although Mary was greatly blessed in the honour given to her of bearing the Son of God, her loving response to God's command, in which her perfect humility and obedience were expressed, was a much greater blessing. Furthermore, although the first honour was uniquely bestowed upon her, the greater blessing is one which all may seek by emulating her:

> ac heo is swaþeah git swyþor eadig,
> for ðan ðe heo Godes word lufað and healt.
> Eac syndon eadige þa ealle þe gehyrað
> þæt halige Godes word and hit healdað mid lufe. (Pope IV. lines 291-94)[23]

but she is yet more greatly blessed because she loves and keeps God's word. In the same way all those who hear the holy word of God and keep it with love are blessed.

To encourage all who have dedicated their virginity to God, Ælfric invites his listeners to look for ways in which they can be like Mary, emphasizing these points rather than the unattainable foreignness of Mary's virtue. He assures them that the pattern of Mary's obedience and love may be followed by virgins even now in such a way that they too may claim for themselves the motherhood of Christ:

> And se ylca is ealra mædena wyrðmynt,
> þe hine lufiað gehealdenre clænnysse,
> and hi magon beon Cristes moddru eac,
> gif hi wyrcað on life his fæder willan. (Assmann III. lines 212-15)

And the same is the honour of all virgins who love him whilst maintaining their purity; they may also be Christ's mothers if in their lives they do his Father's will.

---

23. Compare Assmann III. 185-88; in Augustine, *De sancta virginitate* iii.3.

This bold extrapolation of the idea of Mary's motherhood is found in Augustine's treatise on virginity, *De sancta virginitate* v.5.

For Augustine, Mary is both the foremost member of the church and its type. She is a member of the body of Christ even though she bore him as his mother, and she needs the same salutary aid as all other members of the body, for Christ alone was born without the mortally wounding effects of original sin (*Contra Iulianum opus imperfectum* IV.cxxii). For Ælfric, Augustine's suggestion that Christ is Mary's saviour as well as her Son means that not only is she Christ's mother physically and spiritually, she is also his sister in a spiritual sense:

> And Maria is his modor lichamlice
> and gastlice his swustor and soðlice his modor. (Assmann III. lines 219-20)

> and Mary is his mother bodily, and spiritually his sister and truly his mother.

Mary is therefore mother, member and symbol of the church.

This complex relationship, in which the paradoxes of Mary's fruitful virginity and her relationship with her Son-Saviour are extended to embrace the church and Christ, is the basis of Ælfric's continuing exegesis of the parable of the wedding feast. At this wedding, the church is the bride, but it is also simultaneously the company invited to the wedding. Messengers invite the people to come: the messengers, Ælfric explains, are the prophets and apostles who announced and preached the bridegroom's coming. The invitation declares that all the preparations for feasting have been made. Oxen and fatted fowls have been prepared:

> Hwæt is, 'Mine fearras sind ofslagene, and mine gemæstan fugelas,' buton swilce he cwæde, 'Behealdað ðæra ealdfædera drohtnunga, and understandað þæra witegena gydunge, and þæra apostola bodunge embe mines Bearnes menniscnysse, and cumað to ðam giftum'? (Thorpe XXXV. p. 524. lines 1-5)

> What is, 'My oxen and my fatted fowls are slaughtered,' but as though he said, 'Observe the lives of the Fathers, and understand the discourse of the prophets, and the preaching of the apostles about my Son's humanity, and come to the wedding'?

The guests who come to the wedding discover that it is their wedding, just as much as the bride and bridegroom's, for as they join the celebration, they themselves are made one with the bride:

> Þæt is, 'Cumað mid geleafan, and geðeodað eow to ðære halgan gelaðunge, ðe is his bryd and eower modor.' (lines 5-7)

> that is to say, 'Come with faith and unite yourselves to the holy church, which is his bride and your mother.'

Bringing faith, the guests receive baptism and are thereby begotten to God ('Gode gestrynde'). Children are conceived within this marriage by faith in conjunction with grace (p. 520. lines 30-33).[24] Exactly these two elements, faith and grace, came together in Mary when she conceived her Son.

Another fertile image of the church is that of a building of living stones founded on Christ, the Biblical metaphor of the Messiah as the foundation stone or cornerstone. The church comprises the faithful of all times and places, chosen from Jews and Gentiles. The cornerstone, which is Christ himself, joins members of the old and the new chosen peoples into one community (Pope III. 142-46).[25] Christ as foundation stone supports a building made of living stones:

> Ealle Godes cyrcan sind getealde to anre gelaðunge, and seo is mid gecorenum mannum getimbrod, na mid deadum stanum; and eal seo bytlung ðæra liflicra stana is ofer Criste gelogod. (Thorpe XXVI. p. 368. lines 20-23)

> All of God's churches are counted as one church, and it is built with chosen people, not with dead stones; and all the building of those living stones is founded upon Christ.

---

24. Compare Thorpe IV. p. 74. 35-p. 76. 1; XXXIII. p. 494. 17-19 and p. 496. 22-24.

25. Compare Pope III. 30-36; IV. 180-82.

The image of the living building is one of foundation, construction and interdependence. It speaks of the support offered by one course of stones to the next, all of which are borne by the foundation stone (Godden XL. 125-31).[26]

This is the organic structure of the church described by Augustine when he speaks of the transformation of people into the material of which Christ's church is built. The effect of grace is to render these raw materials suitable for the task: they cannot of themselves become stones of the appropriate quality for the temple. Christians become part of this organic structure when they are spiritually reborn:

> proinde in compagem corporis Christi tamquam in uiuam stucturam templi dei, quae est
> eius ecclesia, nati homines non ex operibus iustitiae quae facturi sunt, sed renascendo
> per gratiam transferuntur tanquam de massa ruinae ad aedificii firmamentum. (*Epistula*
> CLXXXVII.x.33. p. 111. lines 13-18)

> Therefore, it is not by the works of justice which they are about to perform that men
> are born into the totality of the body of Christ as into a living structure of the temple
> of God which is His church, but, by being born again through grace, they are carried
> over as from a ruinous mass into the foundation of the building.

The chosen are pulled out of the pile of rubble and reshaped into suitable material for the building. Christ is the foundation of the living building, which will endure for ever:

> restat autem altera dedicatio uniuersae domus, cuius ipse Christus est fundamentum,
> quae differtur in finem, quando erit omnium resurrectio non moriturorum amplius. (*De*
> *civitate Dei* XV.xix. lines 13-15)

> The other dedication yet remains to be accomplished, the dedication of the whole house
> of which Christ himself is the foundation. This dedication is deferred until the end,
> when there will be the resurrection of those who are to die no more.

---

26. Compare Pope XIV. 232-33; Skeat XVI. 149-53.

The foundation of the church on the faith of Peter is an extension of this idea. Christ gave his disciple Simon the new name to signify the new faith. However, Ælfric is as interested in the appropriateness of the name for Christ as for Peter himself. He is concerned to show that Christ is the true foundation of Christianity, and so in his interpretation he combines the images of Peter, the foundation, and Peter's faith, as typical of the faith of the church, with the image of Christ, the one rock on which both foundation and faith depend:

> Crist is gecweden Petra. þæt is stan. and of ðam naman is gecweden Petrus. eal cristen folc; Crist cwæð þu eart stænen. and ofer ðisne stan þæt is ofer ðam geleafan þe ðu nu andettest. ic getimbrige mine cyrcan; Ofer me sylfne ic getimbrige mine cyrcan. (Godden XXIV. lines 167-71)[27]

> Christ is called 'Petra', that is, the rock, and from that name the whole Christian people is called 'Petrus'. Christ said, 'You are of stone, and upon this rock, that is, upon the faith which you now confess, I will build my church; upon myself I will build my church.'

This may be compared with the explanation offered by Jesus himself in Matthew 16. 18, where Peter is said to be the rock on which the new community is to be built. Ælfric shifts the emphasis from Peter, the foundation, to Christ, the builder and foundation stone. This has the effect of ensuring that the exegesis centres upon Christ rather than on his disciple (or, indeed, the Pope). Moreover, the fact that Ælfric draws attention to Peter's faith rather than Peter's person points the listener away from the individual towards the community of the church: the stress is upon common faith rather than individual prominence or authority. Ælfric also very strongly emphasizes that the church grows through Christ alone, not through the human efforts of his disciples or any other agency.

Another important image for the church, deriving from the Gospels, is that of the kingdom of God. This is the *basileia*, the place of God's rule, in which there is perfect continuity between the church on earth and the church in glory. The presence of Christ is God's kingdom, and his church is the realization of that presence (Pope IV. 174-82). Through the incarnation of the Son God's kingdom has been realized and fulfilled both on earth and

---

27. Compare Godden XL. 86-96, 108-10 and 223-29; Pope XVIII. 152.

in heaven. This means that already in this present life the kingdom is come. Ælfric illustrates this point by reference to the Lord's Prayer, which contains the petition 'Thy kingdom come'. This is not to be understood as a future event so much as an ever-present reality which will be perfected in eternity:

> Æfre wæs Godes rice, and æfre bið: ac hit is swa to understandenne, þæt his rice beo ofer us, and he on us rixige, and we him mid ealre gehyrsumnysse underþeodde syn, and þæt ure rice beo us gelæst and gefylled, swa swa Crist us behet, þæt he wolde us ece rice forgyfan. (Thorpe XIX. p. 262. line 33-p. 264. line 3)[28]

> God's kingdom always was and always will be, but it is thus to be understood that his kingdom shall be over us, and he shall reign in us, and we shall be his subjects with all obedience, and that our kingdom shall be realized and fulfilled, as Christ promised us that he would give us an eternal kingdom.

The perfection of the eternal kingdom is expressed in the image of the heavenly city, Jerusalem, already prepared to receive the elect:

> ure drihten Iesus Christus. se ðe is soð sacerd gelæt þa dædbetendan æfter soðre dædbote to ðære uplican hierusalem. þe he sylf getimbrode. and gearcode eallum ðam þe hine lufiað. (Godden IV. lines 270-73)[29]

> our lord Jesus Christ, who is the true priest, leads the penitents, after true penance, to the heavenly Jerusalem, which he built himself, and prepared for all those who love him.

Augustine's preferred image for the kingdom is the city of God, preeminently the community of saints in its blessed, redeemed, purified state, at last the true church. Yet even

---

28. Compare Thorpe XIV. p. 210. 22-25; XIX. p. 264. 11-15; XXXII. p. 358. 32-35; XXXV. p. 520. 19-23; Godden I. 99; IV. 235-39; V. 37-39; Pope XI. 524-25.

29. Compare Godden XL. 209-12.

on earth the church, as yet unpurified, may truly be called the city of God because its hope is fixed on God, grounded in belief in the resurrection of Christ:

> In spe igitur uiuit homo filius resurrectionis; in spe uiuit, quamdiu peregrinatur hic, ciuitas Dei, quae gignitur ex fide resurrectionis Christi. (*De civitate Dei* XV.xviii. lines 3-5)

> It is in hope, therefore, that a man lives, as 'the son of resurrection'; it is in hope that the City of God lives, during its pilgrimage on earth, that City which is brought into being by faith in Christ's resurrection.

This belief is the national characteristic of the citizens. Those who lack it belong to the earthly city. The two cities, the heavenly and the earthly, are distinguished by their predestined places in the eternal order. The city of God is predestined by grace to reign with God. Those outside the bounds of this city are the reprobate, who will suffer punishment. These will be their final states:

> quas etiam mystice appellamus ciuitates duas, hoc est duas societates hominum, quarum est una quae praedestinata est in aeternum regnare cum Deo, altera aeternum supplicium subire cum diabolo. Sed iste finis est earum. (XV.i. lines 16-20)

> By two cities I mean two societies of human beings, one of which is predestined to reign with God for all eternity, the other doomed to undergo eternal punishment with the Devil. But this is their final destiny.

Even now they are thus distinguished by God. Augustine's understanding of predestination demands that the city of God be the church known to God alone, predestined and elected by grace. For this reason it is possible (and even likely) that some people who are associated with the church on earth and appear to be true citizens will be denied the necessary grace of perseverance: ultimately they will be found to be excluded from the gathering of the elect. It follows, therefore, that the church on earth is not necessarily pure, that purification is still to come. The city of God undeniably exists, even now, but its true composition cannot be ascertained.

This is the basis of Augustine's argument against the Donatists' insistence upon the unique purity of their church. According to his understanding of sin, everyone is impure because of the taint of original sin; the church's only claim to purity is that in heaven the community recognized by God as his own will be purified and blessed with the freedom of sinlessness. The earthly church is merely a foreshadowing of the true city of God. Kelly observes that Augustine's distinction between the true church and the visible one has its root in his early philosophy: 'With his Platonic background of thought this distinction came easily to him, for the contrast between the perfect essence, eternal and transcending sensation, and its imperfect phenomenal embodiment was always hovering before his mind' (Kelly, *Doctrines*, p. 415).

The mixed nature of the church, where the true and apparent members await separation, is depicted in the field of wheat where tares are allowed to grow, or in grain being winnowed to separate it from chaff. The good wheat and the weeds grow together, and will not be separated until the final harvest. This image illustrates how the church, even under God's rule, is an imperfect and manifestly unroyal kingdom, and helps to explain why it cannot be otherwise in the present life. Matthew 3. 2 promises that the grain and the chaff will be separated at the winnowing, but must grow together until then (*Epistula* CLXXXV.16). Moreover the presence of the chaff or tares is no reason to desert the church, Augustine insists to the Donatists: they are not called upon to separate themselves from the good wheat just because there are also tares (*Contra litteras Petiliani*, III.ii.3). Finally, they must acknowledge that the harvest will be gathered over the whole world, at the end of time: 'ager est enim mundus, non Africa, messis finis saeculi, non tempus Donati' ('The field is the world, — not only Africa; and the harvest is the end of the world, — not the era of Donatus', III.ii.3. p. 164. lines 20-22). It cannot be that the church is as restricted as the Donatists would have it.

Even without the challenge of schism, Ælfric sees that the church is only the palest reflection of its ultimate form. Moreover, it is not possible to see who is the clean wheat, to be counted among the predestined, and who the chaff, for whom no provision of grace has been made. They are mixed together (Pope V. 267-70).[30] Purification will come, and after that time the clean wheat will be sheltered from all the tribulations associated with being out in the field:

---

30. Compare Thorpe XXXV. p. 526. 16-20.

se clæna hwæte bið gebroht on Godes berne: þæt is, þæt ða rihtwisan beoð gebrohte to þam ecan life, þær ne cymð storm ne nan unweder þæt ðam corne derie. (Thorpe XXXV. p. 526. lines 28-30)

the pure wheat will be brought into God's barn, that is, the righteous will be brought to eternal life, where no storm nor foul weather comes to harm the corn.

A variation of this metaphor is that of fishing. The Gospels record two particular fishing expeditions, in which Christ directed his disciples where to fish. They teach two different lessons about the nature of the church. On the first occasion, so many fish were caught that the net burst (Luke 5. 6). So it is with the church:

swa fela manna gebugað to geleafan on ðissere andwerdan gelaðunge. þæt hi sume eft ut berstað. ðurh wiðercorennysse and leahtrum heora ðwyran lifes. (Godden XVI. lines 165-67)[31]

so many people turn to faith in this present church that some of them burst out again, because of the reprobateness and the sins of their perverse lives.

The torn net represents the present church, which cannot contain all those who enter. By contrast, the second fishing expedition (John 21. 11), when many fish were caught without straining the net, prefigured the future church; this draught of fish

getacnode soðlice þa gesæligan Christenan,
þe to Godes rice þurh Godes sylfes fultum
eadige becumað to ðam ecan life,
þanan heora nan ne mæg syððan ut aberstan. (Pope XIV. lines 163-66)

truly symbolized the happy Christians who, blessed, attain to God's kingdom through God's own help, to the eternal life, whence none of them can afterwards burst out.

---

31. Compare Pope XIV. 128-31 and 154-57.

All of these images are developed, however briefly, to include some indication of the happiness that awaits the church in its perfected, glorified state. Augustine too looks forward to this time of blessedness. Now the church is burdened with faults and failings, and truly needs to pray for forgiveness: the time will come when sin and death, the trappings of human life, will be no more, and the church will experience the promised perfection and freedom (*Epistula* CLXXXV.ix.38). Ælfric evokes the perfection in glory of the heavenly Jerusalem by comparing it with Solomon's court. The Queen of Sheba, an eminent visitor to that court, had heard much about Solomon's glory, but she was unprepared for the splendour that greeted her arrival. Likewise, the Queen of heaven, the church, awaits the fulfilment of the promise of perfect glory, but cannot possibly imagine it:

> Ne mæg nan eage on ðisum life geseon. ne nan eare gehyran. ne nanes mannes heorte asmeagan. ða ðing þe god gearcað þam ðe hine lufiað. (Godden XL. lines 213-15)[32]

> In this life no eye can see, nor ear hear, nor anyone's heart imagine those things which God is preparing for those who love him.

This consummation is the perfect union of the body of Christ with Christ himself in the kingdom of heaven. Christ will be the source of all existence, or rather, life itself for the faithful:

> and Crist sylf ðonne bið him eallum ælc ðing,
> and him naht wana ne bið, þonne hi hine habbað.
> He is heora rice, and lif, and wurðmynt,
> heora hæl and wuldor, sibb and genihtsumnys. (Pope XI. lines 564-67).[33]

---

32. The reference is to I Corinthians 2. 9 (and Isaiah 64. 4). Compare Pope XI. 554-65; XV. 114-18.

33. I refer to this passage again on page 264. Compare Thorpe XV. p. 238. 4-7; XIX. p. 272. 11-14; Godden XL. 311-17; Pope XVIII. 435-39; Skeat XII. 88-96.

and Christ himself will then be everything to them all, and nothing will be lacking to them, when they have him. He is their kingdom, and life, and honour, their salvation and glory, peace and abundance.

Three groups of images are prominent in these teachings on the nature of the church: body, mother and field. That of the body of Christ is the most important for both teachers: the church is a manifestation of the person of Christ, endowed with holiness and received into Christ's deity. This is especially illuminated by the eucharist, a most powerful expression of unity. The image of maiden and mother is more strongly present in Ælfric's teaching than in Augustine's. The image describes the generation, protection and support of Christians who are gathered beneath a guardian authority; Ælfric, concerned to place his teaching in the context of tradition, responds gladly to this image of the beloved Mother. Finally, both writers look to images to sort out the mixed community of the church. Ælfric's view of the earthly nature of the church, its growth obstructed and its energies dissipated by the presence of tares and chaff, is wholly that of Augustine in his teaching against the Donatists. That apprehension of the imperfect nature of the empirical church directs the mind to the vision of the perfection to come in which Augustine and Ælfric both take great delight. Each acknowledges that heaven's perfection cannot yet be known, and each sees that this earthly stage is necessary before the sublime consummation may take place. Limited understanding now will give way to perfect knowledge in heaven, when indeed the church itself will reach maturity. The eyes of faith are fixed on the glory which awaits the church.

II. BAPTISM

The Donatists forced Augustine not only to reexamine the nature of the church, but also to look again at its membership qualification, the sacrament of baptism. The Donatist claim that only the pure (that is to say, Donatist) priest could baptize with validity impelled him to study how the sacrament worked. Cyprian had taught the need for the rebaptism of schismatics, but Augustine, faced with the same problem, came to a different conclusion. As he understood it, the implication of Cyprian's teaching was no different from that of the Donatist stand: that God's gift was somehow affected by the quality of the minister's life. Augustine found that he could disagree with Cyprian's policy of rebaptism whilst remaining true to him in spirit, because the saint in his humility had prescribed no rules, merely expressed his opinion. Moreover, he said that each bishop was to work as his conscience dictated, that above all unity should be preserved.[34]

In Augustine's understanding, baptism has an intrinsic sanctity, which remains untainted by any kind of external influence. This sanctity is present because it is God's sacrament. From him alone its holiness and power derive:

> cum baptisma uerbis euangelicis datur, qualibet ea peruersitate intellegat ille per quem datur uel ille cui datur, ipsum per se sanctum est propter illum cuius est. (*De baptismo contra Donatistas* IV.xii.18. p. 244. lines 17-19)

> when baptism is given in the words of the gospel, however great be the perverseness of understanding on the part either of him through whom, or of him to whom it is given, the sacrament itself is holy in itself on account of Him whose sacrament it is.[35]

This means that the true mystery of the sacrament is conveyed even by perverse and sinful ministers (19-24).

This is an essential truth if the Christian is to have faith in the saving power of baptism. The Donatist argument that the minister must be pure breaks down easily in the case of a priest who claims to be pure but conceals a sinful nature; according to the Donatist rule baptism administered by him would be invalid, yet no-one could know. It is all very well, Augustine remarks, when one has to judge the suitability of notorious sinners, but what about the secret ones? (*Contra litteras Petiliani* III.xx.23). No: it is far better to trust in the Lord than in any man:

> quod ad baptismum attinet, ne id, quod gratia dei regeneramur mundamur iustificamur danti homini tribuatur: bonum est confidere in domino quam confidere in homine. (III.l.62. p. 214. lines 4-7)

---

34. Cyprian's teaching is described by Augustine in *De baptismo contra Donatistas* II.i.2-iii.4.

35. Quoted in the translation by J.R. King.

As regards the question of baptism, that our being born again, cleansed, justified by the grace of God, should not be ascribed to the man who administered the sacrament . . . 'It is better to trust in the Lord than to put confidence in man.'

The minister remains important, but his role is to administer the sacrament, not to convey purity and justice. These are wholly the gifts of God:

quia hoc non operatur in interiore homine nisi per quem creatus est totus homo et qui deus manens factus est homo. (III.liv.66. p. 220. lines 29-31)

Because these are not accomplished in the inner man, except by him by whom the whole man was created, and who while he remained God was made man.

In addition to these observations about the efficacy of the sacrament, Augustine also studied the nature of the sacramental sign itself. The sign requires the mind to address the concept to which it points:

Signum est enim res praeter speciem, quam ingerit sensibus, aliud aliquid ex se faciens in cogitationem uenire. (*De doctrina Christiana* II.i.1 lines 5-7)

A sign is a thing which, apart from the impression that it presents to the senses, causes of itself some other thing to enter our thoughts.[36]

Speaking generally about the sacramental sign in the context of a discussion about the eucharist, he observes that the sacrament operates on two levels. It has an external, visible appearance or effect which serves as the sign of spiritual transformation perceived only by the mind of faith:

Ista, fratres, ideo dicuntur Sacramenta, quia in eis aliud videtur, aliud intelligitur. Quod videtur, speciem habet corporalem; quod intelligitur, fructum habet spiritualem. (*Sermo* CCLXXII)

---

36. Quoted in the translation by John J. Gavigan.

This, brothers, is called a sacrament, because in it one thing is seen, another understood. That which is seen has bodily species; that which is understood has spiritual effect.

Ælfric endorses the Augustinian doctrine of baptism and draws on Augustine's general findings concerning the nature of the sign itself. Christ instituted the sacrament, first by receiving baptism from John (Mark 1. 9), and then by granting to his disciples the power of administering it (Matthew 28. 19). He received baptism even though he needed no forgiveness of sins, and by this act of humility he opened the way for the greatest and the least to follow him (Godden III. 91-96).[37] Ælfric comments that in receiving the sign he bestowed on it the sanctifying power of his divinity: even the water was transformed into a supernatural element (Pope XI. 17-18).[38] The baptism he passed on was different from the one he had received:

> he forgeaf ðone anweald his apostolon. and eallum gehadedum mannum þæt hi sceoldon fullian mid godes fulluhte. on naman ðære halgan ðrynnysse. (Godden III. lines 214-16)[39]

> to his apostles and all ordained persons he gave the power that they were to baptize with God's baptism in the name of the holy trinity.

As he did with the symbolic actions of breaking bread and sharing the cup, actions already familiar to the disciples, Christ, by this gift of power, took the symbol of conversion and charged it with the presence and might of God. It now conveys 'synna forgyfenys þurh ðone Halgan Gast' ('the forgiveness of sins through the Holy Spirit', Thorpe XXV. p. 352. line 15).[40]

Baptism is one of three important sacramental signs, 'þreo healice ðing' ('three supreme things', Godden III. line 228), which are appointed for cleansing. It is the initiatory act in a life of continuous rededication to God. The second of these signs, the eucharist, is the food

---

37. Compare Thorpe XXV. p. 352. 20-21; Godden III. 197-201; Pope XI. 15-18; XIa. 89-93.

38. Compare Godden III. 97-98; XV. 111-16; Pope XIa. 91-93.

39. Compare Thorpe II. p. 28. 7-8; Pope VII. 130-35.

40. Compare Godden III. 24-25; Pope XII. 72-73 and 93-94.

required for that service. The third essential, without which baptism and the eucharist remain incomplete, is the continuing cleansing of penance, for no-one ever stays free from sin (228-32).[41] Each of the three sacraments is essential for healthy Christian development. It may be said that baptism is the most important because it is the first condition of salvation: it overcomes the disqualifying effects of original sin. In eliminating sin, baptism affords a new relationship with God, a new beginning.

Baptism eradicates both original sin and its attendant condemnation. The sacrament is essential even for the smallest child, because everyone is born with the guilt of original sin:

Þurh Adames forgægednesse, þe godes bebod tobræc,

beoð þa cild synfulle. (Pope XII. lines 134-35)[42]

Through the transgression of Adam, who broke God's command, children are sinful.

Any child who dies without baptism is therefore heathen, and the door of heaven is barred to him (106-8). Even a hurried and informal baptism is infinitely to be preferred to no baptism at all (Fehr I.71. lines 8-10).[43]

Ælfric describes the ceremony of infant baptism in his Epiphany sermon. The child, although unconscious of the statement of faith being made on its behalf, is saved through the faith of its parents and godfather (Godden III. 270-72).[44] The ceremony follows the familiar pattern of repeated questions which the godfather answers. On behalf of the child he renounces the devil, his works and his vainglory; he affirms his belief in the trinity, the unity of God, the resurrection of the body and the reward of heaven: 'He andwyrt ic gelyfe; And se preost gefullað þæt cild mid þisum geleafan, ('He answers, "I believe," and the priest

---

41. Compare Pope IV. 67-71.

42. Compare Godden I. 110-12; XIII. 126-27; Pope XI. 498-500.

43. B. Fehr, editor, *Die Hirtenbriefe Ælfrics in altenglischer und lateinischer Fassung*, Bibliothek der angelsächsischen Prosa, 9 (Hamburg, 1914). Compare *De infantibus*, attributed to Ælfric by Pope (Pope, *Homilies*, p. 56), which urges the earliest possible baptism of a child, lest it die a heathen.

44. Compare Godden III. 252-61; VIII. 123-27.

baptizes the child with this faith', lines 284-85). After the ceremony, paradoxically, the child believes, yet remains ignorant of the faith. Therefore baptism, although a complete sacrament for a baby, must be followed by instruction for the child to be confirmed in the faith confessed for it (287-90).

Like all sacramental signs, baptism possesses two levels of meaning, according to Augustine's definition (*Sermo* CCLXXII). The water of baptism (that which is seen) is transformed invisibly into a medium of spiritual washing (that which is understood); it carries the Spirit's presence and by this mystery acquires a salutary power. The word of consecration represents the moment when an ordinary element is transformed into one with spiritual efficacy:

> þæs halgan gastes miht genealæhð þam brosniendlicum wætere. ðurh sacerda bletsunge.
> and hit mæg siððan lichaman and sawle aðwean fram eallum synnum. ðurh gastlicere
> mihte. (Godden XV. lines 113-16)[45]

> the power of the Holy Spirit draws near to the corruptible water, through the blessing
> of priests, and afterwards it is able to wash body and soul clean of all sins, through
> spiritual power.

This cleansing is the spiritual birth by which the Christian is begotten to God (Pope I. 400-2).[46] Unlike physical birth, which is visible and intelligible to everyone, spiritual birth must be taken upon trust:

> Seo gastlice acennednys, þæt man Gode beo acenned
> on þam halgan fulluhte, þurh þone Halgan Gast,
> is us ungesewenlic, for ðan þe we geseon ne magon
> hwæt ðær bið gefremed on þam gefullodan menn. (Pope XII. lines 123-26)

---

45. I refer to these lines again below on page 189. Compare Godden III. 55-56 and 230-31; Pope XII. 103-5.

46. Compare Thorpe XXXV. p. 520. 30-32; Godden I. 111-17; Pope XII. 71-73, 83 and 135-38.

The spiritual birth, by which a person is born to God in holy baptism through the Holy Spirit, is invisible to us, for we cannot see what has been accomplished there in the baptized person.

The sacrament is endowed with spiritual efficacy which leaves no trace of its operation save on a spiritual plane, perceived only by faith. Although the newly-baptized child appears unchanged, faith perceives a transformation:

> seo halige modor, þe is Godes Gelaþung,
>
> wat þæt þæt cild bið synnfull bedyped
>
> innto þam fante, and bið up abroden
>
> fram synnum aðwogen, þurh þæt halige fulluht. (lines 130-33)

> the holy mother, that is God's church, knows that the child is dipped sinful into the font, and is lifted up washed from sins, through the holy baptism.

The community of the faithful is important here: the new birth is affirmed not merely by the child's godparents but by the whole church. The body of Christ recognizes a new member.

The sacrament of baptism is performed by the priest in the name of the trinity according to the institution of Christ. Ælfric writes that no second baptism should ever be performed, 'þæt seo halige Þrynnyss ne beo swa geunwurðod' ('that the holy trinity be not thus dishonoured', Pope XII. line 90).[47] This is not Augustine's reason. Augustine rejects rebaptism, believing that whatever the shortcomings of the ceremony or the minister, the full sacramental power of baptism is conveyed because it is the gift of God. Provided that the priest baptizes in the name of the trinity, no part of the gift is withheld.[48] Augustine merely adds the qualifier that only when the gift is put to use in the context of the church community does it achieve its potential; until then its grace lies dormant (*De baptismo contra Donatistas* I.xiii.21). Behind Ælfric's reason is the belief that once invoked, the blessing of the trinity may not be repeated without implying that the first was ineffective. He found this emphasis

---

47. Compare *De penitentia* p. 602. 1-3; Godden III. 214-18; Skeat XII. 141-43.

48. That the use of the trinitarian formula was intrinsic to the sacrament is suggested by several passages in *De baptismo contra Donatistas*: III.xv.20; VI.xvii.29; VI.xxxvi.70.

in Bede. Pope identifies the source of this passage as Bede's own statement on rebaptism (*Homeliarum Evangelii* II.18. lines 42-46).[49]

If the reason why baptism may not be repeated has become confused with the passage of time, Ælfric preserves the fundamental point, that the character of the priest has no bearing on the validity of the sacrament. At the same time, he apparently desires to allay fears that the quality of baptism available now may be different from that which was received from the apostles' hands:

> Sume lareowas sindon beteran ðonne sume. swa swa wæron ða apostoli. sume sind waccran swa swa we beoð; Nis hwæðere for ði þæt fulluht ðe we nu mid fulliað. mislic. þæt is. naðor ne betere. ne wyrse. þurh urum geearnungum. for ðan ðe þæt fulluht nis nanes mannes. ac is cristes. se ðe æfre is god þeah ðe we wace sindon. (Godden III. lines 219-24)

> Some teachers are better than others, as the apostles were; some are weaker, as we are. Yet the baptism with which we baptize is not for this reason different, that is, neither better nor worse, according to our merits, because that baptism is not of man, but is of Christ, who is always God though we are weak.

Thus the sins of the priest cannot stand in the way of the forgiveness of God:

> ne se yfela preost ne mæg þurh his agene synna
> Godes þenunga befylan þe of Gode sylfum cymþ,
> for ðan þe se Halga Gast aþwyhð þone hæþenan
> fram eallum his synnum on þam soðan fulluhte. (Pope XII. lines 91-94)

> and the evil priest, through his own sins, cannot befoul God's ministry which comes of God himself, for the Holy Spirit cleanses the heathen from all his sins in the true baptism.

---

49. Pope, *Homilies*, p. 483; notes to lines 78-90.

The task of the priest is to baptize in the name of the trinity: no other details need concern the church (lines 86-89). It is also an error to suppose that because baptism cleanses the sinful soul another baptism is required to cleanse later sins. Even if these sins are very serious indeed they can be cleansed through the sacrament of penance (Godden III. 224-27).

Ælfric's teaching on baptism accords with the conclusions reached by Augustine in his exploration of the sacrament's operation. These state that God alone is responsible for bestowing the grace of baptism, so rebaptism is never necessary, and that the sacrament is effective only within the unity of the church. Ælfric repeats that baptism is required only once, sure that this is true even when baptism is administered by a sinful priest. His additional condemnation of rebaptism on the grounds that it dishonours the trinity is an extension of the same precept. For if a priest's sin cannot damage the sacrament then any instance of rebaptism must imply a lack of faith in the Godhead invoked.

Augustine would have encountered many more adult candidates for baptism than Ælfric. The Holy Saturday ceremony at Hippo was the time for the reception of adult converts, who were welcomed into the church at the culmination of Lenten teaching and cleansing, appropriating for themselves the great celebration of resurrection. However, infant baptism was the long-established norm for the children of the faithful; it was precisely this practice which lent weight to Augustine's teaching on original sin, which has been described as 'a theological justification for an unchallengeable sacramental practice' (Pelikan, *Tradition*, I, p. 317). Ælfric gives his attention only to infant baptism, and so is particularly careful to explain how the sacrament operates in the unconscious spirit of a child. The mystery of baptism seems to have been less puzzling than that of the eucharist. The ritual washing seems to have been readily acceptable as a means of conveying spiritual cleansing. Ælfric offers no discussion comparable to his sermon on the eucharistic sacrifice, in which the precise means by which the sacrament is conveyed is examined. Augustine, prompted by the Donatists, wrote far more about baptism than about the eucharist, but by Ælfric's time this wide-ranging teaching had been reduced to a set of rules. They were properly applied, but perhaps they were not appreciated to the same extent as his doctrine of the body of Christ, so fruitful for the understanding of the community of the church.

III. THE EUCHARIST

In the sacrament of baptism, a natural element, water, conveys a spiritual effect. Externally applied to the body, the water provides a certain amount of real, perceptible, physical cleansing. But its true power and relevance lie in the cleansing of the soul which is effected by the water after it has been consecrated by the priest. Basically the pattern of external, perceptible action and internal, imperceptible effect is true of the eucharist too. But understanding of it is complicated by the words of institution of the supper (Luke 22. 19-20; I Corinthians 11. 24-25). The fact that Christ apparently indicated (and, once his words were translated into Latin, certainly indicated) that the bread and wine were literally equated with his body and blood after his consecration of these simple elements, means that an additional question comes into the discussion of this sacrament: in what way may the elements be said 'to be' the body of Christ? 'Hoc est corpus meum' ('This is my body') is a mysterious and potent statement, and it demands either a resignation to mystery or an extremely detailed and technical explanation.

The former response, accepting the mystery instead of attempting to analyse it, is not improper, for faith necessarily involves the mind in spiritual realities which transcend the physical world. The latter response, approaching the question from a technical point of view, demands a philosophical understanding of matter, and this was gained by the study of Aristotle by Scholastic theologians. Enabled to see matter as having both inward reality and outward manifestation, an invisible substance possessed of externally perceptible accidents, philosophy could make important steps forward in the discussion of the meaning of 'hoc est'. The science and the terminology to express it were both necessary. Neither was available to Augustine, or to the generations of teachers who came before these discoveries but who added their own contributions to the interpretation of the sacrament. These rest on two ways of describing the sacrament, which in the course of time acquired a mutually exclusive appearance although originally each was able to support and inform the other. These were the 'symbolic', largely perceived to be the province of Augustine, and the 'realistic', considered to be that of Ambrose. However, both of these teachers explored both ways of considering the eucharist.[50]

---

50. For a fuller account of these mutually compatible points of view, their ninth-century developments, and the way in which they have been understood by modern commen-

Ambrose's account of the sacrament is very brief and hardly elaborated, whilst Augustine's fuller discussion is found dispersed over various sermons and treatises, and is enhanced by his very important consideration of how sacraments in general may be understood. Because he sees the eucharist as part of a range of sacramental signs experienced by the church, he does not treat it as an isolated phenomenon, but explains it in a way that is consonant with his treatment of other signs. That 'hoc est' makes it proper to say that the bread is the body of Christ, the wine is his blood:

> Panis ille quem videtis in altari, sanctificatus per verbum Dei, corpus est Christi. Calix ille, imo quod habet calix, sanctificatum per verbum Dei, sanguis est Christi. (*Sermo* CCXXVII)

> That Bread which you see on the altar, consecrated by the word of God, is the Body of Christ. That chalice, or rather, what the chalice holds, consecrated by the word of God, is the Blood of Christ.[51]

In addition to this literal assertion of Christ's words, Augustine also explores the spiritual nature of the food received in the bread and the wine. As sacramental signs, they have a spiritual vitality which is perceived by faith, as it were through their physical presence. Simultaneously discerned in the sacrament are what is seen (the elements) and what is understood (their spiritual effect). It is faith which declares the bread and wine to be the body and blood of Christ (*Sermo* CCLXXII). The spiritual effect of the elements is communion with Christ. Indeed the sacrament brings about what it symbolizes, the union of Christ and his limbs, the church:

> Denique ipse dicit: 'Qui manducat carnem meam et bibit sanguinem meum, in me manet, et ego in eo.' Ostendit quid sit non sacramento tenus, sed re uera corpus Christi

---

tators, see Lynne Grundy, 'Ælfric's *Sermo de sacrificio in die pascæ: figura* and *veritas*', *Notes and Queries*, 235 (1990), 265-69.

51. Quoted in the translation by Sister Mary Sarah Muldowney.

manducare et eius sanguinem bibere; hoc est enim in Christo manere, ut in illo maneat et Christus. (*De civitate Dei* XXI.xxv. lines 78-82)[52]

Above all, Christ himself says, 'Anyone who eats my flesh and drinks my blood lives in me, and I live in him.' And thus he shows what it is to eat Christ's body and to drink his blood not just in the outward sacrament but in the reality; it is to live in Christ so that Christ lives in the believer.

For Augustine, therefore, the eucharist may in one respect be understood as a sacramental sign of the body of Christ; in another it is a very literal calling into the present of Christ, for in receiving the sacrament, the body is constituted.

Augustine's teaching concerning the nature of the sacramental sign in the eucharist was mediated to Ælfric through the ninth-century treatise *De corpore et sanguine domini* of Ratramnus. The treatise affirms that 'the inner unseen spiritual reality is the body and blood of Christ; . . . that which is apparent to the bodily senses is bread and wine'.[53] However, Ratramnus also seeks to do something which Augustine never considered necessary, since for the earlier teacher the different levels of reality within which the 'body of Christ' might be discerned have a self-evident coinherence. Ratramnus 'makes a clear distinction between that body of Christ which is in the Sacrament and the flesh which was born, crucified and buried' (p. 228). Here he is apparently responding to the contemporary treatise of the same name written by Paschasius Radbertus, Ratramnus' abbot at Corbie. Paschasius' preferred emphasis is upon the identification of the elements of the sacrament with the crucified, glorified body of Christ.

With these two treatises, a polarization is imposed on ways of looking at the eucharist which for Augustine were entirely compatible. Ælfric's sermon on the sacrament subtly restores that compatibility, and emphasizes that what is needed is an ability to detect the coinherence of several levels of reality. It is most important to allow the eyes of faith to recognize the truth to which the sacrament points. His source is primarily Ratramnus, but he

---

52. Augustine refers here to John 6. 56.

53. D. Stone, *A History of the Holy Eucharist*, 2 vols (London, 1909), I, 228.

takes two exempla from Paschasius, and uses a particularly pertinent insight from Augustine. The effect is a confirmation of the unity of the physical, metaphysical, spiritual and symbolic.

Ratramnus presents a useful discussion of the two levels of reality which may be discerned in the sacrament. Of these, one is the empirical reality of bread and wine. This, he says, may be termed 'veritas' (*De corpore* viii). This in its turn signifies, or points to, a second reality, which may be called 'figura' (vii). Things which possess these two levels might be said to speak one thing openly whilst suggesting another inwardly (vii). In Augustine's terms, these things might all be considered sacraments: they speak internally to the faithful. Augustine's own observations about the way faith penetrates to a deeper mystery are repeated by Ratramnus (ix). This mystery is revealed to the senses of the spirit after the consecration of the elements, now properly called 'the body and blood of Christ' (x).

Ælfric's sermon *De sacrificio in die pascae* discusses the sacrament in these terms. His account of the mystery ('gerynu') is offered 'þy læs ðe ænig twynung eow derian mage. be ðam liflicum gereorde' ('lest any doubt might assail you concerning the living feast', Godden XV. lines 6-7). The historical and typological antecedent of the passover meal shared at the last supper is recalled in a reading from Exodus 12. Ælfric points out that Christians no longer hold the old law 'bodily' ('lichamlice', line 36) but that they need to know what it signifies for them spiritually ('gastlice', line 37). So he explains that the slaughtered lamb by which the Jews commemorated their liberation is a symbol of Christ, recalled in the celebration of mass with the singing of 'Agnus Dei' (38-41). The liberation of the Israelites from death prefigured the liberation of Christians by Christ's passion. Their sharing of the sacrificial flesh, a participation in the sacrifice, prefigured the eucharistic feast. However, as the latter is a symbolic, not a real, holocaust, the participation of the faithful is correspondingly spiritual:

we ðicgað nu gastlice cristes lichaman. and his blod drincað. þonne we mid soðum geleafan þæt halige husel ðicgað. (lines 61-63)[54]

we now partake spiritually of Christ's body and drink his blood when we partake of the holy eucharist with true faith.

---

54. Compare Thorpe XIX. p. 266. 7-8; Godden XII. 212-14.

Ælfric later amplifies this point with reference to Jesus' instructions at the supper which, he says, indicate that the body of Christ is encountered on a spiritual plane in the sacrament:

> Ne het he etan þone lichaman ðe he mid befangen wæs. ne þæt blod drincan ðe he for us ageat. ac he mænde mid þam worde þæt halige husel þe gastlice is his lichama and his blod. (lines 210-13)

> He did not command that we should eat the body with which he was invested, nor drink that blood which he shed for us, but by those words he meant the holy eucharist which is spiritually his body and his blood.

What, then, is the nature of the mystery? How are bread and wine to be understood to be Christ's body and blood? Like Ratramnus, Ælfric emphasizes the ability of the elements to speak through their external appearance to an internal understanding:

> oðer ðing hi æteowɪað menniscum andgitum wiðutan. and oðer ðing hi clypiað wiðinnan geleaffullum modum; Wiðutan hi beoð gesewene hlaf and win. ægðer ge on hiwe. ge on swæcce. ac hi beoð soðlice æfter ðære halgunge cristes lichama. and his blod þurh gastlicere gerynu. (lines 103-7)

> one thing they show externally to human understanding, and another thing they cry within to believing minds. Externally they are evidently bread and wine both in appearance and in taste; but after the consecration, through spiritual mystery, they are truly Christ's body and his blood.

After the consecration of the eucharistic elements a spiritual reality is additionally present and may be discerned by the senses of faith.

In his account of the change discerned by the faithful Ælfric has recourse to Ratramnus' discrimination between literal truth, 'veritas', and spiritual truth, 'figura'. The sacrament works in a way analogous to that of baptism, which has a 'veritas' of ordinary washing, and a 'figura' of cleansing from sin. After baptism, the baptized child is cleansed of Adam's sin, but exhibits no outward transformation. Yet faith insists that a very radical and real change has taken place (107-11). A similar observation may be made of the water of baptism, which has all the empirical characteristics of ordinary water, but in conjunction with certain words has a spiritual power:

> þæs halgan gastes miht genealæhð þam brosniendlicum wætere. ðurh sacerda bletsunge. and hit mæg siððan lichaman and sawle aðwean fram eallum synnum. ðurh gastlicere mihte. (lines 113-16).[55]

> the power of the Holy Spirit draws near to the corruptible water, through the blessing of priests, and afterwards it is able to wash body and soul clean of all sins, through spiritual power.

Literal eyes see the application of ordinary water to the outside of the body. The eyes of faith see a thorough spiritual cleansing of the whole being by means of a spiritual washing. Similarly, Ælfric suggests, the eucharistic elements are created, corruptible things, but in the spiritual mystery they are endowed with salutary power:

> Gif we ða gastlican mihte ðæron tocnawað. þonne undergyte we þæt ðær is lif on. and forgifð undeadlicnysse ðam þe hit mid geleafan þicgað. (lines 121-24)[56]

> If we recognize the spiritual power within it, then we understand that there is life within it, and it bestows immortality upon those who partake of it with faith.

The body of Christ in the eucharist is 'made' differently from the one born of Mary, which was real in the literal sense of the word 'body' : it was made of bone and blood. By contrast, the 'husel' is limbless and soulless, not at all what is brought to mind by the familiar concept 'body':

---

55. Compare Ratramnus, *De corpore* xvii-xviii.

56. Compare Ratramnus, *De corpore* xix.

and nis for ði nan ðing þæron to understandenne lichamlice. ac is eall gastlice to understandenne. (lines 135-36)[57]

and so there is nothing in it to be understood in a bodily way, but everything is to be understood in a spiritual way.

Ælfric suggests that the mystery may be regarded as a promise of the true body of Christ: this is the risen, ascended, reigning Lord knowable only in the reality of heaven. The eucharist promises that future heavenly reality:

Þeos gerynu is wedd. and hiw. cristes lichama is soðfæstnyss; Ðis wed we healdað gerynelice. oð þæt we becumon to þære soðfæstnysse. and ðonne bið þis wedd geendod. (lines 153-55)[58]

This mystery is pledge and symbol; Christ's body is truth. This pledge we possess mysteriously until we come to the truth, and then this pledge will be completed.

The mystery is therefore the means by which the promise of resurrection with Christ, when he will be known in his human and divine natures, may be appropriated by the faithful. They are themselves, in effect, a similar 'wedd' or 'hiw', as Ælfric later demonstrates, because they too can be called the 'body of Christ'. The promise, in each case, is of perfect communion with God, that time of blessedness when the saints will see him face to face.

Because that realization of the promise is held by the mind of faith, anticipating the future reality of which it is the referent, the mystery must itself be understood by faith:

Soðlice hit is swa swa we ær cwædon cristes lichama and his blod. na lichamlice. ac gastlice; Ne sceole ge smeagan hu hit gedon sy, ac healdan on eowerum geleafan þæt hit swa gedon sy. (lines 156-58)[59]

---

57. Compare Ratramnus, *De corpore* lxxii.

58. Compare Assmann V. 155-59, and in Ratramnus, *De corpore* lxxxviii.

59. Compare Ratramnus, *De corpore* lxxxviii.

Truly it is, as we said before, Christ's body and his blood, not bodily, but spiritually. And you are not to wonder how it is done, but to hold it in your belief that it is so done.

Ælfric now offers two miracles to illustrate the transformation which faith recognizes but which the eyes cannot see. They are from Paschasius' *De corpore et sanguine domini* xiv.[60] Ælfric found them in the *Vitae Patrum*. The Paschasian text used these miracle stories to emphasize that the body of Christ (that born of Mary) was literally present in the eucharist. For Ælfric, the miracles seem rather to confirm the two levels of reality in operation. One, that of the spiritual, in which sacrifice is re-presented, is extraordinarily rendered visible. Enhanced vision sees a sacrificial offering in each case.

The first of these miracles is described in the account of a vision imparted to two monks while assisting at mass. Having prayed for some manifestation to confirm their faith, they saw a child lying on the altar as the priest celebrated. An angel offered the child in ritual sacrifice as the bread was broken. When offered to the monks the flesh and blood had changed into bread and wine. They partook of them, 'gode ðancigende þære swutelunge' ('thanking God for the manifestation', line 167). In this miracle the monks' vision confirmed the sacrificial reality of the bread and wine which were physically present before their eyes. Their spiritual sight revealed to them something of the inner meaning of the eucharistic elements. The second miracle resulted from Gregory the Great's request for a sign to confirm the faith of a woman who had doubts concerning the truth of the mystery. To Gregory and the woman the bread appeared as a finger-tip in the dish, whereupon 'þæs wifes twynung wearð ða gerihtlæced' ('the woman's doubt was then corrected', line 173).[61] The miracles allow disbelieving minds access to the faith which Ælfric declares to be essential for an understanding of the mystery. Through faith, the sacrifice which is thereby brought into the present, may be 'seen' and received.

The rather startling physicality of these miracle stories has tended to obscure their meaning in the context of Ælfric's sermon. His citation of these miracles has been taken as

---

60. They may be the work of a later redactor expanding Paschasius' text: Theodore Leinbaugh, 'The sources for Ælfric's Easter Sermon: the history of the controversy and a new source', *Notes and Queries*, 231 (1986), p. 297.

61. Compare Skeat III. 153-62.

proof that he taught the doctrine of transubstantiation centuries before it was affirmed by the Council of Trent.[62] More recently, critics have found in Ælfric's sermon a reconciliation between two antipathetic interpretations, symbolist and carnal.[63] Yet the exploration of the sacrament's different levels of reality offered by the miracles is entirely consistent with Ælfric's sermon as a whole, in which Augustine's 'aliud videtur, aliud intelligitur' is paramount. In the sacrament earthly and heavenly realities, the promise and the promised, coinhere.

That the sacramental sign guides the mind of faith back to participation in the life of Christ is further explored in Ælfric's next point, which is that Christ has always provided himself as spiritual food for his people, according to Paul in I Corinthians 10. The Israelites in the wilderness received the figure of baptism by their passage through cloud and sea; then prefiguring the eucharist they ate manna and drank water struck from the rock. Theirs was also spiritual food and drink, also sacramental, for it fed them miraculously and was a token of the future sacrificial offering of Christ. Ælfric says that the desert manna and water have a spiritual link with the eucharistic sacrifice:

> se heofonlica mete þe hi afedde feowertig geara. and þæt wæter þe of ðam stane fleow hæfde getacnunge cristes lichaman. and his blodes. þe nu beoð geoffrode dæghwomlice

---

62. 'Il n'est pas douteux qu'Ælfric ait cru à la présence réelle; les miracles qu'il rapporte en font foi', Marguerite-Marie Dubois, *Ælfric: sermonnaire, docteur et grammairien: contribution à l'étude de la vie et de l'action bénédictines en Angleterre au Xe siècle* (1942; reprinted Paris, 1943), p. 158.

63. See, for example, Theodore Leinbaugh, 'Ælfric's *Sermo de Sacrificio in Die Pascæ*: Anglican polemic in the sixteenth and seventeenth centuries', in *Anglo-Saxon Scholarship: the first three centuries*, edited by Carl T. Berkhout and Milton McC. Gatch (Boston, 1982), p. 51; C.L. Wrenn, 'Some aspects of Anglo-Saxon Theology', in *Studies in Language, Literature and Culture of the Middle Ages and Later*, edited by Elmer B. Attwood and Archibald A. Hill (Austin, 1969), p. 185; Ratramnus, *De corpore et sanguine domini: texte original et notice bibliographique*, edited by J.N. Bakhuizen van den Brink, second edition, Verhandelingen der Koninklijke Nederlandse Akademie van Wetenschappen, afd. Letterkunde, Niewe Reeks, 87, (Amsterdam, 1974), p. 128.

on godes cyrcan; Hit wæron ða ylcan ðe we nu offriað. na lichamlice. ac gastlice. (lines 186-90)

the heavenly food which fed them for forty years and the water which flowed from the stone betokened Christ's body and his blood, which are now offered daily in God's church. They were the same as those which we now offer, not bodily, but spiritually.

The sacrament is timeless, for it refers back beyond the time of Christ's suffering: he made a sacramental offering of the bread and wine at the last supper, before his death, just as he did for the Israelites in the wilderness, before his birth (191-98). The sacrament's life-giving power holds good even for the Israelites: they consumed the spiritual food for the health of their souls, which received eternal life even though their bodies died (199-208). Ælfric makes the distinction between bodily death, which all suffer, and spiritual death, or eternal death, which is the death of the soul. The sacrament offers protection against this death, because it is the memorial, re-enactment, representation of the one perfect sacrifice of Christ, and the protection so granted operates both back into history and forward into the future (208-20). The body of Christ is life, whenever it is received.

Ælfric completes his exploration of this idea of the coinherence of earthly and heavenly realities with further illustration of how the sacrament unites the body of Christ and his limbs. Recognizing that the body of Christ is the church, as well as the eucharistic offering, Ælfric opens the mystery to embrace this shifting referent: not only is the sacrifice simultaneously given and received, its giver and receiver are also the body of Christ:

Ge soðlice sindon cristes lichama and leomu; Nu is eower gerynu geled on godes mysan. and ge underfoð eower gerynu. to ðan þe ge sylfe sind; Beoð þæt þæt ge geseoð on ðam weofode. and underfoð þæt þæt ge sylfe sind. (lines 229-33)

Truly you are Christ's body and limbs. Now your mystery is laid on God's table, and you receive your mystery, which you yourselves are. Be what you see on the altar and receive what you yourselves are.

This is Augustine's insight.[64] First, the mystery is simultaneously offered and received:

> Si ergo vos estis corpus Christi et membra, mysterium vestrum in mensa Dominica positum est: mysterium vestrum accepitis. (*Sermo* CCLXXII)

> If you are the body of Christ and his limbs, your mystery is placed on the Lord's table: receive your mystery.

Secondly, receiving the sacrament in faith means that the believer becomes what is received: 'Si bene accepistis, vos estis quod accepistis' ('If you have received worthily, you are what you have received', *Sermo* CCXXVII). The sacrament both points to and effects the union of Christ with his church. The heavenly reality of the one body is enacted and brought into the present, such that in the eucharist, which is the promise of eternal life, a momentary perception of that life is granted.

Ælfric's teaching on the eucharist offers a truly Augustinian perception of the mystery which, as he puts it, has life in it. The sacrament, with its earthly elements and heavenly promise, speaks to the mind of faith as the Christian participates in the body of Christ. It offers no small inspiration when the body of Christ identifies itself with the sacrifice, and finds in the eucharist the place where unity is perfectly expressed.

IV. PENANCE

The institution of penance recognizes that Christians continue to sin even after baptism, and that they need the renewed forgiveness of God if they are to continue to grow in the faith. Augustine distinguishes three kinds of penance: the first is a preparation required of all catechumens before baptism (*Sermo* CCCLI.ii.2); the second, performed daily, involving prayer and almsgiving, relates to small sins (iii.5-6); the third is for mortal sins (iv.7). This last penance was imposed by the church annually during Lent, during which time penitents were deprived of the normal rights of church members, including the eucharist. Exclusion from the sacrament would mean a strong sense of exclusion from the church itself, and of

---

64. Probably conveyed by Ratramnus, *De corpore* lxxiii-lxxv.

being cut off from God. That the whole body was felt to be involved in the restoration of penitents seems to have been behind the public nature of the rite: it was not that penitents were to be humiliated, but rather that the community's support might be sought, in intercession and practical assistance, to help them reform.

Augustine recognizes the gravity of the sinners' condition, but assures them that powerful healing is available: 'gravis res, grave vulnus, lethale, mortiferum: sed omnipotens medicus' ('The matter is serious, the wound is serious, lethal, deadly: but the doctor is omnipotent', *Sermo* CCCLII.iii.8). The soul, dead in sin like the body of Lazarus entombed for four days, is brought forth by penance, and restored to life by the forgiveness mediated by the church:

> Elevatus est Lazarus, processit de tumulo: et ligatus erat, sicut sunt homines in confessione peccati agentes poenitentiam. (iii.8)

> Lazarus was raised; he came forth from the tomb: and he was bound, just as men are when they repent of their sins in confession.

At the end of the period of penance the Christian is restored to the community, reconciled with God. The church, with the indwelling love and guidance of the Holy Spirit, acts as the medium for the forgiveness of sins. Because it is essential to be part of the church in order to receive grace and salvation, it is essential to be reconciled to the community after the period of separation, in order to be welcomed back into the sphere of grace.

It should be noted that Augustine, like other teachers before and after him, did not call penance a sacrament.[65] Discussions of early mediæval penance often assume that it was considered a sacrament.[66] The assumption at least recognizes the mysterious nature of

---

65. The number of the sacraments was not fixed: a list containing seven (including penance) was given for probably the first time in the anonymous *Sententiae* (Pelikan, *Tradition*, III, p. 209).

66. For example, A.J. Frantzen, *The Literature of Penance in Anglo-Saxon England* (New Brunswick, 1983); B. Poschmann, *Penance and the Anointing of the Sick*, translated by F. Courtney (Freiburg, 1964); O.D. Watkins, *A History of Penance: being a study of the authorities (a) for the whole Church to A.D. 450, (b) for the Western Church from A.D. 450 to A.D. 1215*, 2 vols (London, 1920), II.

penance, and Augustine's wide generalization relating physical signs to spiritual realities permits and encourages it (*De doctrina Christiana* II.i.1).[67]

Augustine's system was general in the Western church. But a different penitential practice was flourishing in the isolated Celtic church. With no tradition of ecclesiastical penance, here penance was a private affair between priest and penitent. Regular confession was the norm. Manuals ('Penitentials'), known from the sixth century, listed the appropriate penance for each sin in a detailed and extensive tariff. The Penitential was divided into sections dealing with discrete groups of sins according to the classification worked out by Gregory the Great. Penances included fasting, the recitation of Psalms, and the imposition of physical discomfort. Although the system appears to have a more material than spiritual emphasis, the proper purpose of penance was not misunderstood, for the necessity of 'sincere contrition and conversion' was stressed (Poschmann, *Penance*, p. 128). Probably most penitents would have undergone sensible and reforming penances which genuinely encouraged reflection and amendment of life. Confession was an opportunity for counselling and teaching, and correction was expected to follow (Frantzen, *Penance*, p. 152). The tariff system required a knowledgeable and compassionate assessment of the penitent by the confessor to ensure that the penance imposed was appropriate. As a guide to penitential discipline the system could be used wisely and constructively in obtaining a steady improvement in the Christian life. It was this attitude to penance, and the practical system for putting it into effect, that was adopted by the Anglo-Saxon church.

The influence of Gregory the Great upon the early Anglo-Saxon church may have supported the adoption of this system. In his advice to Augustine of Canterbury, as Bede records it, on how to punish a thief who steals from the church, Gregory points out that thieves steal for a variety of reasons and should not be judged as if they were all alike. Punishment should be administered with love, for the sole purpose of delivering the culprit from the fires of hell (*Historia ecclesiastica gentis anglorum* I. xxvii, Augustine's third question). According to Gregory every sin deserves punishment, and invariably receives it, whether through penance or the direct chastisement of God.[68] Fear of punishment, the compunction felt by the sinner sorrowing for his sins, and the Christian's loving desire to be

---

67. Cited above on page 177.

68. F.H. Dudden, *Gregory the Great: his place in history and thought*, 2 vols (London, 1905), II, 419.

obedient to God all combine to produce penitential discipline, at the heart of which is a fine balance between sin and punishment (*Moralia in Iob* IX.xxxiv.54-xlv.69 and XVI.lxviii.82). These themes are found in Ælfric, but without Gregory's intense anxiety about achieving that balance: Ælfric is more ready to embrace forgiveness.

The Celtic system spread to the continent and was reabsorbed by the later Anglo-Saxon church together with the use of public penance for some purposes. In late tenth-century England both were known, but it is clear that the latter was less well-established. Only Wulfstan, as a bishop, has any real interest in the public rite. It is ignored in the Blickling and Vercelli collections, perhaps because of their early date. Ælfric rarely refers to a public penance. Even passages which might presuppose the use of the public rite may merely be alluding to the range of penances which might be undertaken. In a passage which discusses the raising of the three dead as exemplifying the three kinds of 'soul death' which require varying degrees of treatment, Ælfric makes the following observation:

Swa bið eac se digla deað ðære sawle eaþelicor to aræenne, þe on geðafunge digelice syngað, þonne synd ða openan leahtras to gehælenne. Þone cniht he arærde on ealles folces gesihðe, and mid þysum wordum getrymede, 'Þu cniht, ic secge ðe, Aris.' Þa diglan gyltas man sceal digelice betan, and ða openan openlice, þæt ða beon getimbrode þurh his behreowsunge, ðe ær wæron þurh his mandæda geæswicode. (Thorpe XXXIII. p. 498. lines 5-12).[69]

So also it is easier to raise up the secret death of the soul, which sins secretly by assent, than to remedy manifest crimes. He raised up the young man in the sight of all the people, and strengthened him with these words: 'Young man, I say to you, arise.' Secret sins are to be amended secretly, and manifest ones publicly, so that any who had been misled by his wicked actions will be strengthened by his penitence.

A public ceremony may be envisaged here (whether associated with the church or the ecclesiastical courts). But generally, Ælfric's emphasis is rather on private penance, which has a particularly appropriate educational value in the meeting of priest and penitent. Confession

---

69. Compare Thorpe VIII. p. 124. 24-31; A.O. Belfour, editor, *Twelfth Century Homilies in MS Bodley 343*, EETS, 137 (London, 1909), IV. p. 38. 25-27.

The Church and Sacraments

provides the opportunity for spiritual correction and guidance from the wise (Thorpe XIX. p. 268. 2-3). Ælfric advises that a sympathetic spirit is necessary, for a harsh, judgemental attitude is detrimental to the penitent's development:

> Ðu þe styran scealt, þæt he seolf beo irihtlæht, and oðre beon istyrede, ðe þa steor ihyræð . . . Ðe ðe monhatæ bið, ne mæg he wæl styræn; forþan ðe þa halga weræs ðe weron iu lareowæs beoð nu iherode ðurh heoræ liðnysse. (Belfour IV. p. 38. lines 29-31)

> You are to provide counsel so that the person himself may be set right and others who hear the counsel may be guided . . . Anyone who is a hater of people cannot correct well, for the holy men who were teachers in former days are now praised for their gentleness.

Ælfric recognizes that love is necessary for the proper guidance of penitents. The priest is not only the instrument of God's justice, but also, and much more so, the instrument of God's love.

Ælfric's interest in penance is deep and far-reaching. He concentrates on the continuity of the penitential life, its cyclical pattern corresponding to the inability of fallen humanity to avoid sin. Penance is a way of life, a constant striving towards God. God has no need of good deeds, but sees in them the signs of inward conversion: 'He secð godne willan on urum dædum. na his neode' ('He seeks a good will in our deeds, not anything necessary to him', Godden XXVIII. line 58). This recognition of the importance of good will, rather than the actions themselves, stresses the spiritual importance of these actions, and also draws attention to the assurance that in matters of will, the Christian can rely on God to provide grace sufficient for his needs. So the actions of penance are, in fact, signs of the appropriation of grace.

Penance effects a cleansing of the soul which is essential for progress in the Christian life. Although he nowhere explicitly calls it a sacrament, Ælfric associates penance with baptism and the eucharist:

> Þreo healice ðing gesette god mannum to clænsunge. An is fulluht. oðer is husel-halgung. þridde is dædbot mid geswicennysse yfelra dæda. and mid bigencge godra

weorca; Þæt fulluht us aþwehð fram eallum synnum. se huselgang us gehalgað. Seo soðe dædbot gehælð ure misdæda. (Godden III. lines 228-32)

God has established three supreme things as purification for men. The first is baptism, the second is the eucharist, the third is penance with the cessation of evil deeds and a turning to good works. Baptism washes us clean of all sins, the eucharist sanctifies us, true penance heals our misdeeds.

The importance of penance derives from its inseparable association with baptism, which is sufficient for all antecedent sins but cannot cleanse future sins. The eucharist provides spiritual food, and penance provides renewed cleansing after sin. Even really serious sins can be dealt with by penance. It is never necessary to resort to a second baptism:

Þeah ðe hwa wiðsace crist æfter his fulluhte. oððe heafodleahtras gewyrce. ne ðearf he beon eft gefullod. ac he sceal his synna bewepan. and mid soðre behreowsunge gebetan æfter wisra lareowa tæcunge. (lines 224-27)

Even if a person deny Christ after his baptism, or commit deadly sins, he does not need to be baptized again, but he must weep for his sins and atone, with true repentance, according to the teachings of wise instructors.

The term 'behreowsung' ('penitence') describes the necessary sorrow for sins which must precede cleansing or healing. 'Dædbot' ('penance') has at its root an action performed in order to 'cure' or make amends for sin. Its function is atonement, operating by means of external activity on a spiritual plane. A comparison may be made with the eucharist, where the unconsecrated bread and wine have power to nourish only the physical body, but the body of Christ has power to give life to the soul. So also the actions of penance have outward virtue in subduing the flesh, but spiritual virtue in restoring health to the ailing soul. Outward action and inward intention co-operate:

Dædbot mid geswicennysse yfeles. and ælmys-dæda. and halige gebedu. and geleafa. and hiht on gode. and seo soðe lufu godes and manna. gehælað and gelacniað ure synna. gif we þa læce-domas geornlice begað. (Skeat XII. lines 149-52)[70]

Penance, together with abstaining from evil, and almsgiving, and holy prayers, and faith, and hope in God, and the true love of God and men, will heal and cure our sins, if we use these remedies diligently.

Above all, the penitential life is a continuing process of conversion. The new life is characterized by love, and the actions which put this love into practice are particularly effective in providing the cleansing and renewal which are recurrently necessary. Christians who are sensible of the Lord's presence in the poor serve him when they minister to the poor: almsgiving and works of mercy, which demonstrate devotion to Christ and obedience to his commands, are part of the life of active penitence.

True repentance is more important than any outward demonstration of piety, such as fasting. Ælfric does not deny the value of such things, but requires that they should be seen in the proper perspective. The Lenten fast, for example, is part of a penitential pattern of confession, fasting, vigils, prayers and almsgiving which concentrate the Christian's mind on his need of forgiveness and prepare him to celebrate Easter, 'bealdlice mid gastlicere blisse' ('boldly, with spiritual joy', Godden VII. line 6). God requires a spiritual fast:

Nis nan fæsten swa god ne gode swa ge-cweme.

swa swa þæt fæsten is þæt man fulnysse onscunige.

and leahtras forbuge. and forlæte sace.

and mid godum biggencgum. gode ge-cweme. (Skeat XIII. lines 111-14)[71]

---

70. Compare Thorpe X. p. 162. 27-32; XVIII. p. 254. 113-16; XIX. p. 270. 9-12; XX. p. 292. 22-25; XXIV. p. 340. 28-35 and p. 342. 13-15; XL. p. 618. 20-25; Godden XXVI. 101-7; XXVIII. 76-82; XXXI. 99-102; *De penitentia* p. 602. 10-13; Pope III. 148-49; IV. 67-71; VI. 142; XI. 195-99; XIa. 10; XV. 47-54, 120-24 and 160-63; XVI. 94-98 and 109-11; XVIII. 123-24; Skeat XII. 143-45.

71. Compare Thorpe XI. p. 180. 8-12; XXV. p. 360. 11-24; Godden VII. 35-37; Pope II. 167-75; XVII. 174-79.

There is no fast so good nor so pleasing to God as that fast, that a person should shun foulness and refrain from sins, and abandon strife, and please God with good worship.

Genuinely sorrowing for sin and afflicted by its pain, the penitent turns to God for forgiveness like the sinner in the temple. The righteous man praises his own righteousness, but the sinner prays from a true understanding of his own deep unworthiness, conscious of his great need of salvation:

> god ælmihtig. gemiltsa me synfullum; Her is gebed on ðisum wordum. and her is synna andetnys. (Godden XXVIII. lines 40-42)

> 'Almighty God, have mercy on me, a sinner.' Here is prayer in these words, and here is confession of sins.

In the honest appraisal of sin the penitent offers the confession pleasing to God, not the empty vanity of a worldly self-defence. Such a Christian is open to the correction and forgiveness of God. Confession to the priest enables the Christian to receive this correction. Sin is a sickness which needs the attention of a spiritual doctor. This is Ælfric's interpretation of the story of the healed leper whom Christ sent to the temple:

> Swa sceal eac se ðe mid heafod-leahtrum wiðinnan hreoflig bið cuman to Godes sacerde, and geopenian his digelnysse ðam gastlican læce, and be his ræde and fultume his sawla wunda dædbetende gelacnian. (Thorpe VIII. p. 124. lines 11-14)[72]

> In the same way, anyone who is leprous within with deadly sins must go to God's priest and open his secrets to the spiritual physician, and penitently heal his soul's wounds according to his advice and assistance.

---

72. Compare Thorpe VIII. p. 124. 14-19; X. p. 164. 25-28; XIX. p. 272. 4-5; *De penitentia* p. 602. 19-p. 604. 8; Godden IX. 136-41; XIX. 54-59; Pope VI. 209-16 and 258-61; XV. 157-59; Skeat XII. 157-59 and 172-77.

Gregory's anxiety about balancing sin with sufficient penance is not shared by Ælfric. He is confident of the mercy of God, which, working through penance, can achieve the necessary transformation. No sin is so serious that repentance cannot restore baptismal purity. God promises that repentance causes sin to be forgotten (*De penitentia* p. 602. 18-19). This covers all sin, with the single exception of the sin against the Holy Spirit, which can never be forgiven. Because the Holy Spirit is the spirit of forgiveness he can forgive all who repent, but the unrepentant, who deny and reject the gift of this grace, 'sin against' the Holy Spirit:

> Behreowsiendan mannum gemiltsað se Halga Gast,
> ac ðam he ne miltsað næfre þe his gyfe forseoð. (Pope VI. lines 276-77)[73]

> The Holy Spirit has mercy on the penitent, but he never has mercy on those who despise his grace.

The penitent is guaranteed the Holy Spirit's mercy, and need never be anxious about committing the unforgivable sin: simply to be penitent cancels the possibility.

The outward signs of penance indicate an inward contrition, and the forgiveness conveyed by the priest is the sign that God has liberated the Christian from the binding power of sin, to stimulate a return to life. The priest 'unbinds' those who are guided and influenced by the grace of God (Thorpe XVI. p. 234. 2-4).[74] The effect is as miraculous as the raising of Lazarus. The stimulation of grace is nothing less than the gift of life to a corpse:

> Ælc synful man þe his synna bediglað, he lið dead on byrgene; ac gif he his synna geandett þurh onbryrdnysse, þonne gæð he of þære byrgene, swa swa Lazarus dyde, þaða Crist hine arisan het: þonne sceal se lareow hine unbindan fram ðam ecum wite, swa swa ða apostoli lichamlice Lazarum alysdon. (lines 11-16)[75]

---

73. I refer to these lines again below on page 239. Compare Thorpe XXXIII. p. 500. 15-20; Pope VI. 217-20 and 224-27.

74. Compare Thorpe XXVI. p. 370. 12-15.

75. Compare Pope VI. 141, 192-94 and 209-10; in Augustine, *Sermo* CCLII.iii.8, cited above on page 195.

Every sinful man who conceals his sin lies dead in the tomb. But if he confesses his sins through compunction, then he comes forth from the tomb just as Lazarus did when Christ commanded him to arise; then the preacher must unbind him from the eternal punishment, just as the apostles physically released Lazarus.

The disciples put into effect the liberating command of Christ, and released Lazarus. The priest who has heard the penitent's confession is similarly charged by Christ to release him. The church possesses the power of the keys, given to Peter,

> se anweald þe him Crist forgeaf, þæt nan man ne cymð into Godes rice, buton se halga Petrus him geopenige þæt infær. (Thorpe XXVI. p. 368. line 35-p. 370. line 2)

the power which Christ gave him, that no man comes into God's kingdom, unless the holy Peter should open to him the entrance.

Just as Lazarus, raised to life, remained imprisoned in his tomb by the shrouds and stones, and needed the apostles' assistance before his life could begin again, so Christ uses his ministers of the church in this liberating capacity. So it is necessary for the church to release those whom God has forgiven. This thought is found in Ælfric's source for this interpretation, Augustine's commentary on John:

> Sed ut confitearis, Deus facit magna uoce clamando, id est, magna gratia uocando. Ideo cum processisset mortuus adhuc ligatus, confitens et adhuc reus; ut soluerentur peccata eius, ministris hoc dixit Dominus: 'Soluite illum, et sinite abire'. (*In Ioannis Evangelium tractatus* XLIX.24. lines 19-23)

But the confession thou makest is effected by God, when He crieth with a loud voice, or in other words, calleth thee in abounding grace. Accordingly, when the dead man had come forth, still bound; confessing, yet guilty still; that his sins also might be taken away, the Lord said to His servants: 'Loose him, and let him go.'

For Augustine the guilt of sin is not effaced until the church has mediated God's forgiveness. He is speaking of public reconciliation, while Ælfric seems to mean the regular pattern of confession and forgiveness addressed by penitent and confessor, but for each the role of the church is paramount.

Ælfric sees several stages in the penitent's journey to reconciliation. Compunction necessarily precedes confession, for the sinner needs to be impelled to confess. Confession brings the church's power as well as guidance to bear upon the penitent. Penance, the healing medicine, is undergone for the cleansing and restoration of the soul. The participation of the community is once again asserted as the penitent is reconciled to the church: this is the spiritual interpretation of the raising of the young man of Naim, whom Jesus restored to his mother.[76] In his exegesis Ælfric looks at each detail in turn:

> Se ge-edcucoda sitt, þonne se synfulla mid godcundre onbryrdnysse cucað. He sprecð, þonne he mid Godes herungum his muð gebysgað, and mid soðre andetnysse Godes mildheortnysse secþ. He bið his meder betæht, þonne he bið þurh sacerda ealdordom gemænscipe ðære halgan gelaðunge geferlæht. (Thorpe XXXIII. p. 494. lines 14-19)

> The one restored to life 'sits up' when the sinful person is quickened by divine compunction. He 'speaks' when he busies his mouth with the praises of God and seeks God's mercy with true confession. He is 'restored to his mother' when he is associated with the fellowship of the holy church through the authority of the priest.

The penitent is restored to the state of grace and purity given by baptism, and also to full participating membership of the community.

While the penitent is separated from the community he must necessarily be regarded as outside the church. Furthermore, anyone who is unwilling to undergo the penance set by the priest excludes himself from the community of the blessed. The parable of the banquet (Luke 14. 16-24) provides the picture of the man who excuses himself and declines to come: his words seem humble and yet his action is full of pride. Similarly those who refuse to do as the priest bids forgo their place at the banquet (Godden XXIII. 68-70). But Ælfric has no desire to frighten people about penance: rather he seeks to show that it must be understood positively, as a constructive development in response to the guidance of the church. For him, penance is much more than simply an occasional response to sin: it is a way of life. In

---

76. See pages 221-22 for further reference to the raising of the 'three dead'.

advocating this way of life he is not suggesting that people should spend their days fasting, or reciting psalms, or depriving themselves of physical comfort: all these have their value if used in the correct way, but unless they are carefully controlled in the context of the devotional life they are at best sterile and at worst counterproductive in their effect. Rather, Ælfric has in mind the life of almsgiving: the daily exercise of mercy which is both a Christ-like activity and an offering to Christ himself in the person of the poor.

Almsgiving, in Ælfric's teaching, is the embodiment of the positive penitential life. If Christians show generosity in giving to the poor, that same merciful benevolence will be shown to them by God himself:

Cyð mildheortnysse earmum mannum mid þinum begeate. ne forlæt se ælmihtiga god ðe. se ðe ðe to dælere gesette. (Godden VII. lines 101-3)

Show mercy to poor men with your possessions; the almighty God, who has set you as almsgiver, will not abandon you.

The rich do well to remember that before God all are alike in importance. In truth, 'We are all God's poor' ('Ealle we sind Godes þearfan', Thorpe XVIII. p. 254. lines 33-34). When the poor ask for alms,

Hwæt sind þa ðe us biddað? Earme men, and tiddre, and deadlice. Æt hwam biddað hi? At earmum mannum, and tiddrum, and deadlicum. Butan þam æhtum, gelice sind þa þe ðær biddað, and ðaðe hi ætbiddað. (p. 256. lines 1-5)[77]

Who are they that ask of us? Poor, weak, mortal men. Of whom do they ask? Of poor, weak, mortal men. Except for the possessions, those who ask and those whom they ask are equal.

Riches hinder the Christian's progress. Ælfric observes that even on a practical level the rich are overburdened. Literally weighed down with their cumbersome treasures, they are to be

---

77. Compare Thorpe XVIII. p. 256. 13-16; XIX. p. 260. 22-27. Augustine makes exactly these points in *Sermo* LXI.v.8.

pitied. By sharing out the load more fairly, by inviting the help of the poor, who carry nothing, they may free themselves of such unnecessary toil. Additionally, this will reduce the load of sin:

> Forði sceal se rica dælan his byrðene wið þone ðearfan, þonne wanað he ða byrðene his synna, and ðam ðearfan gehelpð. (p.254. lines 31-33)[78]

> Therefore the rich man must share his burden with the poor man; then he will lessen the burden of his sins and help the poor man.

Ælfric suggests that there is a point when riches become sins. When the rich cling to what is rightfully another's, they sin; their attachment to riches means that sin is a way of life for them. They are mistaken if they think their almsgiving benefits only the poor. The poor are the more closely associated with Christ because of their material dispossession, and so they are made the channels of spiritual blessing: in serving the poor, the rich serve Christ (p. 256. line 33-p. 258. line 5).[79] To illustrate this service, Ælfric recounts a story from Gregory in which a leper, carried in pity on the back of a monk to the monastery, is revealed to be Christ. The glory of human nature in Christ, set aside for the piteously degraded form of the leper, should inspire all Christians to pity: Ælfric finds in his example of compassion and love the pattern of Christian response to the poor (Thorpe XXIII. p. 338. 1-4).

Remembering that Christ is yet on earth among the poor, Christians are left in no doubt of the call to service implied by allegiance to Christ. At the moment of judgement they will discover that this service sums up all that may be imputed to them as virtue, and its omission will be imputed to them as sin. In an exhortatory sermon Augustine says:

> audiant homines, digneque considerent quantum sit meritum, Christum pavisse esurientem; et quale sit crimen, Christum contempsisse esurientem. (*Sermo* LX.xi.11)

---

78. Compare Augustine, *Sermo* LXI.vii.12.

79. Compare Thorpe XXIII. p. 330. 17-21 and p. 332. 29-p. 336. 4; XXIV. p. 514. 4-8; XXXVI. p. 550. 12-18; Godden VII. 114-28 and 156-59; XXI. 127-31.

Let men hear and consider as they ought, how great a merit it is to have fed Christ when he hungereth, and how great a crime it is to have despised Christ when he hungereth.[80]

For Ælfric, too, those who were generous in almsgiving are to be welcomed into the kingdom. Those who had compassion on the hungry, the thirsty, the stranger, the naked, the sick and the prisoner will be surprised to hear that in serving these people they have served Christ. But this is indeed the case:

Þæt is soðlice swa to understandenne:
swa oft swa ge ælmessan dydon anum lytlan ðearfan
of Cristenum mannum, þæt ge dydon Criste,
for ðan ðe Crist sylf is Cristenra manna heafod,
and eft ða Cristenan syndon Cristes lima. (Pope XI. lines 430-34)[81]

This is truly to be understood thus: as often as you gave alms to one little poor man among Christian people, you did that for Christ, because Christ himself is the head of Christian people, and again, Christians are the limbs of Christ.

Others will be condemned because their inability to show mercy will be reckoned as sin:

Ðonne andwyrt se Dema þam earmum forscyldegodum:
Soð ic eow secge, me sylfum ge his forwyrndon
swa oft swa ge his forwyrndon anum of þisum lytlum. (lines 448-50)[82]

Then the judge will say to the wretched guilty ones: 'Truly I say to you, you denied it to me as often as you denied it to one of these little ones.'

---

80. Quoted in the translation by R.G. Macmullen.

81. I refer to this passage and to the one which follows again on page 259.

82. Compare Godden VII. 130-173.

The Gospel account of judgement (Matthew 25. 31-46), reveals this separation of the sheep from the goats, the merciful from the unmerciful, to be the moment when the reality of eternal life or eternal death will be blindingly clear. At that moment, nothing more can be done: the Judge's decision cannot ever be changed.

Showing mercy is spiritual almsgiving. Both giving and forgiving are equally necessary in the Christian life. Ælfric associates them one with another in placing together two sayings of Jesus which speak of the blessings they bring:

> He cwæð forgyfað. and eow bið forgyfen; Syllað. and eow bið geseald; Þas twa ælmessana cynn us sind to beganne. mid micelre gecnyrdnysse. (Godden VII. lines 39-41)[83]

> He said, 'Forgive, and you will be forgiven; give, and to you will be given.' These two kinds of alms are to be practised by us with great diligence.

Giving material help will earn reward from God, and the merciful forgiveness of others allows on the last day the possibility of mercy, on which all Christians utterly depend:

> Mildheortnys ana gemundað us on ðam micclum dome. gif we on andwerdum life hi oðrum mannum cyðað; Witodlice ðam bið dom buton mildheortnysse. se ðe nu oðrum demð buton mildheortnysse. (lines 48-51)[84]

> Mercy alone will protect us at the great judgement, if we show it to other people in this present life; certainly he who now judges others without mercy will have judgement without mercy.

---

83. Compare Thorpe XIX. p. 266. 20-31; Belfour IV. p. 34. 7-14 and p. 38. 6-11.

84. Compare Thorpe XXXVI. p. 552. 8-11; Godden XIX. 135-36; XXI. 130-31; XXXII. 63-67; *De penitentia* p. 604. 8-14; Pope XIII. 40-47, 54-55, 67-71 and 101-5; XV. 198-202; Assmann I. 220-23; Skeat XII. 254-57; and in Augustine, *Sermo* LIII.v.5; *Sermo* LXXXIII.ii.2.

Mercy is the active expression of love: love of God directed outwards to others in acknowledgement of a common dependence on the merciful love of God. The parable of the wedding banquet (Matthew 22. 2-14), as well as speaking about the individual's place within the church, also speaks of what he must bring: it extols the wedding garment, without which no guest can be welcome at the wedding.[85] Ælfric's exegesis of the parable, interpreting the garment as love, places great weight upon love as the entry requirement for heaven, suggesting that even baptism might be negated by the absence of love:

> Se Godes Sunu, þe ðurh lufe to mannum becom, gebicnode on þam godspelle þæt ðæt giftlice reaf getacnode, — þa soðan lufe. Ælc þæra þe mid geleafan and fulluhte to Gode gebihð, he cymð to þam gyftum; ac he ne cymð na mid gyftlicum reafe, gif he þa soþan lufe ne hylt. (Thorpe XXXV. p. 528. lines 16-21)[86]

> God's Son, who came to men out of love, indicated in the Gospel that the wedding garment signified true love. Each of those who inclines to God with faith and baptism comes to the wedding, but he does not come with a wedding garment if he does not possess true love.

The guest wearing the wedding garment may be assured of a welcome at the banquet.

It is important to offer penance for sin whilst life remains. This is true even though in Ælfric's view penance may extend after death. In the interim between death and resurrection the sins which were not atoned for in this life must be purged, so that the soul may journey purified to heaven and there obtain the reward of the Christian life. Such purification is available to those whose lives have demonstrated their worthiness. As Augustine himself suggests, no-one who has not in life striven to please God could expect to be forgiven after death for sins not cleansed before death (*Enchiridion* xxix.110. lines 5-9). It is safest to ensure that penance has cleansed the soul, and that true conversion has redirected its energies towards the service of God. Gregory's pattern of the soul's progress from fear to love is repeated by Ælfric:

---

85. Further reference to this parable is made on page 237.

86. In Augustine, see *Sermo* XC.6.

ærest he him ondræt helle wite, and bewepð his synna, syððan he nimð eft lufe to
Gode; þonne onginð he to murcnienne, and ðincð him to lang hwænne he beo genumen
of ðyses lifes earfoðnyssum, and gebroht to ecere reste. (Thorpe IX. p. 140. lines 17-21)

first he dreads the punishment of hell, and weeps for his sins, after he has accepted
God's love again; then he begins to complain, and it seems to him too long until the
time when he is taken from this life's afflictions, and is brought to eternal rest.

Christians must make progress from fear to love if they are to render to God a pleasing
service. Repentance is a step along this road, and it is always met by a merciful response
from God. Indeed, even those close to death may discover this (Pope XIX. 242-45).[87] Mercy
is God's response to the faith represented by even the smallest sign of a repentant spirit.
Anyone who has faith in the saving mercy of God need not fear judgement:

se þe hopað to Criste becymð to miltsunge
huru on Domes-dæg, for þæs Hælendes godnysse.
Se us gelæde to ðam ecan life. Amen. (lines 252-55)[88]

he who puts his trust in Christ will receive mercy, even on judgement day, because of
the saviour's goodness. May he lead us to the eternal life; amen.

In his emphasis on the mercy of God Ælfric takes away the grounds of Gregory's anxiety.
He acknowledges that the fear of punishment is salutary, but it is only the beginning. Even
the most careful calculators of sins and penances could not possibly be sure of covering
everything in their earthly penance: to attempt to deal with sin in this way could lead either
to despair, or to a dangerous self-confidence. Instead Ælfric's concern is to encourage people
to amend their lives to the limit of their capacity, thereby discovering that grace will always
take them further.

The discipline of the penitential life, with all its associated learning and struggling, may
be relied upon in itself to effect something of this change. But the true indicator of the

---

87. Compare Pope XI. 195-99.

88. Compare Pope XV. 41-46 and 227-29.

penitential life is the readiness of the faithful in almsgiving, their generosity in both practical and spiritual ways. Their own merciful actions are essentially the outworking of the grace of perseverance in them, for without this grace they could not do those things which are pleasing to God. If, however, their success in doing good makes Christians think that they are achieving these things by the strength of their own efforts alone, then they are deceived. Ælfric puts it bluntly when he asserts, 'Ne mæg nan man naht to gode gedon buton godes gife' ('No man can do any good without God's grace', Godden XXVIII. line 86). It is grace which co-operates with the Christian's own efforts in learning, developing, correcting and giving, and which will eventually crown those efforts with mercy.

Ælfric's teaching represents an appreciation of penance that has developed out of his understanding of Augustine's doctrine of grace, which lends particular weight to the confidence the faithful may have in the provisions of God's grace. This allows that everything good the Christian can offer to God (such as good works, ready forgiveness and loving service) will be granted by grace. The willing soul will be empowered to be merciful, and as a reward for this almsgiving, will be shown mercy at the last.

4

DEATH AND JUDGEMENT

All must face the death of the body. Ultimately the most important part of the priest's work is the task of encouraging the people in his charge to prepare for death while they still have the opportunity to change their lives for the better. Delay may mean disaster for the soul after death. In addition to the death of the individual, that of the world must also be faced. The end of the world is predicted by Christ in the Gospel of Matthew, where he speaks of the sorrows and fears of those days, and predicts the terrors which will signal that his second coming is imminent (Matthew 24).

For Ælfric, the last days are not far away: in his view a number of the predicted signs have already been accomplished, and the world shows signs of sickening and ageing.[1] He feels very strongly that it is his responsibility to inform the people about the end of the world, and to prepare them for it. Just as he must assist each individual to be ready for death, by encouraging each one to live a life pleasing to God with appropriate penitential devotion, so he must ensure that each one is equipped to deal with the terrors awaiting the world at the end of time. It is important that he provide the factual information available and that the doctrine he teaches them be adequate for a firm grasp of the truth. In the last days Antichrist will be loosed upon the world, free to persecute and deceive for three and a half years, subjecting even faithful Christians to terrible pressure. Only those who are secure in the certainty of the doctrine they hold will be able to withstand the temptation of apostasy.

Augustine's teaching on the experience of the soul after death is inchoate and scattered; the period between the individual death and the end of the world, when judgement will establish the two cities in their permanent homes, holds little interest for him. Although he has faith that Christians will be enabled to deal with whatever awaits them, he offers few firm doctrines. But he does offer numerous suggested elucidations of New Testament predictions, and it was possible for later teachers to refine these into descriptions of what the soul might

---

1. J.E. Cross discusses the theme of the world's ageing in 'Gregory, "Blickling Homily" X and Ælfric's "Passio S. Mauricii": on the world's youth and age', *Neuphilologische Mitteilungen*, 66 (1965), 327-330.

experience; his teaching on the time of judgement also had some bearing on these descriptions. His suggestions were developed by Gregory: the stories recounted in his *Dialogi* provide impressive details of the experiences of the dead. Further details were offered by Bede, in his account of the Visions of Drihthelm and Furseus in *Historia ecclesiastica gentis anglorum*, and Julian of Toledo, in his *Prognosticon futuri sæculi*. Each of these teachers influences Ælfric beyond the sermons which are directly inspired by these works; Augustine, however, remains the foundation of his teaching.

If Augustine shows little inclination to speculate on the experience of the soul after death, he has considerably more to say about the judgement which awaits the soul at the end of time, when it will stand in the general resurrection, reunited with the body. Both he and Ælfric are intensely interested in the interplay of justice and mercy on the day of judgement, when the culmination of God's predestination of the saints will coincide with the final departure of the non-elect. That day will begin the timeless praise to be offered by the elect to God: the purpose for which man was created.

In his homilies Ælfric is careful to discuss both the death of the body and that of the world. He teaches that the death of the individual will lead to some kind of intermediate judgement, for there are specified places where souls are sent to await the general resurrection. The intervening time may be used by some for the completion of penance; the more saintly will be welcomed to a paradisiacal place of refreshment. For each individual, death marks the beginning of a new existence which has been determined by the extent to which the earthly life has been pleasing to God: every Christian must therefore make proper preparation for death by living now a life characterized by almsgiving and penance. After the general resurrection the last judgement will determine for each one an eternity either of rest or of punishment. In principle this will depend both on the service offered to God during the earthly life and on the completion of any expiation allowed to the soul after death, but in practice, it seems that mercy will be shown to those who themselves have shown mercy to others.

I. THE INTERIM BETWEEN DEATH AND RESURRECTION

Ælfric's teaching concerning this interim indicates that significant development has taken place since Augustine addressed the question. Augustine discusses what might happen in this interim rarely and without much detail, neither discounting the possibility of a place of purgation nor assigning to such a place any importance in the overall scheme of salvation. He is far more interested in the day of judgement and its outcome, the eternal life of the saints and the perdition of the damned. Judgement, not the mysterious, undiscovered time before it, is the focus of his attention.

Nevertheless, Augustine made sufficient exploration into what happens to the soul after death to lay the foundation for the imaginative work of later teachers. The development of Augustine's thought has been traced by Ntedika and Le Goff.[2] They locate his early interest in the subject in his personal sense of the importance and value of suffrages for the newly dead. Augustine has little curiosity concerning the actual experience of the soul in its passage from death to new life, but is anxious that each soul should be hastened to the completion of this journey. The prayer for Monica after her death, recorded and shared with others through *Confessiones*, is a clear indicator of Augustine's private need to believe in the contribution of suffrages to the total work of salvation. His prayer gives no impression that he thinks his mother is suffering in a place of punishment from which his intercession may rescue her. Rather she is envisaged as already close to God, able to fight off any devilish challenge with the confident self-defence that Christ has already cancelled her debt (IX.xiii.36. 41-44).[3] Augustine in his prayer takes part in appropriating for her the deliverance already promised by her faith in Christ.

In the *Enchiridion*, again concerned with the question of suffrages, Augustine says that after death the soul dwells in 'abditis receptaculis' ('a hidden retreat', xxix.109. lines 2-3), where it is punished or allowed to rest, according to its merits.[4] In this intermediate state the souls of some of the dead may be assisted by the piety of living friends. Certainly some have no need of such assistance, but there are others who have deserved this help even though they have not been good enough to be released from punishment. Still others have been so wicked

---

2. Joseph Ntedika, *L'Évolution de la doctrine du purgatoire chez St Augustin*, Publications de l'Université Lovanium de Léopoldville, 20 (Paris, 1966); Jacques Le Goff, *The Birth of Purgatory*, translated by Arthur Goldhammer (London, 1984).

3. Le Goff, *Purgatory*, p. 65.

4. Paul the Deacon chose *Enchiridion* xxix.109-111 as a reading for an occasion in memory of the faithful dead, Pars aestiva, 131.

that suffrages will be useless to them. Nothing can change after death where no provision has been made before death. It is wrong, therefore, to expect mercy where none has been earned: 'Nemo autem se speret quod hic neglexerit, cum obierit apud dominum promereri' ('But let no-one hope to obtain, when he is dead, merit with God which he earlier neglected to acquire', xxix.110. lines 15-16). Because the church prays for all, not knowing who merits assistance and who does not, it is inevitable that there will be cases where suffrages will fail to improve the soul's lot, but Augustine supposes dispassionately that they are useful in at least offering a certain consolation to the living:

> Cum ergo sacrificia, siue altaris siue quarumcumque eleemosynarum, pro baptizatis defunctis omnibus offeruntur, pro ualde bonis gratiarum actiones sunt, pro non ualde bonis propitiationes sunt, pro ualde malis etiam si nulla sunt adiumenta mortuorum qualescumque uiuorum consolationes sunt. (lines 24-29)

> Accordingly, when sacrifices, whether of the altar or of alms, are offered for all the baptized dead, these are thanksgivings when made for the very good, propitiatory offerings when made for the not very bad, and at least some sort of solace for the living, even if of no help to the dead, when made for the very bad.

This consolation is derived purely from the hope that the intercession offered may perhaps prove to be helpful, for no-one can have certain knowledge of a soul's destiny after death, nor is it possible to be sure of the quality of a person's life and thus try to predict his chances of salvation. Where they prove useful, suffrages either bring about forgiveness or make the final damnation of the soul less intolerable (29-31). Augustine offers here some small clarification concerning the interim between death and resurrection, but is still primarily interested in the ultimate destination of the soul: only its eternal condition really concerns him.

Gregory the Great, however, with his acute sense of sin and divine retribution, is attracted to the idea of a place where purging punishment may be undergone. Augustine's important classification of the good, the not-quite-good and the bad contains implications for the doctrine of penance. Gregory finds in Augustine's middle category, those for whom suffrages might prove beneficial, a group of people who could hope to complete unfinished penance after death. Their 'hidden retreat' would be a place of rigorous, purifying pains, offering a final opportunity for penance (Dudden, *Gregory* II, p. 426). Only minor sins may be atoned for in this place, however; major sins lead unconditionally to eternal punishment. Moreover, this privilege of extra time is allowed only to those whose lives have demonstrated their worthiness:

> Hoc tamen sciendum est quia illic saltem de minimis nil quisque purgationis obtinebit, nisi bonis hoc actibus, in hac adhuc uita positus, ut illic obtineat promereatur. (*Dialogi* IV.xli.6. lines 44-47)

> In this connection we should also remember that in the world to come no one will be cleansed even of the slightest faults, unless he has merited such a cleansing through good works performed in this life.[5]

Thus the possibility of a time of purgation is itself dependent on the kind of life lived before the death of the body, and is not automatically available. Whilst Gregory acknowledges that the place of mercy, both in the intermediate and in the final judgement of God, should not be forgotten, it is nevertheless unquantifiable and therefore cannot be assumed to have universal effect. For him, the fear of not being able to do enough penance is not quite eliminated by a reminder of God's mercy.

Ælfric's own teaching on the interim between death and judgement includes a translation of Bede's account of the vision of Drihthelm, related in *Historia ecclesiastica*; this makes a careful classification of four types of people who are rewarded for the quality of their lives by rest or punishment immediately following the death of the body. With the intermediate witness of Gregory and Bede, Ælfric can be much more certain than Augustine of the existence of a place where purgation might be undergone. In his preaching on the last days Ælfric encourages the Christian to make appropriate preparations for the soul's journey after death. A realistic evaluation of the soul's standing before God may be hoped for if the terrors attendant upon the return of Christ in judgement are understood. These terrors have reference both to the individual's death and to the time of the general resurrection, because all will be resurrected to face judgement.

---

5. Quoted in the translation by Odo John Zimmerman.

The individual's death is more complex than simply the death of the body, although in earthly life the possibility of the death of the soul is likely to be ignored. Ælfric observes with some incredulity that people are excessively careful of their bodily health, but pay little heed to the health of the soul:

> Ælc man him ondræt þæs lichaman deað,
> and feawa him ondrædað þære sawle deað.
> Þam lichaman men tiliað, þe lange lybban ne mæg,
> and ne tiliað þære sawle þe ne swelt on ecnysse. (Pope XI. lines 118-21)[6]

> Everyone fears the death of the body, and few fear the death of the soul. People take care of the body, which cannot live long, and do not take care of the soul, which does not perish in eternity.

The soul does not perish; nevertheless it may suffer death. This death is eternal. Augustine is equally critical of the common inattention to the needs of the soul (*In Ioannis Evangelium tractatus* XLIX.2. 11-15). He observes around him the typical human folly that is zealous in the cause of bodily comfort and long life, which must come to an end, but is indifferent to the requirements of eternal life, whose joys are freely available and may be possessed inviolably:

> et nos inuicem non accusamus, tam pigri, tam tepidi ad capessendam uitam aeternam, quam si uoluerimus habebimus, cum habuerimus non amittemus; hanc autem mortem quam timemus, etiamsi noluerimus, habebimus' (lines 33-37).

> and we do not accuse ourselves in turn, so sluggish and lukewarm are we about obtaining eternal life, which will be ours if we wish it, and will be imperishable when we have it; but this death which we fear, though we do not want it, we shall have it.

---

6. Compare Pope VI. 143-53.

Ælfric argues that the death of the body should be of no concern to the Christian: it is natural and inevitable, and holds no dangers. The other death, by contrast, is a fearful prospect for those whose lives are stained with sin:

Twegen deaðas synd, swa swa us secgað bec:

an is ðæs lichaman dead, þe eallum mannum becymð,

oðer is ðære sawle dead, þe ðurh synna becymð,

na eallum mannum, ac þam manfullum anum. (Pope XI. lines 129-32)[7]

There are two deaths, as books tell us: one is the death of the body, which comes to all people; the other is the death of the soul, which comes through sins not to all people but to the wicked alone.

The death suffered by the wicked might more accurately be described as separation from eternal life: it is thus a death by negative definition, but it is a living death in which the soul's existence and hence its capacity for suffering are perpetually renewed. Unlike the momentary death of the body, the death of the soul is an eternal condition from which there is no escape. Separated from eternal life the soul is eternally rejuvenated in death, 'æfre geedniwed to þam ecum witum' ('constantly renewed to eternal punishments', line 135). The spectre of death thus raised is quickly replaced by a picture of the other eternity, that of heaven, and the choice offered is clear:

Þysum deaðe ætwindað, swa swa ure Drihten cwæþ,

ða ðe his word healdað, and hi habbað þæt ece lif

mid þam soðan Hælende, þe hi gehyrsumedon on life. (lines 136-38)

As our Lord said, those who keep his word escape this death, and they who obeyed him in life will have that eternal life with the true saviour.

This stark distinction between the saved and the lost has the effect of bringing forward the pronouncements of the last judgement to the time of the individual's death, heightening the

---

7.   Compare Godden XIII. 152-55; XV. 201-6.

sense of crisis to be faced. Here Ælfric seeks to emphasize the division into the saved and the lost which will eventually obtain and encourages no-one to place hope in being almost saved.

Seen from another perspective, every soul is dead until it is brought to life by the work of God in repentance. Ælfric finds in this a pleasing parallel, for while the individual faces two deaths, he is also offered two resurrections, the first in each case referring to this life and the second to the life to come. The resurrection which occurs during the earthly life is that mysterious second, or spiritual, birth out of the death of sin and into the life of God's service (Pope VI. 137-39). Sin is here equated with death, and penance is seen as the means of releasing the soul into life, with the happy possibility of pleasing God:

> for ðam se ðe syngað, hys sawul ne leofað,
> buton heo þurh andetnysse eft acucige,
> and þurh dædbote hyre Drihten gladige. (lines 140-42)

> For the soul of the person who sins does not live, unless it is requickened through confession, and rejoices its Lord by means of penance.

The soul which has undergone the first resurrection may look forward with hope to the second, the general resurrection.

The two resurrections are central to Augustine's discussion of the last days in *De civitate Dei* XX. Here he finds that Christ's promise, that the good will be brought to the resurrection of life and will not come up for judgement (John 5. 22-24), effectively equates judgement with condemnation:

> Ecce hic dixit fideles suos in iudicium non uenire. Quomodo ergo per iudicium separabuntur a malis et ad eius dexteram stabunt, nisi quia hoc loco iudicium pro damnatione posuit? In tale quippe iudicium non uenient, qui audiunt uerbum eius et credunt ei, qui misit illum. (XX.v. lines 116-21)

> Observe that he said here that the faithful will not come up for judgement. Then how will they be separated from the evil by judgement and stand on his right hand, unless in this passage he used 'judgement' for 'condemnation'? For that is the kind of

judgement into which those people will not come who hear his words and put their faith in the one who sent him.

Those who have believed, and done good, move from death to life, whilst those who have done evil are reckoned to be raised to judgement:

> pertinendo ad primam resurrectionem, quia nunc transitur a morte ad uitam, in damnationem non ueniet, quam significauit appellatione iudicii, sicut etiam hoc loco, ubi ait: 'Qui mala egerunt, in resurrectionem iudicii', id est damnationis. (XX.vi. lines 48-52)

This means that by taking part in the first resurrection, which effects the passage from death to life, he will not come up for condemnation, which is what he means by the term 'judgement', as he does also in this other place, where he says, 'Those who have done wrong will rise for judgement.'[8]

Those who face the resurrection of judgement are those who are condemned to die the second death (line 69).

This condemnation to the second death is the result of rejecting the regenerating grace of the first resurrection, that of new life in baptism. Anyone who has lived a dead life, without the new life of Christ, faces a living death after the second resurrection. Thus these two resurrections are the pivotal points for temporal and eternal life:

> ita sunt et resurrectiones duae, una prima, quae et nunc est et animarum est, quae uenire non permittit in mortem secundam; alia secunda, quae non nunc, sed in saeculi fine futura est, nec animarum, sed corporum est, quae per ultimum iudicium alios mittit in secundam mortem, alios in eam uitam, quae non habet mortem. (XX.vi. lines 77-82)

Similarly, there are two resurrections: the first, the resurrection of the soul, which is here and now, and prevents us from coming to the second death; and the second, which is not now, but is to come at the end of the world. This is not the resurrection of the

---

8. Henry Bettenson omits Augustine's last phrase, 'id est damnationis', in his translation.

soul but of the body, and by means of the last judgement it will consign many to the second death, and bring others to the life that knows no death.

The resurrection to life which is the beginning of the life to come is found to be dependent on the earlier resurrection: 'Resurgat ergo in prima, qui non uult in secunda resurrectione damnari' ('And so anyone who does not wish to be condemned in the second resurrection must rise up in the first', lines 52-53).

The first resurrection can be effected by God however seriously the soul has sinned and plunged itself into death. The degrees of the soul's death are exemplified by the three dead raised by Christ. The first death of the soul, the least serious, is represented by the nobleman's daughter (Luke 8. 41-56 and Mark 5. 22-43). This is the secret sinfulness of the soul ('him ys se deað wiðinnan digollice on his sawle', 'death is within him secretly in his soul', Pope VI. line 163). The second, represented by the young man of Naim (Luke 7. 11-16), is the condition of open sinfulness, rendering the soul 'openlice yfele dead' ('openly, evilly dead', line 165). Finally, the one who has been long dead in sin has the characteristics of Lazarus (John 11. 1-45), who had been dead for some days by the time Jesus came to him:

Se ðe gewunolice and unforwandodlice singað,
and hys yfel gewidmærsað þurh yfelne hlisan,
se ys bebyrged on bismerfullum leahtrum,
and he fule þonne stincð on his fracodum dædum. (lines 166-69)[9]

The person who sins habitually and without compunction, and spreads abroad his evil through wicked infamy, is buried in disgraceful sins, and then he stinks disgustingly in his abominable deeds.

The people are assured that however foul this habitual sinning has made the soul, the Lord is able to rescue it from this spiritual death, just as he was able to raise those who had

---

9. Augustine's analysis of the meaning of each raising is in *In Ioannis Evangelium tractatus* XLIX.3. Ælfric uses this exegesis again in Thorpe XXXIII. p. 496. 5-28.

suffered physical death. There is no sin so serious that revivification will not follow (209-16).[10] All that is needed is repentance. Augustine exhorts the people: 'Si peccasti, paeniteat te! et resuscitat te Dominus, et reddet ecclesiae matri tuae' ('If you have sinned, repent, and the Lord will bring you back to life, and return you to your Mother, the Church', *In Ioannis Evangelium tractatus* XLIX.3. lines 18-20). As the young man of Naim was returned, alive, to his mother, so also the Christian is handed back, cleansed, to the church:

> Gyf þu syngodest, þu hit soðlice behreowsa,
> and Crist arærð þe, þæt þu cucu byst on Gode,
> and betæcð þe þinre meder, þæt ys, his gelaþunge,
> on þære þu wære gefullod, and on þære þu scealt geþeon. (Pope VI. lines 192-95)

If you have sinned, be truly penitent and Christ will raise you, so that you will be alive in God, and will entrust you to your mother, that is, his church, in which you were baptized, and within which you are to thrive.

Ælfric makes it clear that although baptism is the sacrament which first restores life to the dead soul, new resurrections are needed to drive away the encroaching influence of death in the new life.

It is in the forgiveness which is received in faith that resurrection to life is found: life is bestowed in the context of faith even in the face of death. The Lord's words to Martha, 'I am the resurrection and the life' (John 11. 25), confirm that faith is life. As Augustine observes, the fact that God is the God of Abraham, Isaac and Jacob, and also the God of the living, proves that the patriarchs live. Faith, therefore, is life, whilst the absence of faith is nothing less than death:

> Crede ergo: et si mortuus fueris, uiues; si autem non credis, et cum uiuis, mortuus es.
> (*In Ioannis Evangelium tractatus* XLIX.15. lines 9-10)

---

10. Compare Thorpe XXXIII. p. 496. 29-33. That this assurance holds good for all sins except the sin against the Holy Spirit is stated in both sermons, Thorpe XXXIII. p. 498. 20-27 and Pope VI. 217-27.

Believe, therefore, and if you die you shall live; if, however, you do not believe, even if you are alive, you are dead.

In his version, Ælfric preserves the force, if not the rhetoric, of this statement, adding one small but significant element:

> ... Se þe on hine gelyfð,
> þeah þe he dead si, he sceal libban swaþeah,
> and se ðe ne gelyfð on hyne, þeah þe he lifes si,
> he ys dead swaþeah þam yfelan deaðe. (Pope VI. lines 363-66)[11]

He who believes in him, though he be dead, yet shall he live, and he who does not believe in him, though he be alive, yet he is dead in the evil death.

Even the living are actually dead if they live without belief, and Ælfric's specification of 'þam yfelan deaðe' makes it quite clear that the death under discussion is the death of the soul, which will continue to eternity.

Approaching the moment of bodily death, the Christian must accept the possibility that no further opportunity of penance may be granted. Penance not completed at death may never be finished. There now comes the intermediate separation of the soul from the body, for, whether rest or punishment is merited at the end of this life, the period between death and the universal resurrection is lived by the soul alone. The body turns to earth and experiences neither pain nor joy (Godden XIII. 156-58). At this moment, the living soul, which has already undergone the first resurrection, is appointed to life, while the dead soul begins its punishment of living death.

The Christian who has been a channel of good works and has gladdened God encounters death as merely a crossing point from one life to the next. For such a person the prospect of judgement holds no fears. Indeed, Ælfric is certain that God's finest servants obtain their reward straight away: the saints journey immediately to be with God. He sends his angels to meet them and to guide them home to rest (Godden XXXVII. 183-201).[12] After the general

---

11. Compare Godden XIII. 159-66.

12. Compare Godden V. 162-66; XXXVII. 170-73; Pope XI. 181-83; XIX. 231-35.

resurrection the saints will not themselves be judged, but will assist the Son in the work of judgement (Pope XI. 361-64). They now await the resurrection with great longing for they will then be reunited with their bodies, and their joy will be complete. Until that moment they dwell in bliss, already close to God.

For Augustine, this continuity of the life of the saints is the one real certainty, although he approaches it in a variety of ways. The common idea is that whatever destiny awaits the sinful, a rewarding rest is certainly promised to the faithful. Augustine teaches that 'diuersas receptiones' ('different receptions') await souls at the moment of death (*In Ioannis Evangelium tractatus* XLIX.10. line 3). Some go to joyful rest, others to torments. These conditions merely anticipate the perfecting of that joy or torment after judgement. Without speculating upon the nature of the torments to be suffered by the wicked, Augustine confidently invites the company of believers to place themselves alongside the patriarchs, saints and martyrs in the peace which precedes the final admission to heaven (12-15). This peace may understood to be merely a sleep, blessed by the absence of the trials of human life: an awakening out of this sleep to true joy is promised (16-18).

In other contexts, Augustine thinks that something finer than sleep is promised in 'Abraham's bosom'. His personal need to believe in the reality of this place and the quality of the new life implied by its protection is attested by his faith, held from an early period, that good friends are kept within its safe confines after their death. In *Confessiones* he speaks of the death of Nebridius, who, after his conversion lived an exemplary, chaste and continent life. Augustine claims this resting place for Nebridius: 'ibi uiuit. Nam quis alius tali animae locus?' ('There he lives, for what other place is there for such a soul?' IX.iii.6. lines 30-31). He trusts that Nebridius' new life carries with it the benefits of sight and knowledge which the faithful so crave: his bodily death has brought him into a new proximity to God which satisfies at last his questioning mind. Further, Augustine has faith that Nebridius, wherever he is, remembers his friend, with the implication that he may do so in intercession:

> Ibi uiuit, unde me multa interrogabat homuncionem inexpertum. Iam non ponit aurem ad os meum, sed spiritale os ad fontem tuum et bibit, quantum potest, sapientiam pro auiditate sua sine fine felix. Nec eum sic arbitror inebriari ex ea, ut obliuiscatur mei, cum tu, domine, quem potat ille, nostri sis memor. (lines 31-36)

There he lives, in the place about which he used to ask me, a poor ignorant man, many questions. Now, he does not place his ear to my mouth, but his spiritual mouth to Thy fountain, and, in proportion to his eagerness, he drinks as much as he can of wisdom, happy without end. But I do not imagine that he can be so intoxicated by it as to forget me, since Thou, O Lord, of whom he drinks, art mindful of us.

In the new state of joy, memory of the old life is not lost. The saints may be relied upon to remember those who have not yet reached their knowledge or fulfilment. Although the place where the saints dwell is a place of great joy, it is not heaven. 'Heaven' is the realization of the rest, joy and knowledge promised by the happy security of 'Abraham's bosom'. It is heaven into which the soul will awaken when it is reunited with the body.

The details of Augustine's account of the transition of the saints from this life to the next vary, for he seems unsure of the extent to which perfect happiness may be ascribed to their new life. However, an idea common to all his discussions of the matter is that the extra dimension to be experienced when the soul and body are reunited represents the achievement of perfection. This is true even where Augustine is willing to concede the possibility that the saints already enjoy completely uninhibited proximity to God. In a discussion about the meaning of the saints' reign with Christ of a thousand years (Apocalypse 20. 6), Augustine does not dismiss the symbolic interpretation that the saints have always reigned with Christ, even in the midst of persecution and death. Theirs is the same triumph as Christ's on the cross: under the new order, death is life, and destruction triumph. But Augustine is even prepared to think of a more literal reign of the saints:

> Sed certe animae uictrices gloriosissimorum martyrum omnibus doloribus ac laboribus superatis atque finitis, postea quam mortalia membra posuerunt, cum Christo utique regnauerunt et regnant, donec finiantur mille anni, ut postea receptis etiam corporibus iam inmortalibus regnent. (*De civitate Dei* XX.xiii. lines 42-46)

> In fact it is certain that the victorious souls of the glorious martyrs, at least, after overcoming all their sufferings and after the end of all their hardships, reigned with Christ, when they had laid down their mortal members; and they are still reigning, until the thousand years are ended, so that they may go on reigning when they have received their bodies, which will then be immortal.

This account of the reign of the saints is seized upon by Gregory, who cannot be satisfied with anything less than immediate and appropriate rewards for them. For him a place merely of peace and refreshment for the saints is inadequate: nothing less than admission to the presence of God could be appropriate for God's finest servants (*Dialogi* IV.xxvi.1. 6-12). Again, they lack only the completion of bliss to be experienced when their souls are reunited with their bodies (xxvi.3. 23-28).

Encouraged by this recognition of the proper joys of the saints, enlarged with details provided by Bede, Ælfric understands the peace of the just to involve an active enjoyment of the interim reward: it is expressed in terms of delightful sensory pleasures. Two categories of people enjoy these pleasures: the good are welcomed to a kind of paradise but the perfect are admitted immediately to heaven. The vision of Drihthelm, related on the authority of Bede (*Historia ecclesiastica* V.xii), has a glimpse of the place where the saints dwell; Drihthelm is not taken there by his angelic guide, but he receives intimations of the beauty of the place:

> Witodlice ða ðe fulfremede beoð on geðohte. on worde. on weorce swa hraðe swa hi of worulde gewitað. swa becumað hi to heofenan rice; Of ðam ðu gesawe þæt micele leoht mid ðam wynsumum bræðe. and þonon ðu gehyrdest ðone fægeran dream. (Godden XXI. lines 87-91)

> Truly those who are perfect in thought, in word, in deed, come to the kingdom of heaven as soon as they depart from the world; from there you saw the great light with the beautiful fragrance, and from there you heard that fair music.

In this place of joy the pure soul awaits the moment of resurrection and judgement. Such a soul has already been admitted to glory: the light, fragrance and music are signs of this. Yet the joy of this soul is not perfect: it enjoys the presence of God in spirit only and longs for its reunion with the body (Pope XI. 243-47).[13] Reunion will effect a transformation:

> and hi beoð þonne gefretewode mid fægerum lichaman,
> and þæt bið þæt oðer reaf ðære ecan myrhðe,
> and hi beoð þonne ece, and æfre undeadlice,

---

13. Compare Godden XIII. 158-59.

ge on sawle ge on lichaman, gesælilice mid Gode,

and heora lichama bið ðonne swiðe leoht and wynsum. (Pope XI. lines 248-52)[14]

and they will then be adorned with beautiful bodies, and that will be that other clothing of the eternal bliss, and then they will be eternal, and ever immortal both in soul and in body, blissfully with God, and their bodies will then be very light and delightful.

For the present, however, the souls must wait in patience for the last judgement. The souls already in bliss pray for judgement to come because they long for the twofold glory of soul and body, but they must wait until the total number of the elect appointed by God is reached (254-60). Even so, the saints already dwell triumphantly with God,

seðe on heofonum is, on ðære he rixað mid eallum his halgum on ealra worulda woruld on ecnysse. (Thorpe XIX. p. 274. lines 14-16)

who is in heaven, in which he reigns with all his saints for ever and ever in eternity.

For the saints, eternal life is already a reality.

Ælfric comments that the souls in bliss enjoy the bright vision of their Creator, and find their gratitude to him enhanced by the sight of the wicked undergoing punishment:

ac hira bliss ne bið na swaðeah gewanod,

þurh ðæt þæt hi geseoð þa synfullan on witum,

ac hi ðanciað þæs ðe swiðor heora Scyppende æfre,

þæt he hi swa ahredde fram þam reðum witum. (Pope XI. lines 264-67)[15]

nevertheless their bliss will not be diminished in that they see the sinful in torments, but they continually give thanks to their creator all the more because he has thus rescued them from the cruel punishments.

---

14. Compare Thorpe XIV. p. 218. 19-29.

15. Compare Thorpe XXIII. p. 332. 21-26 and p. 334. 5-15; in Augustine, *De civitate Dei* XXII.xxx. 93-99.

The souls in bliss will be prompted by the enjoyment of their own salvation to pity the suffering of others, and to intercede for those who are worthy of such intercession, whether they remain on earth or are already suffering punishment (236-39).[16]

If bliss is enhanced by the sight of suffering, it might be expected that suffering would be accentuated by the sight of others in bliss. Ælfric's commentary on the story of Dives and Lazarus (Luke 16. 20-31) comes to this conclusion (Thorpe XXIII. p. 334. 3-5). Gregory says that the wicked are occasionally allowed to see the saints in order to be punished by the sight (*Homeliæ in Evangelia* II.XL.8).[17] Both Gregory and Ælfric read this into the additional suffering of Dives caused by his inability to prevent his brothers suffering as he does. Ælfric decides that Lazarus' reward in heaven could be complete only if he were shown the suffering of Dives. Similarly, Dives' torture must be completed with the knowledge that others must suffer with him:

> forðan ðe se ðearfa nære fullice gewrecen on ðam rican, gif he on his wite hine ne oncneowe; and eft nære his wite fulfremed on ðam fyre, buton he ða ylcan pinunga his siblingum gewende. (Thorpe XXIII. p. 332. line 34-p. 334. line 2)[18]

> for the poor man would not have been fully avenged upon the rich man if he had not recognized him in his punishment; and again his punishment would not be completed in the fire, unless he were to expect the same torments for his brothers.

The suffering souls do not know what is happening 'mid us' (that is, on earth). They do remember their friends and think about them, 'þeah ðe hit naht ne fremige, ne heora freondum ne him' ('although it is of no advantage at all, either to them or to their friends', Pope XI. line 272). This means that souls in punishment are entirely cut off from any whom they might

---

16. Compare Godden XX. 169-71; XXI. 134-36.

17. Gregory's Homily XL is offered in some versions of Paul the Deacon's Homiliary for the Second Sunday after Pentecost, for which Thorpe XXIII is provided. Gregory also says much the same in *Dialogi* IV.xxxiv.4. 38-44.

18. Compare Gregory, *Homeliæ in Evangelia* II.XL.8.

wish to help: they have no means of communication, and their prayers for others are ineffective. Nor does their anxiety for the salvation of others redound to their credit.

For some of these punished souls, and perhaps even for many, the barrier of communication is not entirely sealed: there are some for whom intercession can and will be effective. These are the people who are suffering in order to complete penance begun at the end of their earthly life, or to expiate sins for which they were repentant only at the last. The vision of Drihthelm makes this group generously large. Bede's account of this vision, which may be classed with the imaginative descriptions recounted in Gregory's *Dialogi*, enabled progress to be made beyond the limitations imposed by Augustine's uncertainty in the matter.

In the *Enchiridion* Augustine examines the meaning of Paul's statement that some may be saved as by fire (I Corinthians 3. 10-15). That this fire could be understood as the tribulations suffered in the earthly life, through which some are cleansed, is certainly possible. This is one way in which Augustine interprets Paul's metaphor of the gold, silver or straw buildings raised over the foundation of Christ and tried by fire. His exegesis centres on the degree to which the affections are controlled by the things of this life, in particular by human relationships. Those who build their lives upon Christ may be strong enough to withstand the attractions of earthly pleasures, in which case their building will be secure against the fiery assault of tribulation. Those who are weaker may be attracted by those pleasures, and will be hurt by their loss (xviii.68. 59-73). The fire is not destructive, however, where Christ remains the foundation of the 'building':

> sed non subuertit neque consumit, fundamenti stabilitate atque incorruptione munitum. (lines 73-74)

> but it does not subvert nor consume him, strengthened as he is by his firm and incorruptible foundation.

Augustine follows a similar line of thought in the closing chapters of *De civitate Dei* XXI: the unmarried man who concentrates his mind on the service of God, not caring for the things of this world, builds in gold, silver, precious stones. The married man who loves his wife but does not prefer this affection to his love for Christ builds in wood, hay, stubble. Both build on the same foundation, which is their salvation, though their buildings be of differing quality (XXI.xxvi. 17-67). The fire destroys neither, but proves them:

inuentus est ignis, qui nullum eorum damnet, sed unum ditet, alterum damnificet, ambos probet. (lines 67-69)

There, then, you have this 'fire', as it seems to me, which enriches the one and impoverishes the other; it tests both, while it condemns neither.

Augustine next considers that the fire referred to may be a tribulation to be gone through after this life: he concedes that it is not impossible that a certain number might be saved then by fire: 'Tale aliquid etiam post hanc uitam fieri incredibile non est' ('That some such thing may happen even after this life is not past belief', *Enchiridion* xviii.69. lines 74-75). In *De civitate Dei* Augustine looks at the interim between death and resurrection again to see if this cleansing, saving fire might not fittingly be located in this period. Such a fire may be experienced, he says, by those who construct their buildings of cheap materials. It may also be suffered in combination with cleansing, earthly tribulation (XXI.xxvi. 109-12). This is a possible interpretation of the saving fire: he does not refute it, nor does he give it unqualified approval. A further possible interpretation is that this is the fire which will consume all things in the last days (122-28). Ælfric readily combines these ideas, finding fire in the place of punishment as a means of cleansing, but reserving the 'fire from heaven' for the purifying fire of the last days.[19] In fact, these fires carry out the same task, bringing every soul at last to the throne of judgement through a cleansing fire.

Augustine's reluctance to commit himself on the question of an interim purgation of fire influences Ælfric in spite of the encouragement which Drihthelm's vision and Gregory's *Dialogi* afford. Consequently at no point does he offer to anyone the simple expedient of relying on purification after death. No-one should be satisfied with hoping to be a borderline case, neither wholly good nor wholly bad. A false optimism which relies on the possibility of purgation distracts people from their proper purpose, which is to strive now to be counted among the good who journey immediately to heaven.

Nevertheless, Drihthelm's vision, translated virtually without alteration from Bede, gives grounds for hope. Ælfric's inclusion of this material indicates that although he cannot offer a fully-fledged doctrine of purgatory, he is still unable to accept that the final outcome of human development, in all its complexity, might exclude the possibility of a time of

---

19. See below, pages 252-54.

cleansing. Ælfric accepts on Bede's authority that, in addition to the saints waiting in their bright and fragrant dwelling place, there are two further groups of people who have a final assurance of heaven but who await their reward either in bliss or in purgatorial punishment.

The vision describes a kind of ante-chamber to heaven in which the souls of the not-quite-perfect reside while they await the last judgement, as well as a place of punishment for those who have sins to cleanse before they may gain admission to heaven. The first of these is only slightly less wonderful than the place of bliss glimpsed by Drihthelm:

> Se engel me lædde þærrihte to eastdæle on miccles leohtes smyltnysse into anre byrig. þærbinnan wæs swyðe smeðe feld and brad. mid blowendum wyrtum and grennyse eal afylled. and mid beorhtran leohte þonne ænig sunne scinende; Binnan þam weallum wæron ungerime meniu hwittra manna on mycelra blisse. (Godden XXI. lines 57-63)[20]

> The angel led me immediately to the eastern part in the tranquillity of a great light, into a city, within which there was a very smooth, broad field, all filled with blooming plants and greenery, and shining with a light brighter than any sun. Within the walls were countless multitudes of bright people in great bliss.

Drihthelm, observing this paradise with delight, at first supposes it to be heaven because of the apparent perfection of the scene.[21] He is corrected by the tantalizing glimpse of that yet brighter paradise which is the home of the perfected saints (87-91). The angel promises Drihthelm that if he lives righteously after returning to the body the bright, flower-bearing place will receive him (91-94). Bede and Ælfric conclude Drihthelm's story by describing the ascetic life of monastic devotion which he led after his return to life. If such a life is

---

20. Plummer notes that Bede's original (*Historia ecclesiastica* V.xii) is close to the Apocalypse of Peter, one of the earliest accounts of visions like Drihthelm's, which was primarily transmitted through the *Visio Pauli* (notes to his edition, p. 294). Ælfric, who energetically repudiated the *Visio Pauli* (Godden XX. 1-18), would have been unhappy about the antecedents of Drihthelm's vision had he known them. But he looked upon Bede as a wholly reliable, orthodox source.

21. Ælfric does not say if he regards this place as 'Abraham's dwelling', his name for the place where the righteous awaited the harrowing of hell (Godden V. 143-55).

characteristic of those who attain to the shining meadow, then the life of the saints, who are admitted to the presence of God, must be of still greater purity. The standards are very high, but they are presented in such a way as to encourage people to strive for them, not reject them as impossible.

Although Drihthelm sees a multitude of shining souls enjoying this second level of bliss, it is apparent that those who are found worthy of this ante-chamber are but a small part of the group eventually to be admitted to heaven. More numerous are those for whom a period of purgation is prescribed. Accordingly, Drihthelm's vision also allows him to see a place of punishment, which at first he takes to be hell until the angel corrects him. He sees a valley in which intense heat and intense cold alternate inexorably. The severity of the punishment and its unrelenting pointlessness here serve to underline the intensity of torment to be suffered in hell:

> Seo dene wæs afylled mid manna sawlum. þa scuton hwiltidum of þam weallendum fyre. into ðam anþræcum cyle. and eft of ðam cyle into þam fyre. buton ælcere toforlætennysse. (lines 28-31)[22]

> The valley was filled with the souls of people who rushed from time to time out of the surging fire into the horrible cold, and again from the cold into the fire without any intermission.

The purpose of the cold is merely to reinforce the horror of the fire: there is an implication that without it the sufferers might get used to the heat. Fire characterizes both the temporary punishment of purgation and the eternal punishment of hell, where the flame is dark and terrifying. Fire will also be the instrument of cleansing as the new heaven and new earth are inaugurated at the end of the world. Where light, music and fragrance delineate the heavenly, the hellish is made of fire.

The angel explains that the torturous valley is the place where those who were penitent at the last may expiate the sins of their lives. They failed to show penitence in life, yet when faced with death they sought to be numbered with the saved and not the damned. The price to be paid for belated repentance is the terrible cleansing pain of the fire, which, Ælfric says,

---

22. Compare Thorpe XXXV. p. 530. 35-p. 532. 3.

is so intense that it is greater than any earthly pain. Only small sins may be dealt with here: more serious sins borne unrepented to the next world bring eternal punishment upon the sinner (Pope XI. 220-28). Ælfric's source is the *Prognosticon futuri sæculi* of Julian of Toledo, but the stress on the severity of the fire is Augustine's (*Enarrationes in Psalmos* XXXVII.3. 33-35).[23] Ælfric goes on to say that the period of punishment may be long or short; Augustine says that the maximum term is from death to the day of judgement. Even taking into account the length and intensity of the punishment, this is still to be preferred to the eternal pains suffered by the damned and is therefore to be desired.

Drihthelm's angel says that all the penitent will eventually reach the kingdom of heaven (Godden XXI. 74-77).[24] Indeed some will be delivered from punishment before the last judgement. This will be through the suffrages of others:

> Eac hi sume þurh freonda fultum and ælmysdæda. and swyðost þurh halige mæssan. beoð alysede. of ðam witum ær þam mycclum dome. (lines 77-79)

> Also some of them, through the assistance of friends and almsgiving, and especially through holy masses, will be delivered from punishments before the great judgement.

At the close of his account of Drihthelm's vision Ælfric appends a short exhortatory sermon on the efficacy of the mass for the liberation of souls. He tells the story of Ymma, twice held in captivity. The bonds of the prisoner were repeatedly loosed at the times when his brother, a priest, said mass for his soul. In the story Ymma realizes that his brother's suffrages are responsible for the mysterious way in which the bonds break, and is quite certain that the bonds of 'the other world' would be as easily dissolved (lines 162-66).[25] Ælfric directs any who are interested in further reading to Gregory's *Dialogi*, which is available in an English translation, where they will find multiplied examples of such liberation (176-80).

---

23. Cited by Le Goff, *Purgatory*, p. 68.

24. Compare Godden XL. 275-79; Pope XI. 187-90; Assmann I. 204-7.

25. Compare Thorpe XXIII. p. 334. 30-34; Godden XXI. 131-36; Pope XI. 190, 211-12 and 240-41. Ælfric several times makes the point that masses are the most helpful of all suffrages.

Intercession for the dead is enjoined by the writers of the anonymous Old English homilies, providing the only clue to their expectations of the soul's fate immediately after death. These homilies are ambiguous about the interim between death and resurrection. Whilst they do not claim that there is a place of purgation, this is implied by their teaching that souls benefit from the intercession of others.[26] They do not speculate about purgation, preferring to concentrate their exhortatory energies on the theme of the last judgement and its preceding terrors. The final destiny of the soul is important to them, not the route to judgement: the certainties of damnation have an uniquely persuasive power more useful than speculation in an exhortatory sermon.

Augustine classified the dead in his exploration of suffrages as the very good, the not very good, and the very bad. But all of these are subdivisions of a larger group, the baptized (*Enchiridion* xxix.110. lines 24-29). Augustine is specific here about the essential qualification for salvation: only the baptized may benefit from the intercession of others to bring about an eventual reconciliation with God. Ælfric accepts this principle: in his discussion of the day of judgement he adopts Augustine's analysis of the Gospel account of Christ's separation of the sheep and the goats (Matthew 25. 31-46), and finds that an automatic qualification for eternal damnation is to be heathen: unbaptized (Pope XI. 384-90).

Augustine's 'very bad' are those who will certainly be among the inhabitants of hell after the final judgement. But it runs contrary to human nature to accept that anyone might be so thoroughly bad as to merit no mercy at all. Drawing upon his understanding of justice and grace, Augustine does face this problem of psychology in *De civitate Dei*, in which he condemns the 'misericordes', those who pity the lost because of their unwillingness to accept the facts of God's justice. He says that theirs is a false compassion, all too frequently adopted to comfort those who themselves reject the rigours of penance. Such misplaced pity serves no useful purpose: it merely salves the consciences of sinners (XXI.xviii. 65-67). He notes that all the manifestations of this kind of compassion derive from a basic misapprehension of God's justice: the fact that justice must imply punishment is ignored. One of the strongest arguments for the existence of eternal punishment, he contends, is its corollary of eternal life: if eternal punishment for the wicked is not assured, then neither is eternal blessedness for the elect (40-52). In these arguments there is no indication that intercession might be thought to

---

26. Milton McC. Gatch, 'Eschatology in the Anonymous Old English Homilies', *Traditio*, 21 (1965), p. 125.

rescue people from temporary punishment: the punishments under consideration have reference to the eternal condition of the soul.

Ælfric finds that the 'very bad' are guilty of rejecting the opportunity of repentance. In his discussion of the Lord's Prayer, the petition 'Forgive us our trespasses' offers a clue to the grounds for eternal punishment. Observing that some parts of the prayer have reference both to the present and to the future, he notes that the petition for forgiveness is part of a series of prayers applying only to this life:

> On þyssere worulde we biddað ure synna forgyfenysse, and na on þære toweardan. Se man ðe nele his synna behreowsian on his life, ne begyt he nane forgyfenysse on ðam toweardan. (Thorpe XIX. p. 272. lines 4-7)[27]

> In this world we pray for the forgiveness of our sins, and not in that to come. The person who has no wish to repent of his sins during his life will not obtain any forgiveness in that to come.

Thus impenitent sinners can expect no improvement of their state during the interim after death, and they are condemned to eternal damnation, unless extraordinary circumstances obtain. As for those who repent, some sins will be forgiven in this world, others in the next. Christ himself, by saying that the sin against the Holy Spirit would not be forgiven in this world or in the next (Matthew 12. 32), suggested that some sins at least will be forgiven in the world to come. In this regard the suffrages of others may be of value. The prayers of the saints are understood to be effective, except in the case of those whose condemnation is sure (Godden XXI. 134-36).[28]

Augustine says that the prayers of the saints lose their efficacy once the point of repentance is past. He reasons that the church on earth does not offer supplication on behalf of those who are known to have died impenitent, for such enemies of Christ are judged to be members of the devil's following (*De civitate Dei* XXI.xxiv. 41-42). However, prayer for the living is appropriate while the opportunity of repentance exists:

---

27. Compare Pope XIX. 236-41; Skeat XIII. 309-11; Assmann I. 207-8; in Augustine, *Sermo* LVI.xiv.19.

28. Compare Pope XI. 236-42.

Nunc enim propterea pro eis orat, quos in genere humano habet inimicos, quia tempus est paenitentiae fructuosae. (lines 25-26)

Her reason for praying now for her enemies among mankind is that there is time for fruitful repentance.

Liberation is possible through intercessory prayer only where the soul has not already been assigned to the fire which is eternal. If a soul is thus condemned, nothing will achieve the desired liberation, however long the saints might be implored for their aid.

Augustine has stern words for those who lack the self-discipline to work at their own salvation but hope instead to profit from the zeal and intercession of others. He observes that it is better to place oneself in the company of the intercessors than to rely on the good deeds of others, lest in the end there be too few to effect the rescue of too many (XXI.xxvii. 218-23).

Ælfric, supported by Bede in his acount of Drihthelm's vision, is generous in his estimation of the number who will be saved if they live a good Christian life.[29] Drihthelm's angelic guide is certain that all those who repent, however belatedly, will be saved. Ælfric's confidence in this truth is asserted outside the context of the vision in several other sermons. Repentance in the time of mortal sickness will meet a merciful response from God, he says in the sermon for the Octave of Pentecost:

> Gif se man wolde huru, þonne he seoc bið,
> to Gode gecyrran, and his synna geandettan
> mid soðre bereowsunge, se soðfæsta Dema
> him wolde mildsian, þæt he moste huru
> on Domes-dæge þam deofle ætwindan. (Pope XI. lines 195-99)[30]

---

29. Bede allows Drihthelm's vision to speak with an optimism about the number of the saved that is lacking in his exegetical works.

30. Compare Thorpe XXXIII. p. 496. 22-24, 28-32 and p. 498. 13-18; Godden XX. 218-26.

Nevertheless, if the man should wish to turn to God, when he is ill, and confess his sins with true repentance, the faithful Judge will wish to have mercy on him, so that at last on judgement day he might escape from the devil.

Here it is implied that until the day of judgement the man's soul will be lodged in an insecure condition, but that he will never be condemned to eternal torment with the devil. Punishments may have to be endured first, but repentance now is the truest guarantee of eventual restoration to God.

Indeed Ælfric goes even further than this: again it is in his accounts of visions that he feels free to view salvation with a truly 'post-Gregorian' optimism. In this optimism the role of intercession assumes ever greater proportions, until sometimes it may even be seen to substitute for repentance. Ælfric's sermon on the parable of the wedding feast looks carefully at the fates of two categories of people: those who are welcomed at the great man's feast because they come wearing a wedding garment (interpreted as true love for God), set against those who are cast out of the feast. The latter will suffer all the terrors of hell (Thorpe XXXV. p. 528. 9-p. 530. 22). Ælfric softens the harsh conclusion of the exegesis by recounting a story told by Gregory in which the power of effective intercession is vividly demonstrated. It may overcome even the paralysis of the will brought on by the terror which hell inspires. The story tells of a disobedient brother in a monastery, assailed by a devilish dragon as he lies at the point of death. Lacking the strength to make any gesture of repentance he considers his condition hopeless. Yet the ardent intercession of the brothers effects his release:

Efne ða færlice awyrpte se adliga cniht, and mid blissigendre stemne cwæð, 'Ic þancige Gode: efne nu se draca, þe me forswelgan wolde, is afliged for eowerum benum. He is fram me ascofen, and standan ne mihte ongean eowre þingunge.' (Thorpe XXXV. p. 534. lines 28-32)[31]

Then suddenly the sick man recovered and said with a rejoicing voice, 'I thank God: even now the dragon which was going to swallow me is put to flight through your

---

31. Compare Thorpe IV. p. 66. 29-p. 68. 33; Pope XI. 168-76; in Gregory, *Dialogi* IV.xl.5. 37-42.

prayers. He has been driven away from me, and could not stand against your intercession.'

The efficacy of intercession is always referred to the mercy of God. There is nothing in intercession *per se* which could have any liberating power, yet within the operation of the mercy of God miraculous rescues may be brought off. Another vision retold by Ælfric after Bede is that of Furseus, who was able to observe the struggle for his soul conducted by a legal-minded devil and an angelic advocate of mercy (*Historia ecclesiastica* III.xxix). The devil claims that Furseus has sins which remain uncleansed after death, and calls for justice, but his angel invokes the unpredictable and unquantifiable mercy of God. The devil quite properly protests that this is neither the time nor the place for thinking about repentance, to which the angel responds,

> Nyte ge ða micclan deopnysse godes gerynu. weald þeah him beo alyfed gyt behreowsung. (Godden XX. lines 132-33)[32]

> You do not know the great profundity of God's mysteries: perhaps repentance will yet be granted to him.

Thus, while Ælfric on the one hand seeks to subscribe to the strict conditions applied by Augustine, on the other he wishes to stress God's mercy as the final arbiter, which may override, if God so desire, all other considerations required by justice.

Christ himself provided the precedent for such gracious mercy when he accepted the last-minute repentance of the thief on the cross, and promised that they would be together in paradise immediately (Luke 23. 42-43). Although the penitent man had been a criminal, it is understood that his suffering on the cross eliminated the need for any purgation and allowed him free passage to paradise (Thorpe XXXVII. p. 576. 2-7). The sufferings of the martyrs result in the same immediate entry into paradise (p. 574. 29-34). Ælfric makes the point that this mercy is open to everyone, especially to those who suffer during this life. If they endure persecution because of sin, repentance will release them from future condemnation:

---

32. Compare Thorpe XXXV. p. 532. 26-28; Godden V. 169-71 and 206-9; XXI. 130-31; Pope XV. 115-19.

Gif hwa ðonne for synnum ehtnysse ðolað, and hine sylfne oncnæwð, swa þæt he
Godes mildheortnysse inweardlice bidde, þonne forscyt þæt hwilwendlice wite ða ecan
geniðerunge. (p. 574. line 34-p. 576. line 2)[33]

If then anyone suffers persecution for sins, and knows himself, so that he pray inwardly
for God's mercy, then the temporary punishment will prevent the eternal condemnation.

Although mercy is open to all, there are people who simply reject the opportunity of
forgiveness. The sin against the Holy Spirit, spoken of by Jesus (Matthew 12. 31-32), implies
the rejection of both the forgiveness offered and the impetus towards repentance. By this
rejection the sinner closes the door on the possibility of mercy:

Behreowsiendan mannum gemiltsað se Halga Gast,
ac ðam he ne miltsað næfre þe his gyfe forseoð. (Pope VI. lines 276-77)[34]

The Holy Spirit has mercy on the penitent, but he never has mercy on those who
despise his grace.

The interpretation is Augustine's:

Contra hoc donum gratuitum, contra istam Dei gratiam loquitur cor impoenitens. Ipsa
ergo impoenitentia est Spiritus blasphemia, quæ non remittetur neque in hoc soeculo,
neque in futuro. (*Sermo* LXXI.xii.20)

Against this gratuitous gift, against this grace of God, does the impenitent heart speak.
This impenitence, then, is the blasphemy of the Spirit, which shall not be forgiven,
neither in this world, neither in the world to come.

---

33. Compare Godden XIX. 259-70.

34. Compare Thorpe XXXIII. p. 500. 15-20; Pope VI. 217-20 and 224-27.

By contrast, there are those who show themselves to be 'vessels of mercy' (Romans 9. 23). These are the penitent who have the capacity of mercy and who have not, by the misuse of their free will, cut themselves off from the life of God.

For Augustine, his mother Monica was a model 'vessel of mercy'. The quality of her Christian service gave her son confidence in offering masses for her. Such remembrance had been her own request. Scorning the natural filial preoccupations of her other son, Navigius, concerning the last resting place of her body, she asked for no other service than this spiritual care: 'tantum illud uos rogo, ut ad domini altare memineritis mei, ubiubi fueritis' ('One thing only do I ask of you, that you remember me at the altar of the Lord, wherever you may be', *Confessiones* IX.xi.27. lines 13-14). Monica's request surely fuelled Augustine's own belief that suffrages for a dead person can benefit the soul. Augustine recalls that the sacrament blots out the sentence ('chirographum') written against each person; in her dying request she claimed the sacramental protection made available to her by the sacrifice of Christ (IX.xiii.36. 32-41).

Augustine's prayer for Monica shows that in his own mourning he needed to believe in the value of suffrages for the dead. Holding fast to this belief he begs forgiveness for her sins, and asks that for her, justice may be more than tempered by mercy, 'superexultet misericordia iudicio' ('Let mercy triumph over judgment', IX.xiii.35. lines 24-27). Augustine's sermons exhort the people to be merciful that they might have mercy shown to them, and he now claims this assurance for his mother. In his prayer he invites the wider intercession of all those who read his book, and throws himself, on Monica's behalf, upon the mercy of God, believing that the quality of her life has made his mother a vessel of mercy, worthy of the assistance of prayer after her death.

Ælfric calls the people to repentance and to the exercise of mercy, that their souls will be accessible to the mercy of God now and after death. All that remains is to reinforce the argument with the fear of separation from God's mercy, which begins with the assault of devilish forces at the moment of death. Visions of departing souls confirm that the point of death may involve a struggle between angels and devils, the outcome of which is decisive. Furseus' long account is only one example. Such visions have an other-worldly air of possibility which persuades by its ability to sow doubts in the mind. Moreover Ælfric's dismissal of the popular *Visio Pauli* has the effect of asserting the authority of the visions he feels it is appropriate to cite (Godden XX. 1-18).

Some of these visions encourage sinners to feel that repentance, however hopeless it may appear, is always worth trying. In other cases, the battle between the agents of good and evil is conclusively won by the devils. In one man's vision, devils offer a huge book recording his sins in opposition to the little book of good deeds borne by the angels. The angels concede defeat, and allow the devils to take the soul to damnation (Pope XIX. 183-98).[35] The vision is understood to be a clear prophecy of unavoidable condemnation, but the real purpose of the story is to encourage every Christian to strive for the enlargement of the little book now in the charge of the angels:

Ne fremode his gesyhð him sylfum nan þing,

ac for oðrum mannum him wearð æteowed þæt,

þæt þa beon gerihtlæhte þe ðas rædinge gehyrað,

for ðan ðe ure dæda beoð ealle awritene,

swa yfele, swa gode, on ecum gemynde,

and us eft beoð æteowde on ðam endenextan dæge. (lines 202-7)[36]

His vision was of no advantage at all to him, but it was revealed to him for the sake of others, that they who hear this narrative may be corrected, for our deeds are all recorded, both the evil and the good, in eternal remembrance, and will be revealed to us again on the last day.

The very bad are those who resist all attempts at correction and restoration. They will go straight to hell after death, and will not be offered any further opportunity for penitence:

Ða fordonan synfullan þe deofle gehyrsumodon

on eallum synnum, and forsawon heora Drihten,

and swa geendodon, þa sceolon to helle

swa raðe swa hi gewitað, and ðær wunian æfre. (Pope XI. lines 191-94)[37]

---

35. From Bede, *Historia ecclesiastica* V.xiii.

36. Compare Thorpe XXVIII. p. 414. 1-31; Godden XIX. 204-11; Pope XIX. 208-29.

37. Compare Thorpe XIV. p. 218. 18-19; XXXI. p. 470. 31-34; Godden XIII. 159-62; XL.

The corrupted sinners who were obedient to the devil in all sins, and despised their Lord, and thus came to their end, these must go to hell as soon as they die, and dwell there eternally.

Drihthelm sees the foul flame, in which such souls burn, welling up from the abyss (Godden XXI. 39-44). Judgement day will bring no change in the condition of sinners who are already undergoing punishment in this lowest and darkest of hell's fires. To all others, it will bring great fear, for some will know then for the first time what the judge has decreed for the eternal dwelling of the soul. These will include all those who have lived through the last days; only the dead will have experienced the rest or the torment which may indicate to them the nature of God's final decree.

Ælfric's teaching on the interim between the death of the body and the day of judgement is based on the information given by Augustine, and expanded with the materials provided by Gregory and Bede. The effect of such expansion is to allow Ælfric to be much more dogmatic than Augustine could ever have been on the subject of the soul's journey: ideas which were for Augustine purely speculation, since no proof could be found, are transformed by the testimony of 'eye-witness accounts' into facts of which the teachers are increasingly sure. Ælfric does not speak of 'purgatory', but he has come a long way on the route to giving the locus of cleansing fire a name and a concrete existence.

II. THE LAST DAYS

The last judgement will be heralded by certain specific signs: the Lord himself gave notice of them, with a stern warning about the terrors and difficulties of those times. From one point of view the signs of the approaching end have a useful function, to eliminate complacency:

> He geswutelode hu fela ðrowunga forestæppað þyssere worulde geendunge, gif we God on smyltnysse ondrædon nellað, þæt we huru his genealæcendan dom, mid mislicum swinglum afærede, ondrædon. (Thorpe XL. p. 608. lines 12-15)[38]

258-61 and 279-87; Pope VI. 313-17; XIX. 228-29, 236-41 and 250-51.

38. Compare Thorpe XL. p. 610. 15-18 and p. 618. 20-25.

He made known how many sufferings will precede this world's ending, that, if we are unwilling to fear God in tranquillity, nevertheless, terrified by a variety of afflictions, we should fear his approaching judgement.

There will be both astrological abnormality and spiritual aberration. Terrible apparitions will be accompanied by the most fearsome persecution the world has ever known:

Þonne beoð witodlice swylce gedrefednyssa

swylce næfre ær næran, ne eft ne gewurþað.

Butan God gescyrte þa sorhfullan dagas,

eall manncynn forwurde witodlice ætgædere.

Ac for hys gecorenum he gescyrte þa dagas. (Pope XVIII. lines 248-52)[39]

Then there will certainly be such tribulations as were never before, or will be again. Unless God shorten the sorrowful days, all mankind will surely perish together. But for the sake of his chosen, he may shorten the days.

The evils of the last days will be but the adumbration of the eternal evils to be suffered by the reprobate (Thorpe English Preface p. 4. 10-14).[40] It is possible to look at the last tribulations in another way, of course, for although those days will be fearful, they also hold the promise of great joy for those who keep the faith. Jesus sought to comfort his chosen, reminding them that the signs are the assurance of salvation: 'Look up, and lift up your heads, because your redemption is at hand' (Luke 21. 28);

We ahebbað ure heafda þonne we ure mod arærað to gefean þæs heofonlican eðles. Þa ðe God lufiað, hi sind gemanode þæt hi gladion on middangeardes geendunge, forðan þonne he gewit, ðe hi ne lufodon, ðonne witodlice hi gemetað þone ðe hi lufodon. (Thorpe XL. p. 612. lines 14-18)[41]

---

39. Compare Godden XXXVII. 66-83; Pope XVIII. 345-75.

40. Compare Godden XXXVII. 37-40.

41. Compare Thorpe XL. p. 614. 23-27.

We lift up our heads when we raise our mind to the joys of the heavenly homeland. Those who love God are exhorted that they should rejoice at the end of the world, for when he whom they did not love departs, then certainly they will come upon him whom they loved.

The world's destruction is a mournful prospect only to those who have much to lose thereby; for those whose investment is in the new heaven and earth which will succeed it, the disaster can only bring about the long-awaited rebirth. Christians, for whom this world is an affliction and a torment, fix their hope on the joys of the heavenly 'eðel' ('homeland', lines 28-35). Nevertheless, despite this conviction, the dominant note in Ælfric's sermons about the last days is one of anxiety: he feels responsible for the people's safety, and must fight the expected apostasy. Before all the fears of that time, he says, all present afflictions will fade into insignificance (p. 618. 15-20).

The principal harbinger of the end of the world is Antichrist. Augustine makes it clear that Antichrist's spell of freedom must precede the judgement:

non ueniet ad uiuos et mortuos iudicandos Christus, nisi prius uenerit ad seducendos in anima mortuos aduersarius eius Antichristus; quamuis ad occultum iam iudicium Dei pertineat, quod ab illo seducentur. (*De civitate Dei* XX.xix. lines 91-95)

Christ will not come to judge the living and the dead without the prior coming of his adversary, Antichrist, to seduce those who are dead in soul — although their seduction depends on the judgement of God, which is now concealed.

Antichrist's role is to deceive those who are already dead in the first death, not those who will be raised in the second resurrection. As he observes, Antichrist's persecution is a sign that God already knows the outcome of the lives of those who are dead in the first death: their attack by Antichrist is the beginning of judgement upon them.

Antichrist's name, Ælfric says, may be interpreted 'ðwyrlic Crist' ('perverse Christ', Thorpe English Preface p. 4. lines 21-22).[42] Opposing Christ in all respects, he is Christ's mirror image. He bears a nature uniting man and devilish spirit:

Þonne cymð se Antecrist, se bið mennisc mann and soð deofol, swa swa ure Hælend is soðlice mann and God on anum hade. (Thorpe English Preface p. 4. lines 14-16)

Then Antichrist will come, who is human man and true devil, just as our saviour is truly man and God in one nature.

Here Ælfric implies that Antichrist is an incarnation of the devil. The suggestion that the devil shares with God the power to become incarnate is, however, doctrinally disturbing; Ælfric could not have wished to detract from the uniqueness of the divine, saving incarnation of Christ, even though an interesting parallel with the damning incarnation of Antichrist might have had literary possibilities. Ælfric's later revision of these lines removes the direct juxtaposition of Christ and Antichrist and avoids the question of incarnation. He confines himself to the statement that the devilish nature of Antichrist is due to an indwelling of the devil's spirit. This evil inspiration is an act of taking possession:

ðonne cymð se antecrist se bið mennisc man 7 soð deofol he bið begyten mid forlire of were 7 of wife; And he bið mid deofles gaste afylled. (Corpus Christi College, Cambridge, MS 188, p. 93. lines 19-21)[43]

Then Antichrist will come, who is human man and true devil; he will be begotten in the fornication of a man and a woman. And he will be filled with the spirit of the devil.

Although Ælfric wishes to provide correct information he is less interested in the precise character of Antichrist than in the terrifying effects of the nature which he bears. Antichrist will have magical powers to enable him to perform miracles imitating those of Christ; such

---

42. This interpretation of Antichrist's name indicates that although Ælfric always adopts the spelling 'Antecrist' the name contains the idea of opposition to Christ.

43. My transcript from the manuscript.

miracles will seem dangerously convincing even to the elect. They will increase the tribulations already being suffered by the people:

And se gesewenlica deofol þonne wyrcð ungerima wundra, and cwyð þæt he sylf God beo, and wile neadian mancynn to his gedwylde. (Thorpe English Preface p. 4. lines 16-18)[44]

And the visible devil will then perform countless miracles, and will say that he himself is God, and will compel mankind to his error.

The miracles of Antichrist will make his persecution worse than any previously undergone by the church. The martyrs suffered intensely under the early opponents of Christianity, but they were granted a miracle-working power which was both an encouragement to the suffering and an effective witness to the truth. In the last days, however, such power will be the privilege of the devil, and the faithful will have nothing to reassure them in the face of his triumph (Pope XVIII. 347-65).

The falsehood of Antichrist's miracles will be recognized by all who recall his past deceptions. They will know that the devil can only simulate miracles: as a spirit divorced from the life of heaven, he has none of its power, although he can make a good display out of illusion (Thorpe English Preface p. 6. lines 16-18). He may even be permitted to heal where he has injured, but this is the limit of his power (p. 4. 20-24).

However, the miracle-working Antichrist makes more subtle assaults on Christians in the insinuation of his teaching into the church. His character and purpose constitute true paganism: the heathen ways of the past have never been as offensive as the godlessness of Antichrist (Pope XVIII. 296-99). With sorrow Ælfric records the prophecy that this cancer will reach the heart: the false christ will rehearse his lies at the centre of Christian worship, 'Swa þæt he sitt on Godes temple, and segð þæt he God sy' ('such that he will sit in God's temple, and say that he is God', line 303). Christ warned that others would come claiming to be him, working miracles in an attempt to deceive even the chosen. Ælfric says that anyone who comes before the day of judgement is therefore not Christ, however convincingly the imposter may back his claim with striking miracles and appropriate words. Two things will

---

44. Compare Pope XVIII. 289-95.

guide and sustain the Christian in those days: the first is the conviction that when Christ comes to judge the earth there will be no shadow of doubt that this is truly Christ:

> Ure Hælend Crist ne cymð na to mancynne
> openlice æteowed on þissere weorolde
> ær þam micclan dæge þonne he mancynne demð. (Pope XVIII. lines 383-85)

Our saviour Christ will not come to mankind, openly revealed in this world, before the great day when he will judge mankind.

Christ will reveal himself when he comes: no-one will need to point him out or justify his claim to the title 'Son of Man': the truth will be plain. The second principle to follow is that the deeds of Antichrist will be clearly contrary to the faith taught by Christ and transmitted by the disciples. Never underestimating the difficulty that Christians will experience, Ælfric proclaims that those who keep this faith will be able to see clearly through the dissembling of Antichrist and be strengthened to resist his snares (391-92). Augustine is equally certain that the elect will withstand Antichrist's power. Those who fail during the persecutions of Antichrist cannot truly have been among the elect:

> ex quibus etiamsi aliqui uicti secuti eum fuerint, non eos ad praedestinatum filiorum Dei numerum pertinere. (*De civitate Dei* XX.viii. lines 84-86)

although some of them may be defeated and will follow the Devil, they will not be people belonging to the predestined number of the sons of God.

Ælfric recognizes that the pressure will be strong. The gospel prediction means that all Christians must take seriously the threat to their salvation that the coming of Antichrist will represent. He underlines the importance of keeping the faith, even to death (Pope XVIII. 395-96).

While Ælfric feels all too keenly the sharpness of the tribulation to come, Augustine, nearing the conclusion of *De civitate Dei*, seems almost exultant before it. He looks to the period of Antichrist's persecutions as a time when the power of the church, the body of Christ, will be made manifest. The church will be ready, and empowered to withstand, because Antichrist is permitted his space by God. Antichrist's three and a half years of freedom in the world, when he will have at his command the full force of evil, will in fact demonstrate the extent of the church's triumph over him.[45] Augustine looks to this time with confidence, from the point of view of the victory which has already been won in Christ. Thus even Antichrist's apparent power will reveal the glory of Christ. Imprisoned up until this moment for the sake of weaker Christians, Antichrist is now released, and by implication all Christians will be strong enough to withstand him:

> et soluet in fine, ut, quam fortem aduersarium Dei ciuitas superauerit, cum ingenti gloria sui redemptoris adiutoris liberatoris aspicat. (XX.viii. lines 52-54)

> In the end the Omnipotent will unloose him, so that the city of God may behold how powerful a foe it has overcome, to the immense glory of its Redeemer, its Helper, its Deliverer.

Augustine also offers an exegesis of the fire from heaven which agrees with this triumphant optimism. That fire is the zeal of the saints, who are given the courage to resist Antichrist and his agents. Punning on 'firmamentum' and the solidarity of the saints' response, Augustine enjoys the violence with which they repulse the forces of evil:

> Firmamentum est enim caelum, cuius firmitate illi cruciabuntur ardentissimo zelo, quoniam non poterunt adtrahere in partes Antichristi sanctos Christi. (XX.xii. lines 7-9)

> For the heaven is the 'firmament' through whose 'firmness' these attackers will be tormented with blazing zeal, since they will be unable to draw the saints of Christ to the part of Antichrist.

The burning ardour of the saints will be an instrument of torture to the assailant. Here, Augustine allows a reading which completely reverses the literal meaning of the text, transforming the torturers into victims:

---

45. The three years and six months are prophesied by Apocalypse 13. 5, and supported by other numbers given in chapters 11 and 12.

Et ipse erit ignis, qui comedet eos, et hoc 'a Deo' quia Dei munere insuperabiles fiunt
sancti, unde excruciantur inimici. (lines 9-11)

This zeal will be the fire that devours them, and it will be 'from God', since it is by the
gift of God that the saints are made invincible, and that is what torments their enemies.

Augustine, sensing the triumph of the moment when the city of God will be established
eternally, delights in the excitement and joy of the last day.

Ælfric's attention, by contrast, is concentrated principally upon the fear which will
precede the day of judgement. Nevertheless, he perceives that the persecutions of the last days
will yet have some value for the chosen:

God geðafað eac þæt his gecorenan þegenas beon aclænsade fram eallum synnum þurh
ða ormatan ehtnyssa, swa swa gold bið on fyre afandod. (Thorpe English Preface p. 4.
line 35-p. 6. line 3)

God also permits that his chosen servants will be cleansed from all sins through those
immeasurably great persecutions, just as gold is tried in the fire.

There is an important difference here between Ælfric's suggestion that the persecutions of
Antichrist may have a purgatorial effect and the idea, present in many accounts of the last
days, that a period of fasting may be allowed for the cleansing of the elect who have turned
away from God. Such an idea reflects anxiety concerning the prophecy that Antichrist would
try to deceive the elect; the hope seems to be that the fast would allow those who had
apostatized to return to the fold.[46] But Ælfric's understanding of the prophecy, like
Augustine's, is that the truly elect will remain faithful, though under tremendous pressure.
They will not need a special fast to raise them from the mire of apostasy. The purgatorial
effects of the last tribulations will deal with other, smaller sins, not ultimately damaging to
the life of the soul. The chosen still living in the last days will not have the opportunities of

---

46. Adso mentions this period of fasting in his *Libellus de Antichristo*; R.K. Emmerson,
Antichrist in the Middle Ages (Seattle, 1981), p. 104.

purgation given to those who have died, and the last fire will ensure their purity at the time of judgement.

There are many occasions in the homilies when Ælfric says that earthly tribulations have a purifying effect which will release the sufferer from any further punishment after death.[47] The suffering of poverty is especially noted. The poor may expect to be released from punishment because they have already suffered in this life; no further purgation of their souls is necessary. The story of Dives and Lazarus is the basis for this teaching, and Ælfric tells it with little elaboration: he says the warning is clear, no exposition is necessary (Thorpe XXII. p. 332. 3-4). The short earthly prosperity of the one is contrasted with the eternal blessing given to the other:

> Þa underfeng se welega his gesælðe to edleane to sceortum brice, and þæs ðearfan hafenleast aclænsode hys lytlan gyltas. Hine geswencte seo wædlung, and afeormode; þone oðerne gewelgode his genihtsumnys, and bepæhte. (lines 7-11)

> The rich man received his happiness as a reward, for brief enjoyment, and the poor man's indigence cleansed his small sins. Poverty oppressed and purified the one, his abundance enriched and deceived the other.

For those who have not suffered in poverty, sickness or persecution for the sake of righteousness, a final purification is supplied by the intensely burning fire which will precede the last judgement.

The persecution inflicted by Antichrist upon the faithful will be brought to a sudden end by the coming of Christ in glory. Marshalling all the forces of heaven and the natural world, Christ will appear in triumph, signalling the end of Antichrist's reign of terror:

> Sona æfter þære ehtnysse bið Antecrist ofslagen
> þurh Cristes mihte on hys tocyme,
> and engla werodu beoð astyrede,

---

47. Thorpe XXXI. p. 476. 11-21; XXXVI. p. 554. 4-8; XXXVII. p. 574. 25-p. 576. 7; Godden XIX. 246-70; XXX. 61-63; XXXVII. 202-5; Pope XI. 200-4.

and mid þam Hælende cumað of ðam heofonlican þrymme

swutollice æteowde, swa swa us segð þis godspell. (Pope XVIII. lines 403-7)[48]

Immediately after the persecution Antichrist will be killed through the power of Christ at his coming, and hosts of angels will be aroused, and will come with the saviour from the heavenly glory, clearly revealed, as this gospel tells us.

These lines are a commentary on Matthew 24. 29-30, but they make reference to II Thessalonians 2. 8, where the destruction of 'ille iniquus' ('that wicked one') by the breath of the Lord's mouth is predicted.[49] Ælfric combines the prophecy of astrological calamity with the description of the heavenly host descending. The sun and moon darken 'for ðam ormætan leohte þæs mihtigan Drihtnes' ('before the immeasurably great light of the mighty Lord', Pope XI. line 286). As Christ is the illumination of understanding, his coming in glory with angels bearing the token of his human suffering, the cross, reveals to those who have denied him the darkness of their sin. Although he comes in the glory of his divinity, he comes also in human form, still bearing on his body the marks of torture, by which he may be recognized. This manifestation of suffering combined with glory, the union of human knowledge with divine energy, sheds a penetrating light over all sins (287-95).[50] Ælfric says the light is perceived in different ways by the good and by the wicked:

and he bið swiðe egefull on fyres gelicnysse on ðam micclum dome. þonne he scinð ðam rihtwisum. and byrnð ðam unrihtwisum. (Godden XII. lines 200-2)

and he will be very terrible in the likeness of fire in the great judgement, when he will shine for the righteous and burn for the unrighteous.

Again, fire is at the centre of this judgement scene, striking terror into the hearts of all those who recognize the insecurity of their lives. All are tested by the fire, although not all will

---

48. Compare Thorpe II. p. 28. 14-15; Godden XXXVIII. 179-82.

49. Augustine offers this interpretation of the verse in *De civitate Dei* XX.xii. 15-19.

50. Compare Thorpe XL. p. 610. 6-11 and p. 610. 32-p. 612. 2.

suffer in it. A single fire will carry out in one sweep several tasks: all those living on the earth must die in order that they may be raised, those whose penance has proved inadequate must be purified, and finally a new heaven and earth are to rise like a phoenix from the ashes of the old.

The purifying fire tests the 'buildings' of the faithful, according to Paul's image of the buildings made of materials ranging from precious gold to the meanest straw or chaff. Whatever the quality of the building, each is founded on Christ and because of that foundation will endure. Nevertheless the superstructure is found to be more or less vulnerable depending on the building material involved. Ælfric says that giving an exposition of Paul's text is a fearful task. Its meaning touches every person.

The gold, silver and precious stones are the materials used by God's best disciples, who have nothing to fear. Their buildings are constructed from faith, knowledge, sound doctrine and holy virtue:

> se ðe þyllic weorc getimbrað on godes gelaðunge. ne mæg þæt fyr on domes dæge his getimbrunge forniman. for ðan ðe þæt fyr ne derað þam godum þeah ðe hit tintregige þa unrihtwisan. (Godden XL. lines 242-45)

> the fire on judgement day will not be able to destroy the building of the one in God's church who builds such a structure, for the fire will not injure the good, although it will torture the unrighteous.

This meaning is derived from the physical properties of these materials. Far from being harmed by the application of fire, the precious metals and stones are made more beautiful, passing through the flame without difficulty. So it will be with the righteous, who will suffer no torment, but will instead pass through the fire 'swilce hi on sunnan leoman faron' ('as though they were walking in sunlight', line 250).

The poor builder who is not rich enough to use such costly metals and stones is one whose sins prevent faith and virtues from developing to this precious degree. Superstructures of wood and straw perish in fire. These are light sins which could act as kindling for the building's complete destruction: it is saved only by the quality of the foundation. For such builders, the fire is purgatorial. The sins are not so serious that they can destroy the soul grounded in Christ, but they figure prominently in the lives of ordinary men and women:

Ðas þyllice gyltas ne magon ure sawla ofslean. ac hi magon hi awlætan and gode laðettan. and gif we hi sylfwilles on andwerdum life ne gebetað. we sceolon neadunge on þam witniendlicum fyre hi geðrowian. (lines 269-72)

Offences like these cannot kill our souls, but they can defile them and make them hateful to God, and if we do not make amends for them of our own accord in this present life we must of necessity suffer for them in the punishing fire.

Some sins are simply too terrible to be purged by fire.[51] These are the deadly sins which mean instant dismissal to the place of eternal suffering (279-87).

Ælfric's interpretation of the fire from heaven is one of Augustine's selection of interpretations which are explored in the *Enchiridion* and in *De civitate Dei*.[52] The saving fire proved to be a fruitful image for Augustine, and for his successors who searched avidly through his works for hints concerning the reality of the purgatorial fire. According to an interpretation offered in *De civitate Dei*, the buildings will be constructed in precious or mean materials, according to the attachment of the builder to human relationships. The finest buildings represent the Christian lives of those who love Christ above all others, the poorest, those for whom carnal temptations are irresistible. Nevertheless, all those built on the foundation of Christ will be assured of survival, however drastically the superstructure is reduced (XXI.xxvi. 124-28). Ælfric's use of the metaphor broadens the meaning but the basic idea remains. Augustine's builder in precious materials, who loves the work of Christ above all things, is for Ælfric one who has faith, knowledge, sound doctrine and holy virtue. The builder in mean materials, who is exposed to the temptations of the flesh and enjoys carnal pleasures, is subject to sins which defile the soul and spoil its relationship with God.

The last fire is real, not metaphorical, inflicting intense pain (Godden XL. 272-75). It will carry out or complete all necessary purgations in one of the penal places ('witniendlice stowa', line 275); if this punishment has been adequate there will be no further suffering for

---

51. Gregory the Great adds a further category of builders: those who build in iron, bronze and lead. These represent mortal sins which cannot be destroyed by fire (*Dialogi* IV.xli.5. 39-42). This is derived from Origen (Le Goff, *Purgatory*, p. 57); however, for Origen the purgation of the sins symbolized by these metals is not impossible.

52. Referred to above on pages 229-30.

the cleansed to endure, and they will go forward in the company of those whose purity lends them immunity.

The fire is the signal, with the angel's trumpet blast, for the dead to rise, including those momentarily killed by the flames: this is so that in the general resurrection all may be said to rise from the dead (Pope XI. 296-304).[53] Ælfric takes time to explain the sort of resurrection to be expected, responding to the same curiosity as that already encountered by Augustine. In *De civitate Dei* Augustine discusses at some length the nature of resurrected bodies, finding it necessary to explain, for example, that cannibalized flesh reverts to its original owner (XXII.xx). He also considers the question of the physical mutilation suffered by the martyrs. He decides that although earthly eyes would find the bodies of the martyrs to be disfigured by torture, the heavenly glorification of their bodies will be such that their wounds will be seen by new eyes to be beautiful adornments (XXII.xix). In general, Augustine concludes that all bodies, whether damaged, misshapen or immature, will be granted the stature of an ideal, common state, in which their full potential will be perfectly realized:

> neque in eo quod aptum et congruum dies allaturi fuerant natura fraudetur, neque in eo quod aduersum atque contrarium dies attulerant natura turpetur, sed integretur quod nondum erat integrum, sicut instaurabitur quod fuerat uitiatum? (*Enchiridion* xxii.85. lines 18-22)

> Nature, then, would not be defrauded of anything fitting and harmonious which the passage of days had addded, but rather that which was not yet complete would be completed, just as that which had suffered blemish will be renewed.

God will take care that all will be beautiful and fitting (xxii.89. 77).

Ælfric picks up this theme with support from Julian of Toledo, who finds in Ephesians 4. 13 an indication that the ideal stature is that of Christ: all bodies will be resurrected with the age and stature of Christ at the time of his crucifixion, whether they died in old age or

---

53. Compare Thorpe XL. p. 616. 15-21; Godden XXXIX. 121-31; Pope XVIII. 75-85; in Augustine, *De civitate Dei* XX.xx. 29-65.

in childhood (Pope XI. 305-7).[54] This is not to say that individual characteristics will be distorted or lost, merely that all will realize their potential according to the model of Christ (308-11). The creator's power to raise the bodies of the dead, however they died, is undisputed:

> swaðeah se ælmihtiga God mæg hine eft aræran,
> se ðe ealle þas woruld geworhte of nahte. (lines 336-37)[55]

> nevertheless, the almighty God is able to raise them again, who created all this world out of nothing.

There is no need to enquire into the condition of the bodies of the damned: the question is irrelevant since they will be suffering permanent pain, disfigurement and dissolution, without ever being completely destroyed by the torture (326-31).[56] Ælfric's interest is in the resurrected bodies of those who will live, not of those who will suffer.

Resurrection marks a complete break with the past. All have gone through death, however momentarily, and all have passed through fire, some suffering in it, others experiencing a harmless light. From the moment of resurrection there can be no further cleansing. The risen bodies of the dead are now immutably classified:

> . . . se tima cymð þonne ealle þa deadan
> þe on byrgenum beoð gehyrað swutellice

---

54. Compare Thorpe V. p. 84. 23-25; XVI. p. 236. 23-31; Pope XII. 109-11. Augustine also discusses Paul's comments on the attainment of the stature and age of Christ, but he does not find it necessary to read them literally (*De civitate Dei* XXII.xviii). He thinks rather of the church, the body of Christ, attaining its fullness of stature.

55. Compare Thorpe XVI. p. 236. 8-22; Godden XXXVII. 118-22; XXXIX. 99-104; Pope II. 107-110; VII. 158-61; XI. 246; in Augustine, *In Ioannis Evangelium tractatus* XLIX.1. 5-8.

56. Compare Thorpe XVI. p. 236. 32-34; in Augustine, *Enchiridion* xxiii.92.

Godes Sunu stefne, and gað of heora byrgenum —

to lifes æriste, þa ðe god worhton;

to genyðerunge æriste, þa ðe yfel worhton. (Pope VI. lines 132-36)[57].

the time will come when all the dead who are in their graves will hear clearly the voice of the Son of God, and will come out of their graves, to the resurrection of life, those who did good, and to the resurrection of condemnation, those who did evil.

Resurrection signals the moment of resolution. In the interim between death and resurrection, revealed in Drihthelm's vision, the possibilities of being not-quite-evil or not-quite-perfect are still allowed; at resurrection, Drihthelm's four groups are reduced to two. Ælfric returns to the stark divisions of good and bad, life and condemnation.

III. JUDGEMENT

The angels who accompanied Christ in his triumphant return to earth now gather all his chosen together, purified and ready for the final judgement. The angels guide the elect to their place at God's right hand while the reprobate find their place on his left (Pope XI. 343-46). The moment of judgement brings revelation. For the first time the elect are able to see the Lord with the new eyes of heaven, a perfected vision still denied to the reprobate:

Þonne sitt se Hælend on his heofonlican ðrymsetle,

mihtig and wuldorful, and milde þam godum,

egeslic and andrysne þam earmum synfullum,

and ealle men geseoð swutollice þone Hælend

on þære menniscnysse, ac ne moton swaðeah

ða earman synfullan geseon his godcundnysse;

ða godan ana geseoð þa godcundnysse. (Pope XI. lines 347-53)

---

57. Compare Godden XXXIX. 128-31; Pope XIa. 164-70; Assmann I. 80-84; IV. 87-89.

Then the saviour will sit on his heavenly throne, mighty and full of glory, and gracious to the good, awesome and terrible to the wretched sinners, and all people will see the saviour clearly in the humanity, but yet the wretched sinners will not be able to see his divinity; the good alone will see the divinity.

The elect, fresh from the revivifying fire, have cleansed eyes that can look upon the glory of God and yet live. Those who are to depart to the place of fire have this privileged sight withheld from them. It is striking that the sight of Christ seated in majesty is a joy to the elect, for whom his appearance denotes mercy, while the reprobate see before them only the power of damnation, and are terrified. For them the terrible justice exacted by the visible humanity of Christ remains untempered by the gracious mercy of his invisible divinity.

Augustine also finds that new eyes are necessary for the perfect vision of heaven. Taking hold of the promise that the glass, through which only dark vision is possible, will be cast aside in heaven (I Corinthians 13. 12), he realizes that the resurrected eyes will attain a perfection comparable with all other aspects of the new body. His discussion of the new eyes of heaven indicates that he too thinks that the vision of spiritual things will be confined to the blessed (*De civitate Dei* XXII.xxix. 183-207).

Although the chosen and the reprobate are already in two distinct groups, ranged to the right and left of Christ, they are further subdivided. To the right are, first, the apostles and saints whose lives were of such quality that they merited the heavenly dwelling from the moment of their death:

þæt forme gefylc bið þe we her foresædon,
þe sittað mid þam Hælende on heora heahsettlum;
him ne bið na gedemed, ac hi demað mid Criste
eallum oðrum mannum mihtelice on wuldre. (Pope XI. lines 361-64).[58]

the first company is that of which we have already spoken, who sit on their thrones with the Saviour; they will not even be judged, but they, with Christ, will judge all other men, mightily in glory.

---

58. Compare Thorpe XXVII. p. 394. 20-25 and p. 394. 35-p. 396. 15; Pope IV. 126-28.

Also on Christ's right is a second group, composed of those who were faithful to God, who pleased him with good deeds and almsgiving; their merit is not such that they have escaped judgement, but in being judged they are separated from the wicked and invited to glory (365-70). The third group, already on the Judge's left, is made up of all those who knew about the Christian faith yet persisted in the sinful life. Ælfric concludes that the absence of any sign of God's grace at work in them consigns them to hell:

> hi ne dydon nan god Gode to wurðmynte,
> ne nane ælmessan, ac geendodon on synnum;
> him bið þonne gedemed mid þam deofle to helle. (lines 381-83)

> they did no good in honour of God, nor almsgiving, but ended in sins; they will then be condemned with the devil to hell.

With this group is a fourth, the heathen who remained in ignorance of the love of God, living instead according to the laws of the devil. These too will be punished eternally with the devil (384-90).[59]

These four groups differ from the four identified in the vision of Drihthelm. He saw sinners suffering in the abyss but made no distinction between the impenitent and the heathen; similarly, the two groups welcomed into heaven correspond to three separate communities in Drihthelm's vision: first, there were the saints who were already admitted to bliss; then close by the 'almost-perfect' waited in the flowery meadow; then in the place of fire a third group underwent purgation for small sins. The amalgamation of groups two and three indicates that purgation is completely effective in restoring souls to the state in which God will welcome them. Because of the purgatorial fire a shift occurs in the classification: the boundaries are redrawn.

The newly-rearranged groups, divided two and two, receive judgement from the Lord (Matthew 25. 31-46).[60] To the first two Christ addresses words of welcome: he makes it

---

59. The whole text is paralleled in Thorpe XXVII. p. 396. 17-33. Ælfric took the division into four from Julian, who apparently found it in Gregory (compare *Moralia in Iob* XXVI.xxvii.50-51).

60. The division of the sheep and the goats is also related in Godden VII. 130-73.

clear that the principal criterion in his judgement, in which divinity and humanity play equal roles, is the presence of even the smallest spark of divinely-inspired mercy in the exercise of human compassion. To those who responded to the poor with generosity, as though they were caring for Christ himself, he gives a share in his kingdom (Pope XI. 405-29). Ælfric explains that giving alms to the poor is giving to Christ himself:

swa oft swa ge ælmessan dydon anum lytlan ðearfan
of Cristenum mannum, þæt ge dydon Criste,
for ðan ðe Crist sylf is Cristenra manna heafod. (lines 431-33)

as often as you gave alms to one little poor man among Christian people, you did that for Christ, because Christ himself is the head of Christian people.

To those who failed to give he turns his terrifying, half-visible face, and condemns them for the absence of this spark of mercy (435-48). Their rejection of the poor amounts to a rejection of him:

Soð ic eow secge, me sylfum ge his forwyrndon
swa oft swa ge his forwyrndon anum of þisum lytlum. (lines 449-50)

Truly I say to you, you denied it to me as often as you denied it to one of these little ones.

Mercy and compassion are rewarded by a welcome into the presence of God; but their absence represents a complete denial of Christ. He sends the merciless away.

The judgement of Christ is essentially his examination of each person to see how much of the divine image is preserved. As God and man he possesses the perfect balance of divine and human qualities. He looks for a family resemblance, seeks out those he may call his brothers. Since the proper expression of the divine image in mankind is in loving service offered to God through the care of the poor, this is the distinguishing mark or family characteristic. Acceptance into the kingdom hinges upon recognition. Christ recognizes as brothers those who offered love in this way. The 'sheep' did not realize that they were serving Christ, but they offered their alms as a manifestation of the spark of divinity present

259

as image within them. The 'goats', who did not care for the poor, showed no sign of the spirit of mercy. As a result, they could not see the divinity of Christ when they came before him: they were denied this knowledge of kinship. These the God-man rejects as not belonging to him. In the words of the parable of the wedding banquet, they wear no wedding garment of love (Thorpe XXXV. p. 528. 26-31).[61]

Augustine also looks to almsgiving as the essential virtue sought by Christ at the moment of judgement. Almsgiving is so important, he says, that when they stand before Christ all the merit of the good will consist in their possession of this prime virtue, and all the faults of the reprobate will consist in their lack of it. Those who have been faithful in almsgiving will be welcomed as inheritors with the Son; the rest will be excluded from the kingdom, having no part in its nature. Lacking the right characteristics, they cannot be counted among its people (*Enchiridion* xviii.69. 80-85). Elsewhere he remarks that it is indeed astonishing that Christ's reason for sending sinners into everlasting fire is not that one was an adulterer, another a murderer or thief. It is because they did not give to the poor and hungry. Likewise those who are accepted are welcomed not because they have lived perfect lives, but because they bring with them the virtue of almsgiving which outweighs all the effects of sin. Indeed, since all have sinned, it is impossible that Christ should ask for sinlessness. What he does ask for is a sign of the divine image in the soul, with the incontrovertible evidence of love to reveal the presence of the gift or grace of God. To those in whom he finds this gift he offers no praise of their piety or good works, 'solas eleemosynas imputabit' ('He will impute alms only', *Sermo* LX.x.10).[62] In this reckoning it is merit to have fed Christ, sin to have rejected him (xi.11).

For Ælfric the division into four groups has clear implications for a final ranking of both elect and reprobate. Different degrees of bliss or punishment are allotted to each according to the merit of his life. A range of punishments is prepared to accommodate a variety of sinners, with those who sinned less suffering less, and those who sinned more being apportioned a greater punishment (Pope XI. 493-96).[63] In this scale of 'merit' those who

---

61. Augustine also speaks of the wedding garment of love, for example in *Sermo* XC.6.

62. Quoted in the translation by R.G. Macmullen. Cited again below on page 273.

63. Compare Thorpe XX. p. 294. 1-7; XXXVIII. p. 594. 24-28; in Augustine, *Enchiridion* xxiii.93. 133-37.

have added no sins to the sin of Adam suffer the lightest punishment (497-503). Nevertheless, the condemnation common to all is to suffer in the fire, and to be sensible of absolute separation from God and from the joys of the blessed (504-7).

This community of suffering is emphasized by Augustine in the *Enchiridion*. He concedes the possibility that sometimes certain of the damned will be relieved of their suffering to some degree, as a result of the mercy of God. Yet though their physical suffering might occasionally be alleviated, they will all suffer the permanent spiritual torture of complete separation from God, a torture unimaginably severe. This is the reality of eternal death: 'id est alienatio a uita dei' ('that is, their alienation from the life of God', *Enchiridion* xxix.113. line 73). Ælfric says this experience is intensely painful, but the reprobate will never be able to die and so bring to an end their suffering. They are condemned to a living death, in a terrible parody of life's self-reassertion. This is the second death, in which the soul is lost to eternal life,

> and ne swelt ðeah næfre on ðære hellican susle,
> ac bið æfre geedniwed to þam ecum witum. (Pope XI. lines 134-35)[64]

and yet never dies in the hellish torture, but is perpetually renewed to the eternal punishments.

As those who suffer in hell do not die, so the fire in which they burn is inextinguishable (Godden IV. 265-67).[65]

For Ælfric the damned are faceless: they have lost their individuality and even their humanity through their separation from God. He speaks of them without pity, describing how after the judgement the angels will bundle together the sinful reprobate and toss them into the fire like straw gathered by reapers, and in the fire they will burn amid the sounds of weeping (Pope V. 271-76).[66] Augustine is equally dispassionate in his account of the state of conflict

---

64. Compare Thorpe VIII. p. 132. 15-27; XV. p. 226. 22; XVI. p. 236. 32-34; Pope III. 153-55; VI. 157-59; XXI. 70-71; in Augustine, *Enchiridion* xxiii.92. 127-30.

65. Compare Pope XI. 475-77.

66. Compare Thorpe XXXV. p. 526. 18-27; Pope XVIII. 428-34. J.E Cross discusses this

eternally to be endured by the damned: conflict must necessarily be their lot, for it is the antithesis of peace, enjoyed by the blessed in another place. Theirs is the continually unresolved conflict of sense against pain, where pain maintains a constant assault on the senses. The senses are preserved in order that the body may continue to suffer:

> Ibi autem et dolor permanet ut affligat, et natura perdurat ut sentiat; quia utrumque ideo non deficit, ne poena deficiat. (*De civitate Dei* XIX.xxviii. lines 19-21)

> But in that other life, pain continues to torment, while nature lasts to feel the pain. Neither ceases to exist, lest punishment also should cease.

Both Ælfric and Augustine make the important point that the true torture suffered by the damned is their separation from God. Yet both conceive of this suffering primarily in terms of physical pain. Whilst they are prepared to enter imaginatively into the concept of new bodies for the blessed, wherein the proximity of the saved to God may most perfectly be enjoyed, their understanding of the nature of the damned body seems to be firmly rooted in earthly experience. They do not dwell upon the anguish an eternity of spiritual pain would mean, and they feel no pity for the sufferers.

Corresponding to the eternal suffering appointed for the evil is the eternal bliss to which the good and the newly-cleansed alike are welcomed after the last judgement. While the sinners burn, the justified shine in glory, like the sun (Pope V. 277-78).[67] Again, a hierarchical order may be discerned:

> hi beoð geendebyrde ælc be his geearnungum,
> and eac gewuldrode on þam micelan wurðscipe,
> be ðam ðe hi on life lufodon heora Scyppend. (Pope XI. lines 548-51)[68]

---

homiletic motif in 'Bundles for Burning — a theme in two of Ælfric's *Catholic Homilies* — with other sources', *Anglia*, 81 (1963), 335-46.

67. Compare Pope XI. 570-71.

68. Compare Thorpe XXXVIII. p. 594. 12-14; Godden IV. 299-305; V. 180-82; XXXVIII. 186-88.

they will be ranked each according to his merits, and also glorified in that great glory according to the way in which they loved their creator in life.

Despite the implications of such an order of merit, Ælfric is sure that no envy or enmity will be aroused; rather the blessed will live together in one fellowship ('on anre geðwærnysse', line 552) and perfect peace. Each one will be completely satisfied with the place allocated to him in heaven, desiring nothing more than is given. The dual meaning of 'gife', which embraces both 'gift' and 'grace', is here happily exploited:

and he ne gewilnað nanes wuldres furðor
ofer þæt ðe he hæfð þurh ðæs Hælendes gife. (lines 556-57)

and he will desire no additional glory beyond that which he has through the saviour's gift.

'Þurh ðæs Hælendes gife' may equally be translated, 'through the saviour's grace.' The blessed have been given their eternal bliss by God because of the grace which was found to be active in them. Now their reward is also grace: the glory apportioned to them is in every case a reward for grace.

At the close of *De civitate Dei* Augustine looks forward to the perfection of the saints' bliss as they attain the fulfilment of all their desires. The earthly soul desires to know, to love and to praise God; all these are promised to the saints in heaven, whose knowledge, love and praise will be perfect and inviolable:

Ipse finis erit desideriorum nostrorum, qui sine fine uidebitur, sine fastidio amabitur, sine fatigatione laudabitur. Hoc munus, hic affectus, hic actus profecto erit omnibus, sicut ipsa uita aeterna, communis. (XXII.xxx. lines 33-36)

He will be the goal of all our longings; and we shall see him for ever; we shall love him without satiety; we shall praise him without wearying. This will be the duty, the delight, the activity of all, shared by all who share the life of eternity.

Certainly there will be degrees of honour and glory awarded to the varied ranks of the servants of God. Yet as the angels and archangels now co-exist in perfect peace without envy, so then will all live together without any disruption of the perfect felicity which is the reward of each individual and of the entire heavenly community. For Augustine too this additional benefit is a gift: 'Sic itaque habebit donum alius alio minus, ut hoc quoque donum habeat, ne uelit amplius' ('And so although one will have a gift inferior to another, he will have also the compensatory gift of contentment with what he has', lines 46-48).

Ælfric describes how the energies of all in this perfect bliss are directed towards the praise of God: nothing distracts the saints from their perfect occupation, for they feel no want or need of anything. Their love for God is complete, and it suffers no diminution or interruption: Ælfric describes it as 'buton toforlætennysse' ('without intermission', Pope XI. line 562). The offering of praise is tireless as it is endless, 'butan werignysse' ('without weariness', line 563).[69] In these works of love and praise they are entirely sustained by the person of Christ:

> He is heora rice, and lif, and wurðmynt,
> heora hæl and wuldor, sibb and genihtsumnys. (lines 566-67)

> He is their kingdom, and life, and honour, their salvation and glory, peace and abundance.

For the saints, Christ is not simply the source of these blessings, he is their realization. The saints dwell in the very life of Christ, having his being as theirs, not merely enjoying proximity to his glory. They have this eternally, with no shadow or darkness diminishing the perfect illumination of Christ's person, for in heaven life is experienced as one eternal day ('an ece dæg', line 568).[70] Ælfric, echoing Paul (I Corinthians 2. 9), concedes that the heavenly joys are unimaginable, exceeding all that the mind could possibly desire:

---

69. Compare Thorpe XIX. p. 270. 21-23, 28-31 and p. 272. 1-3; XXI. p. 296. 29-34; Godden V. 284-87; VI. 50-52; XXXVIII. 95-99.

70. Compare Thorpe XXXII. p. 490. 17-23; Skeat XII. 80-91; in Augustine, *De civitate Dei* XXII.xxx. 141-48.

... þe mannes eage ne mihte geseon,
ne eare gehyran, ne heorte asmeagan,
þa micclan mærðe þe se mildheorta Crist
þam eallum behet þe hine lufiað. (Pope XV. lines 115-18)[71]

the eye of man might not see, nor ear hear, nor heart conceive, the great bliss which the merciful Christ promises to all those who love him.

Especially important is the perfection for which the saints longed during the period after death and before the general resurrection, when they lacked bodily communion in the soul's joys. This is now accorded to them. Dwelling with the saviour the blessed now reign in heaven, glorified in both body and soul, freed from all the suffering associated with earthly existence. They also rest in complete assurance that this bliss cannot be taken from them: after the final judgement the populations of heaven and hell are eternally fixed (Pope XI. 214-15).[72] In this secure freedom the perfection of humanity promised by the person of Christ is realized in all. By his ascension to heaven as Son of God and Son of Man he draws the saints up after him, his humanity opening to them the fullness of divine life and giving them a share in his kingdom. Thus they are raised to the apotheosis of human potential and then lifted even higher by their association with the one who perfectly equates human and divine in himself. Ælfric's sermon closes with the affirmation of these joys and with a doxology which grounds them in the worship of the Trinitarian God:

and hi be twyfealdan beoð þonne gewuldrode
on sawle and on lichaman, and hi scinað æfre
swa beorhte swa sunne on heora Fæder rice.
Se ðe leofað and rixað mid his leofan Suna

---

71. Compare Thorpe XIV. p. 218. 23-29; XVI. p. 238. 3-7; XXI. p. 296. 31-34; Godden XXXVIII. 92-94; XL. 213-15; Pope XVIII. 439; Skeat XII. 92-96.

72. Compare Pope XXI. 66-71; in Augustine, *Enchiridion* xxix.111. 33.

and ðam Halgan Gaste, on anre godcundnysse,

an ælmihtig God, a butan ende, AMEN. (lines 569-74)[73]

and they will then be doubly glorified, in soul and in body, and they will shine for ever as brightly as the sun in the kingdom of their Father, who lives and reigns with his beloved Son and the Holy Spirit, in one godhead, one almighty God, for ever, amen.

Ælfric's teaching on death and judgement is strongly influenced by the teachers who succeeded Augustine. Of particular importance are Bede's account of Drihthelm's vision of the purgatorial places and Julian's narrative of the events that presage the end of the world. Gregory's *Dialogi* must also carry much of the responsibility for the confidence Ælfric places in some accounts of visions which supplement biblical prophecy with imaginative detail. Yet his teaching has an Augustinian foundation, exemplified by the *Enchiridion* and the closing books of *De civitate Dei*. These works, however, at least to some extent, acknowledge that nothing much can be known about the future life: as a result *De civitate Dei* offers an almost overwhelming quantity of interpretations and ideas. Later teachers adopted these so readily that Augustine's exploratory thinking became definitive: suggestions acquired the secure status of doctrine.

This security is what Ælfric requires. He discerns the need for clear orthodox teaching, the firm foundation on which faith may confidently be built. Good teaching is an urgent requirement whether or not the end of the world is close at hand: Ælfric's sense of responsibility for each person means that any delay is unacceptable. If the signs of the world's ageing are to be interpreted as indicating that the last days are approaching, this urgency is the greater because of Ælfric's fears of apostasy. He is to be commended for his rejection of uncertain sources, such as the highly detailed *vita* of Antichrist available in Adso's writings.[74] He refers to authoritative sources throughout. His teaching on eschatology can properly claim to be Augustinian, for although sometimes great distances have been crossed in the intervening centuries, the signposts to the teaching Ælfric adopts are all there in Augustine.

---

73. Compare Godden XL. 313-17; Pope II. 109-14; XI. 246-56; XII. 113-15; XVIII. 422-23 and 435-39.

74. See Emmerson, *Antichrist*, p. 77.

6

CONCLUSION

It was never Ælfric's intention to write a new theology. Primarily a teacher, his purpose was to liberate the souls entrusted to him from the dangers of ignorance, and in so doing, to ensure that he had discharged the duty bestowed upon him as a priest. Ælfric considered himself merely a translator, but he was much more than that, shaping the received doctrines of the church into a manageable body of teaching which could readily be believed, understood and learnt. To do this required both an intelligent reading of the texts and a compassion for people born of a sense of their worth as individuals. The intelligent reading included an overarching, guiding theology, which I suggest may be identified as the Augustinian doctrine of grace.

Within this doctrine it is possible to make sense of the relationship of God and mankind, and especially the redemption achieved by the God-man on behalf of his spiritual brothers and sisters; it also allows a coherent doctrine of the church, within which the sacraments are all part of a continuous building up of the community and the individual, that recreation through the Son which mirrors the initial process of creation. In particular, it allows an understanding of the last things in which the emphasis is placed on the realization of the divine image in the human soul, where enough of the image is preserved for the gestures of mercy to demonstrate the soul's 'family likeness' to the merciful God. Ælfric's compassion for people not only compels him to provide for their education, but also insists that for each one a hope of finding that family likeness is maintained to the end. Simultaneously he strives, according to his own sense of responsibility, to mediate the useful learning of books, and he rests in the merciful provision of grace appropriate to each one's needs.

A comparison of Ælfric's teaching with Augustine's reveals that such an overarching theology guides him just as it guided Augustine. Whether or not Augustine is Ælfric's direct source (in terms of the work before him, or remembered by him, as he writes), Augustine's theology is his primary source, and this applies even in the doctrines where Ælfric has at his disposal more detail than Augustine left behind.

In his doctrine of God he is a faithful transmitter of Augustine's understanding of the trinity and unity of God, appreciating especially the place of love within the Godhead as its unifying and sustaining force. He teaches these things simply and directly, using Augustine's analogies as a means of building up the listener's comprehension to the point where the analogy of the mind is intelligible and valuable. The bright vision of realized faith is effectively conveyed. So, too, is the sense which is so strong in Augustine of the mystery of divinity: not even the wisest can penetrate it to the full, and, whilst every Christian may learn something of it here and now merely by looking at the divine image in human creation, a complete understanding of the mystery must await the resurrection. Looking forward to that fulfilment, Ælfric is very conscious that the signs are pointing clearly to the end of the world. For Augustine, the last days are still in the future even if the reign of the saints has already begun. For Ælfric, the last days are the present time, a fact proved by the accomplishment of various prophecies but manifested most of all in the sinful lives of men and women. In his treatment of the last days, Ælfric relies to a very large extent on the colourful account provided by Julian of Toledo. But Julian's work does not contradict Augustine, and the foundation ideas from *De civitate Dei* and the *Enchiridion* are strongly present. They are recognizable amongst the mass of detail which has accrued.

In Ælfric's teaching on the last days, Augustine's ideas are extrapolated from the point at which he left them to accommodate the needs of another time and place. In a different way Augustine provided the formative doctrines of church and sacrament for later centuries. Ælfric's treatment of the sacramental life of the church shows him to be the inheritor of those doctrines. The church's understanding of each of the three sacramental bases of the faith, baptism, eucharist and penance, owes something, sometimes a great deal indeed, to the advancement in Augustine's own understanding brought about by his encounters with schismatics. Each of these signs is treated differently by Ælfric, and his reliance on Augustinian doctrine varies accordingly.

In the case of baptism, Ælfric has no political need, as Augustine had, to argue for only one baptism. He has no converts from schismatic churches to deal with. He makes the point that baptism must not be repeated apparently because this is something which must be set down about baptism, rather like a law which continues on the statute books long after the necessity for it has disappeared. But the fact that baptism need not be repeated is rooted in an important doctrinal point, for it reflects Augustine's discovery that the power of the sacrament resides exclusively in God who bestows it, not the minister who mediates it. Also relevant to Ælfric's account of baptism is Augustine's general discussion of the nature of the sacramental sign, in which he discovers that the outward action or symbol is of value only in that it points the Christian to the spiritual truth contained. The sign makes use of outward symbol to guide the mind to levels of reality which would otherwise be much more inaccessible.

In this respect the elements of the eucharist fulfil the same function as the water of baptism, operating as the tangible and visible medium of spiritual reality. As in the case of baptism, a verbal formula serves as an additional 'outward symbol', for neither Augustine nor Ælfric would argue that the words of blessing themselves have an intrinsic spiritual efficacy: to do so would suggest that these formulae had magical powers. All that the words do is to represent the presence and power of God. Uniquely, in the case of the eucharist, the words of consecration also have the function of calling attention to the moment when Christ's body and blood are made mysteriously present. The priest's words signify the moment when the sign has attained its full sacramental potential. Ælfric's teaching on the eucharist is so deeply imbued with this sense of the power of the mystery that again he may be said to mediate Augustine's own understanding of the sacrament, even though his access to it is primarily through Ratramnus' ninth-century treatise. That Ælfric recognizes Augustine's inspired identification of the church and the sacrament in the body of Christ confirms his ability to perceive the coinherence of different levels of reality in the eucharist. Here, again, as with Ælfric's teaching on death and judgement, Augustinian doctrine mediated by others is supported and enhanced by direct reference to Augustine himself.

Penance works in conjunction with baptism and the eucharist to cleanse and to sanctify. As it does in the mysteries of baptism and the eucharist, outward action in penance guides the Christian towards spiritual growth. Without the spiritual import of the sign, water, bread and wine are of no more benefit to the believer than ordinary washing or an ordinary meal. Similarly, without the spiritual dimension of co-operation with grace, resulting in conversion and growth, the outward discipline of the penitential life is of minimal benefit. Most striking in Ælfric's teaching about penance is the sense that it is not so much a Lenten activity, a medicine against the disordering effects of sin, or a cancellation of debts, but it is rather a way of life which involves positive direction and conversion. In this respect Ælfric draws again on Augustine's general understanding of signs, and also refers directly to specific points made by Augustine in his sermons, especially his emphasis upon almsgiving as the essential characteristic which is found to identify the true inhabitants of the kingdom of heaven. Both teachers conclude that no-one can be welcomed into the kingdom without the virtue of almsgiving, regardless of other evidence of piety or goodness, and that however bad the sinner, the only sin that will be counted on the day of judgement will be the omission of almsgiving.

For Ælfric, the Christian life is indistinguishable from the proper exercise of penitential discipline: his emphasis on living a life which is pleasing to God is a theme to which he has constant recourse in his homilies. No-one, however, is expected to live such a life without the assistance of grace. Indeed, the necessity of grace for every good work is clearly asserted by Ælfric, echoing this most fundamental of Augustine's teachings. Thus in emphasizing the propriety of the life of mercy (manifested in almsgiving and forgiveness), Ælfric maintains a truly Augustinian stance whilst approaching the question of Christian *mores* in a pragmatic and helpful way. Nothing Ælfric demands of Christians is impossible, because sufficient grace has already been provided by God. All that they have to do, whether consciously or unconsciously, is to appropriate that grace for themselves, co-operating with grace by loving all whom the church identifies as brothers.

It is curious that in his theology of grace Ælfric is at once most Augustinian and most independent. He has made this doctrine his own. It is impossible not to be struck by the compassion inherent in Ælfric's flexible account of grace. Energetically rehearsing Augustine's pronouncements, right down to a momentary stringency to which only the strictest Augustinian of the ninth century would have subscribed, he also allows a gentler view to come forward. In collocating predestination and mercy in the loving mind of God he permits all of Augustine's emphasis upon justice to stand, whilst at the same time he insists that mercy is unquantifiable, unfathomable. The angel who speaks for the disputed soul, standing his ground against the devil, is right:

Ne tæle ge to dyrstelice. for ðan ðe ge nyton godes digelan domas . . . Æfre bið godes mildheortnys mid þam men. þa hwile ðe ðær bið gewened ænig behreowsung . . . Nyte ge ða micclan deopnysse godes gerynu. weald þeah him beo alyfed gyt behreowsung. (Godden XX. lines 127-33)

Do not make your accusations too presumptuously, for you do not know God's secret judgements . . . God's mercy is always upon the man while repentance may still be looked for . . . You do not know the great profundity of God's mysteries: perhaps repentance will yet be granted to him.

Conclusion

In this response to a not impertinent call for justice, Ælfric places the emphasis upon mercy: this is the basis of every relationship with God until mercy is rejected. The only obstacles to salvation are the ones erected by mankind. God places no such difficulties in the way.

In his account of grace, Ælfric is very close indeed to Augustine. At the same time he seeks also to broaden the parameters of salvation according to Augustine's own perception of the love of God, but in a way that Augustine himself is not completely able to see. Ready though he may be to ascribe to God the love which is beyond human comprehension, Augustine is apparently not ready to allow that this love, rather than divine justice, might be understood to be the prime mover in salvation. His assessment of predestination is characterized by a logic pursued to its end, but that pursuit is itself very much confined by the limits of human understanding. Ælfric, on the other hand, with his simple but strong recognition that prescience differs from predestination, is free to choose a different emphasis, which reveals that love is a stronger force than judgement. His understanding of predestination allows that 'godes digelan domas' are judgements in which mercy is active.

This independence of Ælfric is the more commendable when it is seen how closely he models his teaching on Augustine; indeed he never avoids even the harshest of Augustine's doctrines. Augustine's teaching of a predestination to punishment finds a place in Ælfric's most condemning pronouncement. Unlike Augustine, however, Ælfric thinks that this predestination applies uniquely to the Jews: they, of all people, have most conclusively condemned themselves. Of their own volition and determination, they have excluded themselves from the love of God. Their sin was in their collusion with the devil in engineering the death of Jesus. One might even say that their action, sheer rejection as it was, constituted the first 'sin against the Holy Spirit', for in their proud insistence that the sin was one they wanted to bear for themselves (and even transfer to their children), the Jews were rejecting the forgiveness available from God through the Spirit. They therefore placed themselves in the category of those who could not be saved, because they refused to receive the salvation offered to them.

The rejection of God's Son by the Jews is a factor which must have been seen by God in his prescience, in which all time and all events are eternally present, but not predestined by him, according to Ælfric's understanding of the difference between the two. Just as God knew the gracious quality of Jacob and Esau's love and service before they lived, and arranged his response accordingly, so too must the action of the Jews have been accommodated in God's plan for mankind as he 'meditated' upon the solution to the problem of sin.

271

So it is that Ælfric's statement about the condemnation of the Jews may properly be reconciled with his more generous view of God's desire for salvation. His account of God includes the idea that God responds in love to the disaster of sin. The 'meditating' God, therefore, is not one who can be taken by surprise or forced to change his plans, but a God who freely places the constraints of love upon his actions. So also might love be expected to define God's approach to judgement.

This interpretation is most clearly carried through in Ælfric's account of the last judgement and the division of the saved and the lost. Ælfric fits his teaching into the context outlined by Julian of Toledo, using the broad divisions already established by Bede in the Vision of Drihthelm. But to find the single most important factor in ascertaining the final destination of any one soul, he turns again to Augustine. Augustine's quite startling assertion about the supreme importance of almsgiving effectively confirms that Ælfric's own emphasis upon mercy is the proper one.

Augustine's anxiety about the proper recognition of the justice of God is such that he condemns the 'misericordes', those who search for possible loopholes in the rigid justice ascribed to God (by Augustine), as people who are merely looking for salves for their own consciences. These are Christians who want an easy life: the realities of God's judgement do not fit with their own requirements. The 'misericordes', in Augustine's view, all have in common the mistaken idea that God is not serious when he threatens judgement. Augustine is surely right to find in fear and laziness the source of their protestations. But at the same time he may be wrong to confine his interpretation of divine judgement to the little room bounded by imperfect human perceptions of perfect judgement. The 'misericordes' apparently want God to relax the rules (as those rules were codified by Augustine). Ælfric rejects this idea: his merciful God is not one who allows people to escape without doing their duty, or who affords entrance into his heaven to those who have not merited its reward. It is merely that by the time of the last judgement all of God's mercy and all of his justice are focused on the single issue of almsgiving.

It is in the context of a sermon, rather than a treatise, that Augustine is most inspired by the idea that almsgiving, the practical application of mercy, sums up the Christian response to God. He echoes the expected surprise around him when he admits how incredible it sounds that, in the end, the sinner will not be condemned because he has committed this sin or another, but that he will be classified as 'sinner' because the blessing of almsgiving is missing. Similarly, it sounds too simple to be true that all the saintly qualities of the rest are effectively meaningless. But in fact, this is the case. Only almsgiving counts: 'illis quos coronaturus est, solas eleemosynas imputabit' ('to those whom He is about to crown, He will impute alms only', *Sermo* LX.x.10).[1] Indeed the crown is to be bestowed not because one has remained sinless, and so escaped punishment, but because almsgiving has effected the necessary cleansing:

> Non ergo itis in regnum, quia non peccastis: sed quia vestra peccata eleemosynis redemistis. (x.10)

> Ye shall therefore go into the kingdom, not because ye have not sinned, but because ye have redeemed your sins by alms.

These assurances from Augustine are entirely in keeping with Ælfric's expectations of salvation. Ready to ascribe to God the willingness to save all men, Ælfric makes the qualification for mercy not predestination, as Augustine in his works on grace might have suggested was the case, but almsgiving, as Augustine concedes in this sermon. These are essentially the same doctrine, seen from different points of view, for Augustine teaches that every soul predestined to grace is provided with everything necessary for the service of God, which must include almsgiving. Ælfric's preferred stress is on almsgiving itself, and he gives the impression that it is within everyone's God-given capacity to offer this service to God whom he encounters in the person of the poor man. Those who fail to offer even the smallest kindness to Christ in this guise have only themselves to blame, and their condemnation is just and righteous, as the salvation of the redeemed is merciful.

Such an understanding of the nature of grace emphasizes that each Christian wins mercy as a prize for exercising mercy. Thus, Christians are busy about their own salvation as they do good for others. In exhorting the people to such business Ælfric is never asking them to struggle by themselves, but always to recognize the involvement of grace at every stage. He also suggests, however, that because grace is necessarily involved, then even Christians who do not understand grace and are not conscious of appropriating it to themselves are actually doing so all the time they are busy with good works. Whether or not they notice the Spirit's gracious bestowal of gifts is irrelevant: they are nevertheless receiving those gifts by actively

---

1. Quoted in the translation by R.G. Macmullen.

making use of them. Wearing the garment of love, therefore, they are welcomed to God's banquet and recognized as friends, even if they had not realized that they had been invited to the wedding.

Ælfric and Augustine both see the value of good works as the active expression of devotion to God, but both also suggest that devotion itself may be generated by such active service. Simply wearing the garment of love, the Christian is brought by the means of grace into the presence of God himself. Ælfric shows how the garment fits everyone who chooses to wear it: the offering of love is one that all can make, however poor. He says that such a gift is worth incomparably more than earthly treasures: it is 'se goda willa, þa ða eorðlican sceattas unwiðmetenlice oferstihð' ('the good will, which immeasurably exceeds earthly treasures', Thorpe XXXVIII. p. 584. lines 3-4). The good will which all can bring is manifested in love for friends and enemies and in helping any neighbour. Such practical realizations of love are a spiritual offering of the highest order:

> Hwæt is ænig lac wið þisum willan, ðonne seo sawul hi sylfe Gode geoffrað on weofode hire heortan? Be ðisum cwæð se sealm-scop, 'In me sunt, Deus, uota tua, quæ reddam laudationes tibi:' 'God Ælmihtig, on me synd þine behat, þa ic ðe forgylde ðurh herunga.' (lines 10-14)

> What is any offering by comparison with this will, when the soul offers itself to God on the altar of its heart? Of this the Psalmist said . . . 'Almighty God, your promises are within me, which I will repay to you in praise.'

Ælfric's use of this verse in illustration of his point makes the 'sacramental' action of almsgiving, that is, giving in love, a gift of the same kind as the spiritual offering of the self which characterizes the eucharist. In that sacrament, the sacrifice is the sign of the offering made on the altar of the heart, and is purely an offering of what has already been received. In Ælfric's interpretation of the Psalmist's words, the good will's works of love are equated with 'the promises' of God: the will offers back to God the things already possessed according to his promises. At the same time, the psalm verse is also made to equate the good actions of the will with praises: so the gift of good works, however humble or seemingly uninspired, is itself a sacrifice of praise to God.

Not all of Ælfric's listeners would have thought in this way about such a verse and examined it in relation to their own faith, linking penance in this spiritual interpretation with the eucharist. Here Ælfric speaks in a way which is intelligible to all on a certain level, but which points to the depths of meaning that may be found in the psalm verse. Any listener could hear in the verse cited a confirmation of what Ælfric had been saying; the more thoughtful listener might be taken beyond the use of these words as a proof-text and made to think both about the spiritual reality of the Christian's gift to God and of the prevenient grace present in the 'promises' which make that gift possible.

Ælfric's doctrine of grace informs and shapes his whole response to the relationship of God and mankind. It is fitting that he should follow the Doctor of Grace with this energy, since he had absorbed so much of what Augustine taught in other spheres. In receiving Augustine's teaching on grace he is able to add to it truths learned from him about love, that force which is at the heart of the Godhead. Love is manifested, in those with whom God dwells, in almsgiving. This, of all things the most pleasing to God, is drawn from grace, and is at the last rewarded by grace.

BIBLIOGRAPHY

ABBREVIATIONS

ACW   Ancient Christian Writers: The Works of the Fathers in Translation, edited by J. Quasten and J.C. Plumpe (1946-)

CCCM   Corpus Christianorum Continuatio Medievalis (Turnhout, 1966-)

CCSL   Corpus Christianorum Series Latina (Turnhout, 1953-)

CSEL   Corpus Scriptorum Ecclesiasticorum Latinorum (Vienna, 1866-)

EETS   Early English Text Society (Original Series unless Supplementary Series is specified)

FC   The Fathers of the Church: A New Translation, edited by L. Schopp, D.J. Deferrari and others (Washington, 1947-)

LF   A Library of the Fathers, Translated by Members of the English Church, edited by Marcus Dods (Oxford, 1840-57)

PL   *Patrologia Latina*, edited by J.-P. Migne (Paris, 1841-64)

Thorpe   See below, Primary Sources: II. Old English Works

WAA   *The Works of Aurelius Augustine, Bishop of Hippo: a new translation*, edited by Marcus Dods (Edinburgh, 1871-76)

PRIMARY SOURCES: I. LATIN WORKS

Ambrose, *De fide ad Gratianum Augustum*, CSEL, 78, edited by O. Faller (Vienna, 1962)

— *De mysteriis*, CSEL, 73, edited by O. Faller (Vienna, 1955)

— *De sacramentis*, CSEL, 73, edited by O. Faller (Vienna, 1955)

Anselm, *Cur Deus Homo*, in *Sancti Anselmi Opera Omnia*, edited by F.S. Schmitt, 2 vols (Stuttgart, 1968), I

Augustine, *Confessiones*, CCSL, 27, edited by L. Verheijen (Turnhout, 1981); translated by Vernon J. Bourke, FC, 21 (Washington, 1953)

— *Contra Iulianum (opus imperfectum)*, Books I-III, CSEL, 85.1, edited by Michaela Zelzer (Vienna, 1974); remainder in PL, 45

— *Contra litteras Petiliani*, CSEL, 52, edited by M. Petschenig (Vienna, 1909); translated by J.R. King, WAA, 3 (Edinburgh, 1872)

— *De anima et ejus origine*, CSEL, 60, edited by C.F. Urba and J. Zycha (Vienna 1913); translated by Peter Holmes, WAA, 12 (Edinburgh, 1885)

— *De baptismo contra Donatistas*, CSEL, 51, edited by M. Petschenig (Vienna, 1908); translated by J.R. King, WAA, 3 (Edinburgh, 1872)

— *De catechizandis rudibus*, CCSL, 46, edited by I.B. Bauer (Turnhout, 1969)

— *De civitate Dei*, CCSL, 47-48, edited by B. Dombart and A. Kalb, 2 vols (Turnhout, 1955); translated by Henry Bettenson, Penguin Classics (Harmondsworth, 1984)

— *De correptione et gratia*, PL, 44; translated by John Courtney Murray, FC, 2, second edition (Washington, 1950)

— *De diversis quaestionibus ad Simplicianum*, CCSL, 44-44A, edited by A. Mutzenbecher, 2 vols (Turnhout, 1970-75)

— *De doctrina Christiana*, CCSL, 32, edited by J. Martin (Turnhout, 1962); translated by John J. Gavigan, FC, 2, second edition (Washington, 1950)

— *De dono perseverantiae*, in The *'De dono perseverantiae' of St Augustine: a translation with an introduction and a commentary*, Catholic University of America Patristic Studies 91, edited by Sister M.A. Lesousky (Washington, 1956)

— *De fide et symbolo*, CSEL, 41, edited by J. Zycha (Vienna, 1900)

— *De Genesi ad litteram*, in *La Genèse au sens litteral*, Bibliothèque augustinienne, Oeuvres de St Augustin, 48-49, translated with an introduction and notes by P. Agaësse and A. Solignac, 2 vols (Paris, 1972, 1970); translated by John Hammond Taylor, ACW, 41, 2 vols (New York and Ramsey, 1982)

— *De gratia Christi et de peccato originali*, CSEL, 42, edited by C.F. Urba and J. Zycha (Vienna, 1902); translated by Peter Holmes, WAA, 12 (Edinburgh, 1885)

— *De gratia et libero arbitrio*, PL, 44; translated by Robert P. Russell, FC, 59 (Washington, 1968);

— *De libero arbitrio*, CSEL, 74, edited by W.M. Green (Vienna, 1956)

— *De natura et gratia*, CSEL, 60, edited by C.F. Urba and J. Zycha (Vienna, 1913); translated by Peter Holmes, WAA, 4 (Edinburgh, 1872)

— *De nuptiis et concupiscentia*, CSEL, 42, edited by C.F. Urba and J. Zycha (Vienna, 1902); translated by Peter Holmes, WAA, 12 (Edinburgh, 1885)

— *De ordine*, CSEL, 63, edited by P. Knoll (Vienna, 1922)

— *De peccatorum meritis et remissione*, CSEL, 60, edited by C.F. Urba and J. Zycha (Vienna, 1913)

— *De praedestinatione sanctorum*, PL, 44; translated by Peter Holmes and Robert Ernest Wallis, WAA, 15 (Edinburgh, 1876)

— *De sancta virginitate*, CSEL, 41, edited by J. Zycha (Vienna, 1900)

— *De trinitate*, CCSL, 50-50A, edited by W.J. Mountain, 2 vols (Turnhout, 1968); translated by Stephen McKenna, FC, 45 (Washington, 1963)

— *De vera religione*, CSEL, 77, edited by W.M. Green (Vienna, 1961)

— *Enchiridion*, CCSL, 46, edited by E. Evans (Turnhout, 1969); translated by Bernard M. Peebles, FC, 2, second edition (Washington, 1950)

— *Enarrationes in Psalmos*, CCSL, 38-40, edited by D.E. Dekkers and J. Fraipont, 3 vols (Turnhout, 1956)

— *Epistulae*, CSEL, 34, 44, 45, 57, 58, edited by A. Goldbacher, 5 vols (Vienna, 1895-1923); translated by Sister Wilfred Parsons (Letters 165-203), FC, 30 (Washington, 1955)

— *In Ioannis Evangelium tractatus*, CCSL, 26, edited by D.R. Willems (Turnhout, 1954); translated by John W. Rettig, Tractates 1-10, FC, 78 (Washington, 1988), Tractates 11-29, FC, 79 (Washington, 1988); and by James Innes, Tractates 38-124, WAA, 11 (Edinburgh, 1874)

— *In Epistolam Ioannis ad Parthos tractatus*, PL, 35

— *Sermones*, CCSL, 41 (Sermons 1-50), edited by C. Lambot (Turnhout, 1961); remainder in PL, 38-39; translated by Sister Mary Sarah Muldowney (selection) FC, 38; by R.G. Macmullen (51-183), LF, 16, 2 vols (Oxford, 1843-44); and by Quincy Howe, Jr., *Selected Sermons of Saint Augustine* (London, 1967)

Bede, *Historia ecclesiastica gentis anglorum*, edited by Charles Plummer (1896; reprinted Oxford, 1966)

— *Historia ecclesiastica gentis anglorum*, edited and translated by B. Colgrave and R.A.B. Mynors (Oxford, 1969)

— *Homeliarum Evangelii*, CCSL, 122, edited by D. Hurst (Turnhout, 1955)

— *In Lucae Evangelium expositio*, CCSL, 120, edited by D. Hurst (Turnhout, 1960)

Cæsarius of Arles, *Sermones*, CCSL, 103-104, edited by G. Morin, 2 vols (Turnhout, 1953)

Gregory the Great, *Dialogi*, book IV, Sources chrétiennes, 265, edited by A. de Vogüé (Paris, 1980); translated by Odo John Zimmerman, FC, 39 (Washington, 1959)

— *Homeliæ in Evangelia*, PL, 76

— *Moralia in Iob*, CCSL, 143, 143A and 143B, edited by M. Adriaen, 3 vols (Turnhout, 1979-85)

Julian of Toledo, *Prognosticon futuri sæculi*, PL, 96

Ratramnus of Corbie, *De corpore et sanguine domini: texte original et notice bibliographique*, edited by J.N. Bakhuizen van den Brink, second edition, Verhandelingen der Koninklijke Nederlandse Akademie van Wetenschappen, afd. Letterkunde, Niewe Reeks, 87, (Amsterdam, 1974)

Paschasius Radbertus, *De corpore et sanguine domini*, CCCM, 16, edited by Bede Paulus (Turnhout, 1969)

— (=Pseudo-Jerome), *Epistola ad Paulam et Eustochium*, PL, 120

Thomas Aquinas, *Summa Theologiæ*, 60 vols: Volume 58, 3a. 73-78, edited and translated by William Barden (London, 1965) and Volume 59, 3a. 79-83, edited and translated by Thomas Gilby (London, 1975)

— *Summa Theologiæ: a concise translation*, edited by Timothy McDermott (London, 1989)

PRIMARY SOURCES: II. OLD ENGLISH WORKS

Assmann, Bruno, editor, *Angelsächsische Homilien und Heiligenleben*, Bibliothek der angelsächsischen Prosa, 3 (Kassel, 1889), reprinted, with a supplementary introduction by Peter Clemoes (Darmstadt, 1964)

Belfour, A.O., editor, *Twelfth Century Homilies in MS Bodley 343*, EETS, 137 (London, 1909)

Bethurum, Dorothy, editor, *The Homilies of Wulfstan*, corrected reprint of 1957 edition (Oxford, 1971)

Crawford, S.J., editor, *Ælfric's Exameron Anglice; or, The Old English Hexameron*, Bibliothek der angelsächsischen Prosa, 10 (Hamburg, 1921)

Fehr, B., editor, *Die Hirtenbriefe Ælfrics in altenglischer und lateinischer Fassung*, Bibliothek der angelsächsischen Prosa, 9 (Hamburg, 1914)

Förster, Max, editor, *Die Vercelli-homilien zum ersten Male herausgegeben: I: Halfte* (Homilies I-VIII), Bibliothek der angelsächsischen Prosa, 12 (Hamburg, 1932)

Godden, Malcolm R., editor, *Ælfric's Catholic Homilies, the Second Series: Text*, EETS, Supplementary Series, 5 (London, 1979)

279

MacLean, G., editor, 'Ælfric's version of *Alcuini Interrogationes Sigeuulfi in Genesin*', *Anglia*, 6 (introduction) (1883), 425-73; *Anglia*, 7 (text) (1884), 1-59

Morris, R., editor, *Old English Homilies and Homiletic Treatises . . . of the Twelfth and Thirteenth Centuries*, EETS, 29, 34, 2 vols (London, 1868)

— editor, *The Blickling Homilies of the Tenth Century*, EETS, 58, 63, 73, 3 vols (London, 1874-80)

Napier, A.S., editor, 'De Infantibus', *Anglia*, 10 (1888), 154-55

Pope, J.C., editor, *The Homilies of Ælfric: a supplementary collection, being twenty-one full homilies of his middle and later career for the most part not previously edited, with some shorter pieces, mainly passages added to the second and third series*, EETS, 259-260, 2 vols (London, 1967-68)

Skeat, W.W., editor, *Ælfric's Lives of Saints: being a set of sermons on saints' days formerly observed by the English Church, edited from British Museum Cott. MS Julius E.vii with variants from other manuscripts*, EETS, 76, 82, 94, 114, 4 vols (London, 1881-90); reprinted as 2 vols (London, 1966)

Szarmach, Paul, editor, *The Vercelli Homilies IX-XXII*, Toronto Old English Series, 5 (Toronto, 1981)

Thorpe, Benjamin, editor, *The Homilies of the Anglo-Saxon Church: the first part, containing the Sermones Catholici or Homilies of Ælfric, in the original Anglo-Saxon, with an English version*, 2 vols (London, 1844-46) (Volume I is cited as 'Thorpe', Volume II is used only for *De penitentia* and this text is cited under that title)

SECONDARY SOURCES

Aulén, G., *Christus Victor: an historical study of the three main types of the idea of atonement*, translated by A.G. Hebert (London, 1931)

Babcock, W.S., 'Augustine and Paul: the case of Romans IX', *Studia Patristica*, 16, part 2, edited by E.A. Livingstone (Berlin, 1985), 473-479

— 'Augustine and Tyconius: a study in the Latin appropriation of Paul', *Studia Patristica*, 17, part 3, edited by E.A. Livingstone (Oxford, 1982), 1209-15

Bibliography

Backhouse, Janet, D.H. Turner and Leslie Webster, *The Golden Age of Anglo-Saxon Art: 966-1066* (London, 1984)

Bakhuizen van den Brink, J.N., 'Ratramn's Eucharistic Doctrine and its Influence in Sixteenth-century England', *Studies in Church History*, 2, (1965), 54-77

Barré, H., *Les homiliaires carolingiens de l'école d'Auxerre*, Studi e Testi, 225 (Vatican City, 1962)

Bentley-Taylor, David, *Augustine: wayward genius* (London, 1980)

Bloomfield, M.W., *The Seven Deadly Sins: an introduction to the history of a religious concept, with special reference to mediæval English literature* (1952; reprinted East Lansing, Michigan, 1967)

Blunt, John Henry, editor, *Dictionary of Sects, Heresies, Ecclesiastical Parties, and Schools of Religious Thought* (London, Oxford and Cambridge, 1874), republished (Detroit, 1974)

Boase, T.S.R., *Death in the Middle Ages: mortality, judgment and remembrance* (London, 1972)

Bonner, G., 'Les origines africaines de la doctrine augustinienne sur la chute et le péché originel', *Augustinus*, 12 (1967), 97-116

— 'Augustine and Modern Research on Pelagianism', The St Augustine Lecture 1970, Villanova, Pa (Villanova, 1972)

— 'The Church and the Eucharist in the Theology of St Augustine', *Sobornost*, 7th series, no. 6 (1978), 448-461

— 'Christ, God and Man in the Thought of St Augustine', *Angelicum*, 61 (1984), 268-294

— 'Augustine's Doctrine of Man: image of God and sinner', *Augustinianum*, 24 (1984), 495-514

— *Saint Augustine of Hippo: life and controversies*, revised reissue (Norwich, 1986)

Bosworth, J. and T.N. Toller, *An Anglo-Saxon Dictionary* (Oxford, 1898); *Supplement* by T.N. Toller (Oxford, 1921); *Enlarged Addenda and Corrigenda* by A. Campbell (Oxford, 1972)

Bouhot, J.-P., *Ratramne de Corbie: Histoire littéraire et controverses doctrinales* (Paris, 1976)

Boyer, C., *Essais sur la doctrine de St Augustin* (Paris, 1932)

Brook, V.J.K., *A Life of Archbishop Parker* (Oxford, 1962)

Brown, Peter, *Augustine of Hippo: a biography* (London, 1967)

— 'Pelagius and his Supporters: aims and environment', *Journal of Theological Studies*, n.s., 19 (1968), 933-114

Burnaby, John, *Amor Dei: a study of the religion of St Augustine* (London, 1938)

Chadwick, Henry, *Augustine* (Oxford, 1986)

Clayton, Mary, 'Delivering the Damned: a motif in Old English homiletic prose', *Medium Ævum*, 55 (1986), 92-102

— 'Homiliaries and Preaching in Anglo-Saxon England', *Peritia*, 4 (1985), 207-42

— *The Cult of the Virgin Mary in Anglo-Saxon England*, Cambridge Studies in Anglo-Saxon England, 2 (Cambridge, 1990)

Clemoes, P.A.M., 'The Chronology of Ælfric's works', in *The Anglo-Saxons: studies in some aspects of their history and culture, presented to Bruce Dickins*, edited by P.A.M. Clemoes (London, 1959), pp. 212-247. Corrected reprint: 'The Chronology of Ælfric's Works', *Old English Newsletter*, Subsidia, 5, (Binghamton, New York, 1980)

— 'Ælfric', in *Continuations and Beginnings: studies in Old English literature* edited by Eric G. Stanley (London, 1966), pp. 176-209

Collins, Marie, Jocelyn Price and Andrew Hamer (editors), *Sources and Relations: studies in honour of J.E. Cross, Leeds Studies in English*, n.s., 16, (1985)

Crawford, J., 'Evidences for Witchcraft in Anglo-Saxon England', *Medium Ævum*, 32 (1963), 99-116

Cross, F.L. and E.A. Livingstone, *The Oxford Dictionary of the Christian Church*, second edition, corrected and revised (Oxford, 1985)

Cross, J.E., 'Ælfric and the Medieval Homiliary — objection and contribution', *Scripta Minora Regiae Societatis Humaniorum Litterarum Lundensis* (1961-62), part 4, 3-34

— 'Aspects of Microcosm and Macrocosm in Old English Literature', *Comparative Literature*, 14 (1962), 212-47

— 'Bundles for Burning — a theme in two of Ælfric's *Catholic Homilies* — with other sources', *Anglia,* 81 (1963), 335-46

— 'Gregory, "Blickling Homily" X and Ælfric's "Passio S. Mauricii": on the world's youth and age', *Neuphilologische Mitteilungen*, 66 (1965), 327-330

— 'Ælfric — mainly on memory and creative method in two *Catholic Homilies*', *Studia Neuphilologica*, 61 (1969), 135-55

— 'The Literate Anglo-Saxon — on sources and disseminations' (Sir Israel Gollancz Memorial Lecture), *Proceedings of the British Academy*, 58 (1972), 67-100

Cunliffe-Jones, H., editor, *A History of Christian Doctrine* (Edinburgh, 1978)

Danielou, Jean, *The Bible and the Liturgy* (London 1960)

Davies, J.G., editor, *A New Dictionary of Liturgy and Worship* (London, 1986)

Denzinger, Henry, *The Sources of Catholic Dogma*, translated by Roy Deferrari (St Louis, 1955)

Dewart, Joanne McW., 'The Christology of the Pelagian Controversy', *Studia Patristica*, 17, part 3, edited by E.A. Livingstone (Oxford, 1982), 1221-1224

Dix, Gregory, *The Shape of the Liturgy*, second edition (London, 1945)

Dubois, Marguerite-Marie, *Ælfric: sermonnaire, docteur et grammarien: contribution à l'étude de la vie et de l'action bénédictines en Angleterre au Xe siècle* (1942; reprinted Paris, 1943)

Duchesne, L., *The Early History of the Church, from its Foundation to the End of the Fifth Century*, translated by Claude Jenkins, 3 vols (London 1914-1924), III

Dudden, F.H., *Gregory the Great: his place in history and thought*, 2 vols (London, 1905), II

Dunn, J.R., 'An Index and Analysis of Major Themes in Ælfric's Homilies, the Trinity, the Sacraments, Eschatology, Heresy' (unpublished PhD dissertation, University of Colorado at Boulder, 1976)

Eliade, Mircea, editor in chief, *The Encyclopedia of Religion*, 15 vols (New York, 1987)

Eliason, Norman and P.A.M. Clemoes, editors, *Ælfric's First Series of Catholic Homilies: British Museum Royal 7 C. xii fols. 4-218*, Early English Manuscripts in Facsimile, 13 (Copenhagen, London and Baltimore, 1966)

Emmerson, R.K., 'Antichrist as Anti-Saint: the significance of Abbot Adso's *Libellus de Antichristo*', *American Benedictine Review*, 30 (1979), 175-90

— *Antichrist in the Middle Ages* (Seattle, 1981)

Evans, G.R., *Augustine on Evil* (Cambridge, 1982)

— *The Thought of Gregory the Great* (Cambridge, 1986)

Evans, R.F., *Pelagius: inquiries and reappraisals* (New York, 1968)

— *One and Holy: the Church in Latin Patristic thought*, Church Historical Series, 92 (London, 1972)

Ferguson, John, *Pelagius: a historical and theological study* (Cambridge, 1965)

Frantzen, A.J., *The Literature of Penance in Anglo-Saxon England* (New Brunswick, 1983)

Frend, W.H.C., *The Rise of Christianity* (London, 1984)

— *The Donatist Church*, second edition (Oxford, 1985)

— *Saints and Sinners in the Early Church: differing and conflicting traditions in the first six centuries* (London, 1985)

— *The Making of Orthodoxy: essays in honour of Henry Chadwick* (Cambridge, 1989)

Focillon, Henri, *L'An Mil* (Paris, 1952)

Förster, Max, *Über die Quellen von Ælfric's Homeliae Catholicae; I: Legenden* (Berlin, 1892)

— 'Über die Quellen von Ælfric's exegetischen Homiliae Catholicae', *Anglia*, 16 (1894), 1-61

Gatch, Milton McC., 'Two Uses of Apocrypha in Old English Homilies', *Church History*, 33 (1964), 379-91

— 'Eschatology in the Anonymous Old English Homilies', *Traditio*, 21 (1965), 117-65

— 'MS Boulogne-sur-Mer 63 and Ælfric's First Series of *Catholic Homilies*' *Journal of English and Germanic Philology*, 65 (1966), 482-90

— *Death: meaning and mortality in Christian thought and contemporary culture* (New York, 1969)

— 'Some Theological Reflections on Death, from the Early Church Through the Reformation', in *Perspectives on Death* edited by Liston O. Mills (New York, 1969), pp. 99-136

— *Preaching and Theology in Anglo-Saxon England: Ælfric and Wulfstan* (Toronto, 1977)

Gilson, Étienne, *The Christian Philosophy of St Augustine* (Paris, 1929), translated by L.E.M. Lynch (London, 1961)

Godden, Malcolm R., 'Old English Composite Homilies from Winchester', *Anglo-Saxon England*, 4 (1975), 57-65

— 'The Development of Ælfric's Second Series of *Catholic Homilies*', *English Studies*, 54 (1973), 209-216

Gneuss, Helmut, 'A preliminary list of manuscripts written or owned in England up to 1100', *Anglo-Saxon England,* 9 (1981), 1-60

Graef, Hilda, *Mary: A History of Doctrine and Devotion*, 2 vols (London, 1963), I

Grégoire, Réginald, *Les Homeliaires du moyen age: Inventaire et analyse des manuscrits*, Rerum Ecclesiasticum Documenta, Series Maior: Fontes, 6 (Rome, 1966)

Grundy, Lynne, 'Ælfric's *Sermo de sacrificio in die pascæ: figura* and *veritas*', *Notes and Queries*, 235 (1990), 265-69

Halvorsen, N., 'Doctrinal terms in Ælfric's Homilies', *University of Iowa Humanistic Studies*, 5 (1932), 3-98

Hanson, R.P.C., *The Search for the Christian Doctrine of God* (Edinburgh, 1988)

Hazlett, Ian, editor, *Early Christianity: origins and evolution to AD 600* (London, 1991)

Healey, Antonette diPaolo and R.L. Venezky, editors, *A Microfiche Concordance of Old English*, Dictionary of Old English Project, Centre for Medieval Studies, University of Toronto (Toronto and Delaware, 1980)

Hennecke, E., *New Testament Apocrypha*, edited by Wilhelm Schneemelcher, translated by R.McL. Wilson, 2 vols (Philadelphia, London, 1965), II

Hefele, C.J. von, *History of the Christian Councils, from the Original Documents*, translated and edited by W.R. Clark and H.N. Oxenham, 5 vols (Edinburgh, 1871-96), IV, edited by H.N. Oxenham (1895)

Hill, Joyce, 'Ælfric's use of Etymologies', *Anglo-Saxon England*, 17 (1988), 35-44

— 'Ælfric and the Smaragdus Problem' (unpublished paper delivered at Kalamazoo, May 1991: forthcoming)

Hill, W.J., *The Three-Personal God* (Washington, 1982)

Hughes, A., *Mediæval Manuscripts for Mass and Office* (Toronto, 1982)

James, M.R., *The Apocryphal New Testament* (Oxford, 1953)

Jedin, H. and John Dolan, editor, *Handbook of Church History*, 3 vols, III: *The Church in the Age of Feudalism* by F. Kempf et al., translated by Anselm Biggs (London, 1969)

Kelly, J.N.D., *Early Christian Creeds*, second edition (London, 1960)

— *Early Christian Doctrines*, fifth edition (London, 1977)

— *The Athanasian Creed*, The Paddock Lectures for 1962-63 (London, 1964)

Ker, N.R., *Catalogue of Manuscripts containing Anglo-Saxon* (Oxford, 1957)

King, Edward B. and Jacqueline T. Schaefer, editors, *Saint Augustine and his Influence in the Middle Ages* (Sewanee, Tennessee, 1988)

Kirwan, Christopher, *Augustine* (London and New York, 1989)

Klauser, T., *A Short History of the Western Liturgy: an account and some reflections* translated by John Halliburton, second edition (Oxford, 1979)

Knowles, David, *The Evolution of Medieval Thought* (London, 1962)

— *The Monastic Order in England: a history of its development from the times of St Dunstan to the Fourth Lateran Council, 940-1216*, second edition (1963; reprinted Cambridge, 1966)

La Bonnardière, A.-M., 'Le verset paulinien *Rom.*,v,5, dans l'oeuvre de saint Augustin', in *Augustinus Magister*, Congrès International Augustinien, 3 vols (Paris, 1954), I and II (Communications), pp. 657-665

— editor, *Saint Augustin et la Bible*, Bible de tous les temps, 3 (Paris, 1986)

Ladner, G.B., *The Idea of Reform: its impact on Christian thought and action in the Age of the Fathers* (Cambridge, Mass, 1959)

Lambert, M.D., *Mediæval Heresy: popular movements from Bogomil to Hus* (London, 1977)

Lapidge, Michael and Helmut Gneuss, editors, *Learning and Literature in Anglo-Saxon England: studies presented to Peter Clemoes on the occasion of his sixty-fifth birthday* (Cambridge, 1985)

Leclercq, J., 'Tables pour l'inventaire des homiliaires manuscrits', *Scriptorium*, 2 (1948), 195-214

Leff, Gordon, *Medieval Thought: St Augustine to Ockham* (London, 1959)

Le Goff, Jacques, *The Birth of Purgatory*, translated by Arthur Goldhammer (London, 1984)

Leinbaugh, T.H., 'Ælfric's *Sermo de Sacrificio in Die Pascae*: Anglican polemic in the sixteenth and seventeenth centuries', in *Anglo-Saxon Scholarship: the first three centuries*, edited by Carl T. Berkhout and Milton McC. Gatch (Boston, 1982) pp. 51-68

— 'The sources for Ælfric's Easter Sermon: the history of the controversy and a new source', *Notes and Queries*, 231 (1986), 294-311

Letson, D.R., 'The Form of the Old English Homily', *American Benedictine Review*, 30 (1979), 399-431

Macy, G., *The Theologies of the Eucharist in the Early Scholastic Period* (Oxford, 1984)

Markus, R.A., 'St Augustine on Signs', *Phronesis*, 2 (1957), 60-83

— *Saeculum: history and society in the Age of Augustine* (Cambridge, 1970)

— *Augustine: a collection of critical essays* (New York, 1972)

— *From Augustine to Gregory the Great* (London, 1983)

Marrou, H.I., *St Augustine and his Influence Throughout the Ages*, translated by Patrick Hepburne-Scott (New York and London, 1957)

Martimort, A.G., editor, *The Church at Prayer*, 4 vols, II: *The Eucharist* by Robert Cabié, translated by Matthew J. O'Connell (London, 1986)

Mascall, E.L. and H.S. Box, *The Blessed Virgin Mary* (London, 1963)

McEntire, Sandra, 'The Doctrine of Compunction from Bede to Margery Kempe', in *The Medieval Mystical Tradition in England*, Exeter Symposium IV, edited by Marion Glasscoe (Cambridge, 1987)

McKitterick, Rosalind, *The Frankish Church and the Carolingian Reforms 789-89* (London, 1977)

McNeill, J.T. and H.M. Gamer, *Mediæval Handbooks of Penance* (New York, 1938)

Meaney, Audrey L., 'Ælfric and Idolatry', *Journal of Religious History*, 13 (1984), 119-135

Mersch, E., *Le Corps mystique du Christ*, third edition (Paris, Brussels, 1951)

Mortimer, R.C., *The Origins of Private Penance in the Western Church* (Oxford, 1939)

Ntedika, Joseph, *L'Évolution de la doctrine du purgatoire chez St Augustin*, Publications de l'Université Lovanium de Léopoldville, 20 (Paris, 1966)

Ogilvy, J.D.A., *Books Known to the English, 597-1066*, Mediæval Academy of America publication no. 76 (Cambridge, Mass., 1967)

Palmer, P.F., 'Sacrament of Penance', *New Catholic Encyclopædia* (Washington, 1967)

Patout Burns, J. and G.M. Fagin, *The Holy Spirit* (Wilmington, Delaware, 1984)

Pegis, Anton C., *Basic Writings of St Thomas Aquinas* (New York, 1945)

Pelikan, Jaroslav, *The Christian Tradition*, 5 vols, I: *The Emergence of the Catholic Tradition, 100-600* (Chicago, 1971); III: *The Growth of Medieval Theology, 600-1300* (Chicago, 1978); IV: *Reformation of Church and Dogma, 1300-1700* (Chicago, 1984)

— *The Mystery of Continuity: time and history, memory and eternity in the thought of Saint Augustine* (Charlottesville, 1986)

Polman, A.D.R., *The Word of God According to St Augustine*, translated by A.J. Pomerans (London, 1961)

Portalié, E., *A Guide to the Thought of St Augustine*, translated by R.J. Bastian (Chicago, London, 1960)

— 'Augustin', in *Dictionnaire de théologie catholique*, edited by A. Vacant and E. Mangenot, I, 2268-2472

Poschmann, B., *Penance and the Anointing of the Sick*, translated by F. Courtney (Freiburg, 1964)

Powers, J.M., *Eucharistic Theology* (London, 1968)

Rahner, K., *The Church and the Sacraments*, translated by W.J. O'Hara (Edinburgh, London, 1963)

Raynes, Enid M., 'MS Boulogne-sur-Mer 63 and Ælfric', *Medium Ævum*, 26 (1957), 65-73

Reinsma, Luke M., *Ælfric: an annotated bibliography* (New York and London, 1987)

Richards, Jeffrey, *Consul of God: the life and times of Gregory the Great* (London, Boston and Henley, 1980)

Rigby, Paul, *Original Sin in Augustine's 'Confessions'* (Ottawa, 1987)

Rist, J.M., 'Augustine on Free Will and Predestination', *Journal of Theological Studies*, n.s., 20 (1969), 420-47

Rowe, Trevor, *Augustine: pastoral theologian*, Fernley-Hartley Lecture, Bristol 1974 (London, 1974)

Rusch, W.C., *The Later Latin Fathers* (London 1977)

Russell, J.B., *Dissent and Reform in the Early Middle Ages*, Publications of the Centre for Medieval and Renaissance Studies, 1 (Berkeley and Los Angeles, 1965)

— *Lucifer: The Devil in the Middle Ages* (Ithaca and London, 1984)

Sawyer, P.H., *Anglo-Saxon Charters* (London, 1968)

Schiller, G., *Iconography of Christian Art*, 2 vols, translated by J. Seligman (London, 1971), I

Scragg, D.G., 'The Corpus of Vernacular Homilies and Prose Saints' Lives before Ælfric', *Anglo-Saxon England*, 8 (1979), 223-77

Sisam, Kenneth, *Studies in the History of Old English Literature* (Oxford, 1967) (corrected reprint of 1953 edition)

Smalley, Beryl, *The Study of the Bible in the Middle Ages* (Oxford, 1952)

Smetana, Cyril L., 'Ælfric and the Early Mediæval Homiliary', *Traditio*, 15 (1959), 163-204

— 'Ælfric and the Homiliary of Haymo of Halberstadt', *Traditio*, 17 (1961), 457-69

Southern, R.W., *The Making of the Middle Ages* (London 1953)

Spindler, R., *Das Altenglischer Bussbuch* (Leipzig, 1934)

Srawley, J.H., editor, *St Ambrose 'On the Sacraments' and 'On Mysteries'*, translated by T. Thompson, with introduction and notes by J.H. Srawley (London, 1950)

Stanley, Eric G., *The Search for Anglo-Saxon Paganism* (Cambridge and Totowa, New Jersey, 1975)

Stone, D, *A History of the Holy Eucharist*, 2 vols (London, 1909)

Sullivan, J.E., *The Image of God: the doctrine of St Augustine and its influence* (Dubuque, Iowa, 1963)

Swete, H.B., editor, *Essays on The Early History of the Church and Ministry* (London, 1918)

Szarmach, Paul E. and Bernard F. Huppé, *The Old English Homily and its Background* (Albany, New York, 1978)

Szarmach, Paul E., editor, *Sources of Anglo-Saxon Culture*, Studies in Medieval Culture, 20 (Kalamazoo, 1986)

TeSelle, E., *Augustine the Theologian* (London, 1970)

Tixeront, J., *History of Dogmas*, translated from the fifth edition by H.L.B., 3 vols (St Louis and Freiburg, 1910-16)

Traherne, Jr, Joseph B. 'Cæsarius of Arles and Old English Literature: some contributions and a recapitulation', *Anglo-Saxon England*, 5 (1976), 105-119

Vacant, A. and E. Mangenot, compilers, *Dictionnaire de théologie catholique*, 15 vols (Paris, 1909-50)

Warner, Marina, *Alone of all her Sex* (London, 1976)

Watkins, O.D., *A History of Penance: being a study of the authorities (a) for the whole Church to A.D. 450, (b) for the Western Church from A.D. 450 to A.D. 1215*, 2 vols (London, 1920), II

Wetzel, James, 'The Recovery of Free Agency in the Theology of St Augustine', *Harvard Theological Review*, 80 (1987), 101-125

White, Caroline L., *Ælfric: a new study of his life and writings*, Yale Studies in English, 2 (London, 1898), reprinted, with a supplementary classified bibliography prepared by Malcolm R. Godden (Hamden, Connecticut, 1974)

Whitelock, Dorothy, M. Brett and C.N.L. Brooke, *Councils and Synods, with other Documents Relating to the English Church, I: A.D. 871-1204, part 1, 871-1066* (Oxford, 1981)

Williams, N.P., *The Ideas of the Fall and of Original Sin* (London, 1938)

Willis, G.G., *St Augustine and the Donatist Controversy* (London, 1950)

Wrenn, Charles L., 'Some Aspects of Anglo-Saxon Theology', in *Studies in Language, Literature and Culture of the Middle Ages and Later: studies in honour of and presented to Rudolph Willard*, edited by E. Bagby Attwood and Archibald A. Hill (Austin, 1969), pp. 182-89

Zettel, P.H., 'Ælfric's Hagiographic Sources and the Latin Legendary Preserved in BL MS Cotton Nero E.i and CCCC MS 9 and Other Manuscripts' (unpublished D.Phil. dissertation, University of Oxford, 1979)

'Saints' Lives in Old English: Latin manuscripts and vernacular accounts: Ælfric', *Peritia*, 1 (1982), 17-37